D0897599

LINDSAY'S PROMISE

Mayor Lindsay and his press secretary, Woody Klein

Lindsay's Promise

THE DREAM THAT FAILED

A Personal Account by WOODY KLEIN

The Macmillan Company

Collier-Macmillan Ltd., London

The author wishes to thank New York magazine for permission to use in somewhat different form excerpts from an article he wrote entitled "Why One of the Worst Slums in New York Hasn't Been Torn Down," which was published in that magazine on May 6, 1968.

The Macmillan Company
866 Third Avenue, New York, N.Y. 10022
Collier-Macmillan Canada Ltd., Toronto, Ontario

Library of Congress Catalog Card Number: 73–114327

First Printing

Printed in the United States of America

TO

Audrey and Wendy

Acknowledgments

The initial encouragement I received from Robert Markel of The Macmillan Company helped to make this book possible.

I am indebted to many people in the Lindsay Administration who contributed to this book, particularly those who responded to my inquiries and who helped to gather vital information.

In addition, I would like to express my thanks to Valorie J. De Bella, who meticulously typed out the final manuscript; and to Mrs. Lillian Lehman, who carefully proofread the book.

I would also like to thank George F. Willison, the noted author and historian, who contributed several constructive suggestions.

My special appreciation goes to my long-time friend Edward J. Silberfarb, a former City Hall reporter for the New York *Herald Tribune* and a former colleague in government, for reading and criticizing the entire manuscript. His counsel was invaluable.

Above all, I am deeply grateful to my wife, Audrey, for her patience, understanding and assistance. She helped me to shape the book from the beginning, and edited the manuscript in its various stages. Without her at my side, this book would never have been written.

Contents

"I cannot promise you a peaceful, quiet Administration. I cannot promise you that you will not continue to hear the howls of the power brokers. I cannot promise you the ominous silence of unanimity. But I can promise you change and reform and progress."

MAYOR JOHN V. LINDSAY, *February 21, 1966*

Prologue

"Sometimes people call me an idealist. Well, that is the way I know I
am an American. America is the only idealistic nation in the world."
— WOODROW WILSON, 1919

DURING MY YOUNGER years, I believed that the world, the nation,
my city around me could be—indeed, must be—changed for the
better. I grew up filled with the dreams and hopes of Franklin
Delano Roosevelt. I was stirred by Harry S. Truman's boldness,
moved by Adlai E. Stevenson's intellect and wit, impressed by
Dwight D. Eisenhower's honesty and goodness, and deeply in-
spired by John F. Kennedy's courage, character and style.

By the time I was thirty-five years old, therefore, it seemed
logical and natural for me to be entering public life in New York
City at the side of a friend for whom I had felt considerable affection and respect for seven years—John V. Lindsay. I was comfortable in 1965 with the concept that the highest form of public

service in the United States was as an elected or appointed official at some level of government.

Before joining John Lindsay, I had spent nearly a decade as a newspaper reporter writing about the social problems of New York's slums. My professional and personal interests had centered on the Negro and Puerto Rican ghettos, and I devoted all of my time to the causes of civil rights and equal justice. I used my position as a newspaper reporter to try to awaken everyone I could to the need for improving the social, economic and political climate in New York City. I was deeply troubled by the fact that more than one million people were trapped in poverty-plagued tenements in the biggest city in the world.

When John Lindsay announced his candidacy for Mayor in May of 1965, I felt the time had come for me to put my typewriter aside and help bring about the reforms for which I, and many other people, had been fighting for decades. I had read Jacob Riis' books about slum conditions at the turn of the century in New York and, despite the apparent lack of progress in the intervening years, I still firmly believed that New York could be a "slumless" city. But to remain on the sidelines as a journalist-observer would no longer be satisfactory. So I decided to try and help Lindsay get elected.

When I joined John Lindsay, I began what I thought would be an exciting, rewarding and productive political career filled with opportunities to help the new Mayor solve some of the overwhelming problems confronting New York.

The times, the events and the people we encountered all combined to make our task far more difficult than I had ever imagined it would be. Nevertheless, in gathering perspective during the course of writing this book, I have concluded that the time I spent with John Lindsay was far from wasted. I came away having learned a great deal about politics and the conflict among people who hold power in municipal government.

Even though I know as well as anyone the weaknesses of John Lindsay as a man and as a Mayor, I also know his many fine points. It is not my purpose in this book to reflect any discredit upon a friend whom I still admire and respect, but rather to try and relate my own personal reactions to the thirty-three months I spent in the political arena.

It is because I want to pass along to anyone who is interested in knowing what it is really like inside politics that I decided to write this book. The experiences that are related in the following pages are, of course, singularly subjective. At the same time, many newspaper accounts of major events are also included since my role in the Administration was to deal with the news media. Press reaction to our policies and programs helped us measure our progress by reflecting the public's changing moods.

I feel it was a privilege to have shared the beginning of a potentially significant reform movement in New York, even though it has not yet succeeded. In this, I recall the words of Justice Oliver Wendell Holmes, Jr., who once said: "I think that, as life is action and passion, it is required of a man that he should share the passion and action of his time at peril of being judged not to have lived."

WOODY KLEIN

Westport, Connecticut
January, 1970

LINDSAY'S PROMISE

1 *"Together we can make New York the great Empire City again."*

A POLITICAL THUNDERBOLT struck New York City on May 12, 1965. John V. Lindsay, the handsome young Republican Congressman from the 17th ("Silk Stocking") District in Manhattan's fashionable upper East Side, disclosed that he was considering running for Mayor.

The incumbent Democratic Mayor, Robert F. Wagner, was tired, apathetic and ineffective after twelve long years in office. But up to the time of Lindsay's hint he would enter the race, no Republican of major stature had tried to wrest City Hall away from the Democrats since Fiorello La Guardia had last triumphed in 1941.

The *New York Times* broke the news on the morning of May 12 with a lead story headlined:

LINDSAY, IN SHIFT,
CONSIDERS RACE
AGAINST WAGNER

A 'Yes' Expected

Congressman 'Deeply
Troubled' about the
City, Says Aide

The forty-three-year-old Lindsay, six feet four inches tall, with light brown hair and blue eyes, cast a new and fresh image on politics in a cynical city. A man who enjoyed sports—ice skating, skiing, swimming, tennis and sailing—he was an acceptable "blue blood" who looked every bit the part of the Ivy League, Yale Law School graduate that he was. His credentials also included membership in the St. James Episcopal Church, the Citizens' Committee for Children of New York City, the Council on Foreign Relations, Board of Advisors of the Young Men's Christian Association, Board of Directors of the New York City Mission Society and the Yale Corporation (Board of Trustees). An attorney, he was also a member of the New York City, New York State and American Bar associations.

Add to this his educational background—Yale University and the Yale Law School; his military experience—gunnery officer on a destroyer with duty in the Mediterranean, the invasion of Sicily, in the Southwest Pacific and in the Western Pacific; his home life—married to the former Mary Anne Harrison, a Vassar graduate; father of four children, three girls and a boy—and the picture of John Lindsay as an "instant hero" was complete. (See Appendix, pages 301–303.)

At about noon on that same day—May 12, 1965—I was having lunch in Frank's Restaurant on 125th Street in Harlem. It was sunny and pleasant outside—the temperature was about 70 degrees. I was on an assignment for my newspaper, but my mind was preoccupied with the news about Lindsay.

I had been moved all morning to do something about this story. I had spent nine years as a newspaperman writing about decaying living conditions in New York City. During that time I had come to know John Lindsay casually, but well enough to like him and to believe that he was exactly what New York needed. I had written hundreds of stories and columns criticizing Mayor Wagner for his inertia, for failing to attack the slum blight that was spreading throughout the city. I had been an angry, impatient young reporter. The election of an attractive, fresh person like John Lindsay seemed like a very exciting idea to me, even though I realized he was a long shot.

I finished lunch and then began looking for the nearest Western Union office. I had made up my mind. It was time to get involved with the political processes about which I had been writing for so many years. At 304 St. Nicholas Avenue, not too far from Frank's, I found Western Union. I scribbled a hurried message on the telegram form and addressed it to "Rep. John V. Lindsay, House Office Building, Wash., D.C." The message read: "Urge you to run. You will win. Glad to help in any way. Letter follows. Warmest regards. Woody Klein."

When I returned to the *World-Telegram* in lower Manhattan at 125 Barclay Street, the other reporters were talking about Lindsay's prospects, if he should decide to run. Several old political writers didn't give him much of a chance against Bob Wagner. "He's an Ivy Leaguer who's never been outside of the Silk Stocking district," said one veteran reporter. "What the hell does he know about running New York?"

Despite the generally cynical reaction around the newsroom, my enthusiasm had not diminished. The first thing I did when I returned to the third-floor city room was to sit down and type out a letter, addressing it "Personal and Confidential" to Lindsay's Washington office. I wrote:

DEAR JOHN,
Should you decide to run, I would be very happy to make any and all material I have at my command available to you. I would want to assist in any way possible, especially in civil rights and housing. I just want you to know that you can count on me. This letter follows a telegram I sent earlier.

Best personal regards,
WOODY KLEIN

I later learned that the *Times* story had been "planted" by Robert Price, a thirty-three-year-old attorney and Lindsay's manager during his campaigns for Congress, who had telephoned *New York Times* reporter Tom Ronan the day before, on May 11, after talking with some of Lindsay's closest friends and potential bankrollers. Lindsay had been wavering during the previous week and on Friday, May 7, he had talked at length with Price about running. Over that weekend, Lindsay struggled with himself as he pondered his future in his Washington home. On Monday, May 10, he had received encouragement from Governor Rockefeller and Senator Javits, but he had still not made up his mind. Nevertheless, Price's message to Ronan on the 11th was: Lindsay is ready to run. The carefully constructed story, leaked skillfully by Price, had put Lindsay on the front page and it had served as a trial balloon that was to receive tremendous spontaneous support.

That night, as I made my way home, I thought about my friendship with the man who had just shaken New York City's political world.

I had first met John Lindsay in 1958 when he ran for Congress as an insurgent after upsetting the County Republican machine and Frederic R. Coudert, Jr., the incumbent GOP Congressman, by 2,077 votes in a primary. Lindsay, a thirty-seven-year-old newcomer to politics from Manhattan, went on to win the general election by 7,700 votes over the Democratic-Liberal candidate, Anthony B. Akers. I had a drink with Lindsay at a midtown hotel while I was covering his campaign. I was impressed with his warmth, charm and candor as we talked about his chances of winning. He seemed optimistic and carefree; he laughed a lot and was eager to answer my questions. It was a pleasant meeting.

Two years later, when Lindsay was running against William J. vanden Heuvel, a thirty-year-old contemporary of mine whom I had known during my college days, I was assigned by my paper to cover the Lindsay race once again. In the two years since I had last covered a Lindsay campaign, I had been in touch with him on issues affecting housing problems in New York City. My newspaper had played a major role in exposing conflict-of-interest in the city's Robert Moses-managed Title I middle-income housing program. One of the biggest problems had been the refusal of the city's housing officials, including Moses, to tell the press and the public how they were choosing sponsors, sites, builders and all the other key parts of the multimillion-dollar housing program. A group of newsmen, including myself, had urged several New York Congressmen to amend the Title I section of the Federal

Housing Act of 1949 to make it mandatory for all potential sponsors to disclose their financial backgrounds and to divulge a complete projection of estimated rentals in future projects. Lindsay had introduced the amendment and it became law.

He also had introduced legislation to reform the restrictive McCarren-Walter Immigration Act, and had worked for health insurance for the aged. His liberal record was a source of great concern to the Republican wing in Congress, but Lindsay, nevertheless, stuck to a dogged go-it-alone course which won him many admirers in New York, including myself. I was even more impressed with Lindsay as a political phenomenon in 1960 when he won by 26,000 votes, taking 59.8 percent of the ballots in the 17th Congressional District. This was in the same year that Senator John F. Kennedy was elected to the Presidency, carrying Lindsay's district easily. What made Lindsay's victory even more remarkable was that vanden Heuvel had been billed as housing adviser to Senator Kennedy.

Lindsay's Congressional campaign in 1962 was less newsworthy. He won an expected victory, beating New York University law professor Martin B. Dworkis (Dem.-Lib.) by 53,000 votes. It was the largest plurality he had ever garnered, but it was an "off year" politically and everyone expected Lindsay to win handily.

About the time that Lindsay's third term in Congress got under way in 1963, I began writing a book about the cause of slums in New York. On January 27, 1963, I wrote him a letter asking him to write the foreword to the book. In early February, we met in his Congressional office at 30 West 44th Street to discuss the project. He was enthusiastic. He seemed relaxed and happy. After a half hour or so I rose to leave. He put his arm around me and gave me a bear hug, then slapped me on the back. "It was good to see you again," he said. "Let's get together again soon and have a drink. I want to talk to you about some of the public-housing projects. Some of the tenants write to me and tell me they're having real problems." Since I was spending almost all of my time writing about housing problems in the city, I agreed to meet him anytime. Several weeks later he telephoned me at my office and asked me to go with him on an informal, off-the-record tour of several housing projects in Harlem. We talked to many of the tenants. I was impressed with the fact that he had followed through his request and had done so without the benefit of any publicity.

In the meantime, I had received a letter from him dated February 6, 1963. "I can't tell you how flattered I am that you want me to write the foreword for your book," he had written and confirmed that he would do so after seeing the manuscript.

By pure coincidence, as I read Lindsay's letter on February 7, I turned to a story in the *New York Times* on an inside page, which carried this headline:

LINDSAY GAINING
STATUS IN HOUSE

———

Some Suggest That He Run
for City or State Office

———

"In his 15 years in Republican politics," the article said, "he had never shown a lack of confidence or a reluctance to battle both within and without his party." The news story pointed out, however, that Lindsay sometimes found himself in conflict with the House Republican leadership and that "the frustrations implicit in being a Liberal in a Conservative House, as well as a Republican in a Democratic House, have led Mr. Lindsay's friends to suggest that he take his widely acknowledged talents back to New York State in search of political advancement."

"Two possibilities arise," the article continued. "The Republican nomination for Mayor of New York City in 1965 and for Governor in 1966. Both involve serious political risks, as they offer major challenges. . . . At this date, Mr. Lindsay is merely musing about such prospects, as he spends a good many evenings speaking at the Republican and other functions in New York City and occasionally upstate."

Lindsay and I exchanged more letters during the summer of 1963 and we met again to discuss the manuscript of my book. Early in 1964, he took exception to a paragraph in an edited version of the foreword he had written. He did not want the term "Silk Stocking" used to describe his district. "I know it is fun to do it," he wrote, "and especially in this context it is useful for contrast. But I don't wish to be a party to perpetrating the myth because it just isn't so. It always astonishes me how many bright people, political scientists included, have no idea of either the boundaries or the contents of the 17th Congressional District." Lindsay said his district contained the most varied mixture of people and incomes and living conditions of any Congressional District in the United States.

Lindsay declared his intention to run for reelection relatively early in 1964—on June 20. Although his opponent that year, Mrs. Eleanor Clark French, was a liberal and a member of the City Human Rights Commission, she had little chance of upsetting the popular incumbent. The entry of a third, Conservative Party, candidate, Kieran O'Doherty, also appeared to make little difference in this election. The only concern in the Lindsay camp was that Lyndon Johnson was expected to crush Barry Goldwater by such a lopsided margin that any Democrat, including Mrs. French, running on the same ticket as President Johnson, couldn't help but benefit.

The outcome surpassed even the most optimistic expectations of Lindsay followers. Lindsay was reelected by a plurality of more than 70,000 votes.

I remember that election night of 1964 in the Madison Room of the Hotel Roosevelt. Lindsay was in a mellow, thankful mood. He thanked Bob Price—"my old friend and campaign manager" —and he predicted that the outcome of his reelection would "have a major effect on the future of the Republican Party." I asked Mary Lindsay if she felt John should go on to higher office. "Of course he should go on," she replied matter-of-factly. "John has brought integrity and decency into politics in New York."

Six months later—in May 1965—I was witnessing the opening of Lindsay's campaign to capture New York City's highest office. And I was certain that if he could win the mayoralty, he would not only change the city but would begin a brilliant national career.

On May 13, assisted by Bob Price's lightning-fast contacts with political and press figures alike, Lindsay found himself and his entire family on the 8:30 A.M. flight from Washington to New York for the official announcement of his candidacy and the kickoff of his campaign in each of the city's five boroughs. His announcement was dramatic and timely. "I, for one," he declared, "cannot stand by while the decline and fall of New York continues headlong." He said he was entering the race "because conscience and duty compel me and because I believe that with proper leadership our city can once again be restored as the Empire City of the world. Cities are for people and for living and yet under its present tired management, New York City has become a place that is no longer for people or for living." Without mentioning Mayor Wagner by name, Lindsay assailed the Democratic Administration. He charged that "in these long years of one-party rule in New York, we have seen its strength diminish, its pre-eminent place among world cities lost, and its people beset with hopelessness and despair."

The new candidate, who toured the five boroughs on the day he declared his candidacy, added: "We have seen our city lose its spirit and its power to lead. Its banners no longer lift as a symbol of proud citizenship. There is no leadership, and in such a vacuum of leadership there is no standard, no tone, no quality of excellence." Lindsay told his audiences in each borough that he would wage the most intensive campaign "in the modern history of the city."

Lindsay received a large turnout in each of the boroughs, first at the Concourse Plaza Hotel in the Bronx and, as the day went on, the crowds increased in size. By the time he reached the St. George Hotel in Brooklyn, people were lining the streets in campaign-sized crowds and they were pressing him for handshakes and autographs. From the day Lindsay announced, to June 10, 1965, the day Robert F. Wagner dramatically withdrew from the mayoral race, Lindsay captured the headlines and the imagination of the public.

On Tuesday, May 25, I felt the need to do something more than just sit around and dream of what would happen if John Lindsay replaced Bob Wagner. I had not received a response to my telegram and letter to Lindsay, but Bob Price had telephoned me and told me he wanted to talk to me at the Roosevelt as soon as I could stop by.

I went up to the hotel in the late afternoon of that day in May, ostensibly on a story for the *World-Telegram* about the "Lindsay brothers." Lindsay had three brothers and all were already involved in the campaign. I had called Harry O'Donnell, who was in charge of press relations for the campaign (on leave from the Republican State Committee), and made arrangements to obtain information at the Roosevelt on the Lindsay family. The eldest of the brothers, George N., then forty-five, was soft-spoken, almost shy. He was put in charge of coordinating research and developing issues in the campaign. David A. Lindsay, forty-three, John's twin (fraternal), was also a little circumspect, but less shy than George. He could be found at the Roosevelt from time to time, but he preferred to advise John privately. Both of these brothers were lawyers. The youngest brother, Robert ("Rod"), thirty-nine, was vice-president of the Morgan Guaranty Trust Company. The Lindsays' older sister, Mrs. Eleanor V. Schieffelin, forty-seven, was not involved in the campaign. Later in the summer, in a tragic accident, she drowned in her swimming pool at home in Long Island.

While I was at the Roosevelt I had an opportunity to speak with Bob Price. He said he wanted to improve the research in the campaign. "We need to hit the issues hard. We need someone who knows where the weaknesses are and who knows how to exploit them. We need somebody to take over George Lindsay's group and make them work. How about it?" he asked. I told him I didn't know if I had the time.

"I'll pay you. How much do you want? Two hundred and fifty a week? Three hundred a week? You name it," Price responded.

"I didn't come up here to make any money off the campaign," I said.

"Come on, nobody works for nothing," Price replied.

"You manage Lindsay's campaign for nothing, don't you?" I said.

"I had to take out a loan to run this one. But that's the way I do things. Why don't you take a leave from your paper and join us in the campaign?" he said.

"I'll think it over. I want to talk to John about it, too."

"Fine. Now how about a good story for tomorrow's paper? I have one here I promised a man on the *Tribune,* but if you want it I'll give him something else," Price went on.

And so our conversation went: blunt and to the point. He wasted neither motion nor words. Price, the balding, tight-lipped, quick-minded architect of John Lindsay's previous Congressional victories, was fully in charge of this campaign and he left no doubt about it even to a friendly visitor on his first trip to campaign headquarters.

I left Price's office a little confused as to what a working newspaperman can—and should—do to help a friend who was running for Mayor. My beat included many activities in which the Mayor's office was involved—housing, civil rights, social welfare. I was told by colleagues that it was not unusual to find newsmen on the payroll of political candidates. Still, in good conscience, I felt I had only two clear alternatives: to take a leave from my newspaper and work for Lindsay for pay, or continue as a reporter and work for Lindsay as a volunteer nights and weekends.

I decided to try and get a leave of absence. I was convinced that I was doing the right thing in deciding to help Lindsay. Meanwhile, Lindsay continued to make news, including one speech from which the *Times* had selected its "Quote of the Day" for May 26. It read: "I'm running as Lindsay. As Fiorello La Guardia said, there's no Republican or Democratic way to clean the streets." And on June 11, Lindsay came up with a suggestion that minority groups be allowed to participate in the "decision-making process" at City Hall. He said he believed that was the only way to change the climate that had led to the riots of the summer before. He said minority group leaders "desperately want the dignity of responsibility . . . they do not merely want to be a delegation to City Hall; they want to be part of City Hall." This was to become one of his major campaign themes and it made me feel good to know that Lindsay had what I considered an enlightened and liberal concept of how to deal with the city's racial tensions.

Lindsay called me one night in late June at Spring Valley, New York, where I was spending the summer. He said he was happy to know that I wanted to help him. I suggested he telephone Richard D. Peters, editor of the *World-Telegram,* with the request for my leave. Lindsay agreed. I told Peters he would be hearing from Lindsay about the tentative plan for a leave of absence. However, Peters said he did not want me to take a leave. He told me I was needed at the paper and he also said he felt my "usefulness" to the newspaper would be impaired when I returned because I would have publicly taken sides in a major political campaign.

Lindsay and I discussed Peters' decision. Despite a personal plea from Lindsay, the *World-Telegram* editor stuck to his position. I spoke to Lindsay a second time from Spring Valley. He advised me not to leave my job and we agreed I would help him on nights and weekends.

By June 29, I had firmly committed myself to help research and help write two of Lindsay's major "position papers"—on housing and civil rights. I had also met at the Roosevelt in George Lindsay's suite on several occasions with other people on civil rights, and I had started to attend a series of evening meetings on housing, which were held in the offices of *The Reader's Digest* in the Pan Am building rather than at Hotel Roosevelt campaign headquarters across the street because some of the people attending the meetings were still working in the Wagner Administration. Lindsay's Democratic running mate for Comptroller, Milton Mollen, "chaired" the sessions on housing. Among those who contributed were Robert Seaver, who had served as Mollen's public relations man when Mollen was Wagner's housing coordinator. The technique Lindsay's managers were using was to reach out in every profession and bring in the best ideas from everywhere, especially from well-known people who were willing to contribute.

During the third week in June, I spoke with Richard R. Aurelio,[1] one of Lindsay's most talented campaign aides, who was on loan from the staff of Senator Jacob K. Javits. Aurelio said Lindsay was scheduled to appear before the United Council of Harlem Organizations on Saturday morning, June 26, and that he needed some ideas for a speech. Over a long weekend in Spring Valley, I hammered out 18 one-paragraph ideas that could be fitted into an overall theme for a program to avoid a repeat of the violence that had hit New York the summer of 1964. Lindsay offered a ten-point program "to help relieve the summer tensions and frustrations in the slums and neighborhoods of our city." He said: "I deeply believe that if we are to make progress, we must recognize that the tensions in our slums truly constitute a crisis." This was the speech in which he first touched on the subject of the Police Review Board. He urged that it be expanded from three police officials to include an additional staff of four "outstanding citizens." One of my suggestions which he used was that the Mayor should appoint an assistant "whose primary and only responsibility this summer would be to keep in intimate touch with the moods, tensions and strains of the slum neighborhoods." The concept was simple: establishment of antennae that would be tuned round-the-clock to trouble spots so City Hall could respond before any damage was done.[2]

As the campaign moved into late summer and early fall, Lindsay was beginning to emerge, I thought, as the man who could save New York. His white papers on housing, parks, narcotics, labor, air pollution, crime, education, employment and business, finance, transportation, water supply, welfare and other vital subjects caught the public's imagination, despite the fact that the campaign went unreported in the daily newspapers from September 16 to October 10 because of a citywide newspaper strike.

As I continued reporting on the mayoral campaign, one of my best sources for news was Charles G. Moerdler, the thirty-year-old president of the Young Republican Club. Moerdler, an articulate and bright attorney, had taken up the battle cry for better housing conditions in New York. Beginning in April with a report on "Wagner's Slums," Moerdler and his associates revisited scores of slum buildings about which I and other reporters had been writing for years. He issued periodic reports before and after Lindsay declared his candidacy. I wrote stories about these reports.

By the time Labor Day arrived, I had been hearing from Moerdler almost daily. His club had branched out into the poverty and welfare fields; it was attacking the Democrats on all fronts. Moerdler, a young man who spoke quickly and with forcefulness, invariably wore a blue pin-striped suit and vest. He was impressive, both in appearance and in what he said, because he made it a point to do his homework on each of the issues he raised—particularly housing.

As I became more involved with Moerdler, my telephone at the *World-Telegram* was also ringing with story tips from Bob Price. On September 8, Price called to tell me that William F. Buckley, the Conservative Party candidate, and some of his colleagues had been responsible for smashing windows of several Lindsay storefronts in Brooklyn and Queens.

"How do I know this is true?" I asked Price.

"Because I'm telling you," he said.

"I'll have to verify it, before I can print a story like that," I replied.

"Look, if you don't want it, I'll give it to the *Post* or the *Tribune*. I promised those guys some exclusives, too," he said.

"I want it," I replied, "but I want someone who saw those windows smashed to talk to me."

"Well, Connie [Constantine Sidamon-] Eristoff has all the information," he snapped. "Call him up right now."

I decided to go up to the Roosevelt, after advising my city editor of the tip from Price, and get the facts confirmed. Eristoff gave me what I needed and after further confirming reports of damage with the police, I wrote the story for the next day's first edition. The headline all the way across page one read: HATE TACTICS HIT LINDSAY. My story began: "Rep. John V. Lindsay and his campaign workers throughout the city are being victimized by 'vicious right-wing hate tactics,' a source close to the Republican-Liberal candidate disclosed today." I went on to name the locations and reveal, for the first time, that Lindsay's life had been threatened in late June, that he had been given a bodyguard on July 3 and that the guard had been taken off him on August 17.

No sooner had the first edition hit the streets when Buckley called a press conference to deny that he had any knowledge of such vandalism. He further charged Lindsay's people with fabricating the whole story. I was sent by my paper to cover the Buckley press conference. When it was over, I went to the telephone and tried to reach Lindsay, who, by this time, had heard about Buckley's denials. Lindsay himself, when pressed about my story, said he had no firsthand knowledge himself that the damage had been done by Buckley's people.

I tried to reach Price, but he was unavailable. Then I reached Oliver Pilat, who had left the *New York Post* to serve as second-in-command to Harry O'Donnell in Lindsay's press department. Pilat refused to get a message to Lindsay and told me that "the candidate cannot be bothered right now." He seemed to be angry that I even wanted to speak with Lindsay. I finally deduced that Price had given me the story without checking with Lindsay.

Apparently, Price's "trial balloon" stories were accepted by the press. As it turned out, he was the best source of information at the entire Lindsay headquarters, much to the distress of Harry O'Donnell, whose official job it was to give out all of the information to the news media. But Price's technique was working. Lindsay was coming across as a man who cared, a man who wanted to cut across party lines and who wanted to appeal to all New Yorkers. As a campaign manager, Price had been called the best. He was. A curious combination of frankness, crudeness and shrewdness won him many friends among the working reporters hungry for a story each day.

Only once did Price "feed" me a lead that did not pan out. One day he called to tell me that Frank Costello, the underworld character, was "definitely seen" at the Summit Hotel, headquarters of Comptroller Abraham D. Beame, the Democratic candidate for Mayor. Price gave me the names of several prominent Democrats who would confirm, Price said, that Costello had met with Beame. I called every one of them. Nobody confirmed the tip and, of course, I could not write the story. Price urged me to, anyway, but I told him it would be journalistically foolhardy without any sources.

Meanwhile, Lindsay's appeal to Democratic voters who might normally vote for Abe Beame was growing rapidly. Much of Lindsay's campaign material reflected the Fusion and Independent theme which Price knew would be Lindsay's only chance of upsetting Beame. One flyer in particular played upon a Democrat's loyalty and love for John F. Kennedy. It likened Lindsay to the late President. "Sometimes party loyalty asks too much," it said at the top, quoting John Kennedy. The leaflet went on to explain: "John Kennedy, confronted with corruption in the Massachusetts Democratic Party, had once told Arthur Schlesinger, Jr.: 'Sometimes party loyalty asks too much . . . nothing can be done until the [Massachusetts Democratic] Party is beaten—badly beaten. Then there will be a chance of re-building.'" The Lindsay campaign material also reminded voters that Franklin Delano Roosevelt had crossed party lines to support Republican-Fusion candidate Fiorello La Guardia for Mayor.

In support of this theme, the *New York Post*'s James A. Wechsler wrote on September 16, 1965, in his column:

There are lifelong Democrats who find themselves unable to vote for any man guilty of any form of association with the Republican Party. . . . I sympathize with their condition, even while clinging to the hope that it is not incurable. . . . I can hardly quarrel with the proposition that John Lindsay would be a formidable national figure if he successfully grappled with the appalling problems of this city. But it is a poor specimen of a liberal who decides we dare not give Lindsay the chance because he might one day be running against Hubert Humphrey or Robert Kennedy. The year is 1965; New York cries out for a new era. And that is what this battle is all about.

I continued my own reporting on the campaign and in mid-October I served as a member of a panel questioning Beame and Lindsay at a public meeting in Town Hall on health and welfare issues. The meeting was under the auspices of the Community Council of Greater New York. Called "Face the City," it was a debate that did not generate much news, but which pitted me and other reporters in the newsman's role against both Beame and Lindsay. There were five panelists and each of us only had time to ask two questions because of the candidate's lengthy answers during the one-hour meeting. I asked: "Mr. Lindsay, violence in the streets in New York is on everybody's mind these days. The crime rate in our city has gone up steadily. What would you do, if elected Mayor, to make New York a safer place?"

Lindsay offered an answer that reflected the fact that he had been well briefed on the subject. "You're right," he responded quickly. "It has gone up 15 percent over the last year alone, 30 percent in the last ten years—major crime has gone up. The double padlock is the symbol in New York City! People have pulled the shades down and gone into isolation. While the rest of the country moves forward, New York retreats." He said he would modernize New York City's Police Department with "computerized electronic equipment" which would relieve the police of paper work and free them to patrol the streets. Lindsay added: "And if our people will stop turning their backs on their neighbors, that might help too." He was given a tremendous ovation by the audience.

Less than a week later, I decided to use my weekly column in the newspaper to review what Lindsay had pledged up to then—especially some of his statements that had not received much attention during the newspaper strike which was over on October 10. My column of October 26, 1965, one of the last I ever wrote for the newspaper, listed all of Lindsay's major statements and urged New Yorkers to vote for him.

I mentioned Lindsay's housing program in this column. Of all the projected programs, his housing white paper entitled "A Program for New York's Housing Crisis," was the one with which I was most familiar because I had written most of it myself. It was the first time in all of the nine years I had been a newspaper reporter that I had really put myself to the test of thinking about a solution for a major city problem. Most of my time as a reporter had been spent simply "exposing" problems. I found writing the housing white paper an immensely difficult job which took most of the summer. Fortunately, I had the assistance of Milton Mollen, and a small team of intelligent, knowledgeable men who contributed technical economic and real estate statistics and other information. The white paper called for an 11-point, four-year program for action on the city's housing shortage. The heart of his program was a pledge by Lindsay to build 160,000 low and middle income apartments during his four-year term. I had devoted many long nights and weekends helping to prepare the housing paper which had been released to the press on Thursday, October 7—while the newspaper strike was still underway. It did not, as a result, get much attention on radio or television, and few people at the time were really aware of the recommendations. Nevertheless, I felt we had committed to paper a set of housing goals which—if carried out—would go a long way toward helping to solve New York's decades-old housing shortage.

Lindsay's final theme in the campaign was simply this: "Friends, fellow New Yorkers, we have the possibility of creating something new and exciting and hopeful for New York. If you give me your trust, give me your confidence, together we can make New York the great Empire City again."

On November 2, Election night, 1965, I was assigned to write the story of the race for City Council President. I sat most of the evening in the *World-Telegram* city room and waited for the results to trickle in. I was in a pensive mood that night. It was to be my last as a newspaper reporter, after eleven years, nine of which I had spent in that city room. During the newspaper strike, when I worked for CBS, I had been offered a job as an investigative correspondent for WCBS-TV, the local CBS affiliate in New York. I had loved newspapering, but with strong rumors of a pending merger with the *Journal-American* and with the prospect of a new career in a media which I had enjoyed as a sideline, I had decided to give television a try on a full-time basis. I made my decision to accept the TV job many weeks before the election with the knowledge that if Lindsay won I could always join him at a later time.

As Election night wore on and the race between Lindsay and Beame seesawed back and forth, it became clear that Queens County District Attorney Frank D. O'Connor was piling up a major victory over Timothy W. Costello, Lindsay's Liberal Party running mate for City Council President. O'Connor was to triumph by more than 400,000 votes and my story the next day reflected the fact that he had actually received more votes than Lindsay, who squeaked by Beame with a slim 102,407 plurality out of 2.6 million votes. Lindsay received 1,149,106 votes; Beame, 1,046,699 votes; and Conservative Party candidate William F. Buckley did surprisingly well with 341,226 votes. The results were, nevertheless, viewed as a stunning victory for John Lindsay who had emerged from Manhattan's "Silk Stocking" district and captured New York without any formal party clubhouse organization.[3] I was so pleased by his victory that I wrote him a letter offering to help him in City Hall and two weeks later he wrote back thanking me for my offer and stating he would be in touch with me further.

The week after the election I began working at Channel 2, appearing occasionally on the 6 P.M. and 11 P.M. local news broadcasts with stories about civil rights, housing and other municipal subjects. My assignments required me to work a long day—sometimes from 9 in the morning to midnight. On Tuesday, November 23, at about 7 P.M. I was sitting at my desk at WCBS-TV at 524 West 57th Street when the phone rang.

"This is John Lindsay, Woody," the familiar voice on the other end of the line said. "What are you doing tonight? How about meeting me for a drink so we can talk?"

"Fine. Where?" I said, knowing I was not scheduled to appear for the 11 o'clock news.

"At the Waldorf. I have to drop in there for a short meeting.

I'll meet you there and we can take a walk. I'll see you there about 10."

"Good. I'll be there, John," I said. I had some idea of what Lindsay wanted to talk about because I had met with Price at the Roosevelt in the days immediately after Lindsay's victory to discuss a possible job with Lindsay. Price had said at the time he wanted me to become part of the new Administration. "Which agency do you want?" is the way he put it, and he then proceeded to describe a few housing commissionerships. I told him I was not certain I wanted to run a city agency, but rather if I did come into the Administration I would want to do something related to journalism. We talked about the job of press secretary. I told him I might be interested. "But anybody can do that job," he said. "Why don't you take a commissionership? That's where the real challenge is. Run your own shop." We had agreed to talk more about it. I went away feeling fairly certain that the logical man for Lindsay's press aide was Harry O'Donnell, who had held the same job for former Governor Thomas E. Dewey. O'Donnell had been in charge of the press for Lindsay during the campaign and he was by far the best political public relations man in New York.

In the ensuing weeks—before Lindsay telephoned me at CBS —reports of who was being considered for the press secretary post filtered back to me. There was the obvious speculation about O'Donnell. But O'Donnell had never gotten along well with Price because Price never checked with him before "leaking" stories to newsmen. As a result, there were now reports that O'Donnell did not want to work for Lindsay if Price did. And, during this time, Lindsay was publicly trying to persuade Price to be his Deputy Mayor.

With all this in the back of my mind, I took a taxi over to the Waldorf in time to catch the end of a meeting at which Lindsay had just spoken. Ollie Pilat was there, shepherding Lindsay around, introducing him to a number of people. So was Sid Davidoff, the heavy-set poker-faced young Lindsay aide who had served at his side almost twenty-four hours a day during the campaign. It was a clear and cold night as Lindsay and I broke away from the crowd surrounding him and headed across Park Avenue to begin our walk.

"I had no idea things were as bad as they are in New York," Lindsay said to me as we reached Madison Avenue. "This is a hell of a job I've got for myself and I'll need all the help I can get." He then continued to talk about what he had learned about New York during his long street campaign. It was not a pleasant summary.

As we reached 38th Street and Madison, he put his hand on my shoulder, looked me in the eye for the first time since we had left the Waldorf, and said: "Price tells me you want to work for us. He says you'd be interested in the press job. I think that would be fine. You can do it and I think you have the right credentials. I want to do away with the old image. I want to change this town and you can help me."

As we turned to cross Madison Avenue and head back toward the Waldorf, I told Lindsay what I expected from the job of press secretary. I told him I would have to know what was happening inside City Hall, I would have to be present at meetings where important decisions were being made, and that he would have to "level" with me at all times. I told him I could only be useful to him and the press if I was informed myself. He nodded in agreement, qualifying this only by saying: "There may be some times when I will want to be alone, or go somewhere, and I won't tell anybody—not even you."

"As long as you can be reached by telephone. But you won't be able to disappear in this job, John," I added. "The Mayor of New York is too visible—no matter where he is."

As we returned to the Park Avenue entrance of the Waldorf, it was past 11 o'clock. Lindsay, his hands in his pockets, looked at me once more and said, suddenly: "I've known you for a long time, Woody, but I don't know how old you are."

"I'm thirty-five," I replied. "Why do you ask?"

"A little old for this Administration," he smiled, "but I think I can use you. How about it? Is it a deal?" He stuck out his hand and, as I shook it warmly, I replied: "I think so, John. Just give me a few days to think about it. I want to talk it over with my wife."

We agreed that I would call him the following Friday night—November 26—in New Haven, where he was scheduled to spend the weekend at a friend's house before attending a meeting of the Yale Corporation Board of Trustees.

On that Friday night I told John Lindsay I would accept his offer.

2 *"I hope we can keep the press fat, satisfied and comfortable."*

I WAS STANDING at John Lindsay's side in the Madison Room of the Hotel Roosevelt on the morning of November 30, 1965. The lights of the TV equipment were shining in our eyes. The room was filled with reporters from radio, television and the newspapers. I recognized among them many of my friends, men and women I had known for years as fellow newsmen. Lindsay looked a little nervous. He took a piece of paper out of his pocket and placed it on the lecturn in front of him. Then, as soon as the room became quiet, he began:

"Well, ladies and gentlemen of the press, I'm delighted to announce that I am today unburdening myself of some chores and I am adding to my staff Woody Klein who is known to all of you. Woody has agreed to take on the job of press officer or press secretary, whatever title he wishes to put on it. And it pleases me no end to make the announcement. As you know, I regard public information as a terribly important and very serious aspect of the Mayor's job and the government of the City of New York. . . . I'm delighted that Ollie Pilat, a man for whom I have the greatest affection, admiration and regard, has agreed to stay on with me also, at least until I take office on January 1. So between the three of us, Woody and Ollie and I, I hope we can keep the press fat, satisfied and comfortable."

When the question period began, Paul Weissman, of the *Herald Tribune*, asked the Mayor-elect: "In the scale of press secretaries involved in government, Bill Moyers [Press Secretary to President Johnson] is obviously in a policy-making position, and there are others who are merely mechanics and issue press releases. Where would you place your concept of this job?"

Lindsay responded: "Mr. Klein's role, I can assure you, will be far more than that of a mechanic. I shall want him to be an intimate part of the Lindsay team, or the Cabinet. And his duties will be very broad. To be a proper and complete press man, I would think that he'd have to have total knowledge of everything I'm doing and what the other officers of the Administration are doing. He will coordinate the system of making information public in all city agencies."

Within twenty-four hours after Lindsay had announced I was to join him, I found myself alongside Ollie Pilat in a tiny, third-floor room in the Hotel Roosevelt. Newspapers were scattered all around the room. There were a few file cabinets, several telephones and typewriters. This was press headquarters—a converted hotel room in which as many as a dozen newsmen at a time congregated to wait for news from the Mayor-elect. The first statement I released came in answer to a reporter's question: What is Lindsay doing to avoid a possible transit strike December 31? I talked with Lindsay and released the following paragraph:

STATEMENT BY MAYOR-ELECT JOHN V. LINDSAY: There cannot be a strike. I assume that Mayor Wagner will do all he can to try and settle this dispute. I shall remain available to assist in any way possible for the sake of the people of New York.

There was a campaign atmosphere at the hotel. It was as if Lindsay were still running for Mayor. Every few minutes some excited, young campaign worker would rush into the press office with some rumor and ask if it was true. Fortunately, Ollie Pilat was a veteran professional newspaperman who had been in the campaign and knew how to calm people down. At sixty-one, he had somehow withstood the rigors of walking the streets with Lindsay and now he was helping to break me in. I was also assisted by a tireless, young Lindsay campaign worker, Edith Radley, whom Lindsay had assigned to continue working with me after we moved to City Hall.

In the early days of December, my time was taken up with the scores of requests for information from newspaper reporters, radio and TV newsmen; magazine and book writers; and foreign journalists. There were two or three reporters from each of New York's six daily newspapers assigned to cover the Roosevelt and find out what the Mayor-elect intended to do about New York's problems. I arrived at the press room at about 8 every morning and remained until 10 or 11 at night—sometimes later. Ollie Pilat and I then took turns receiving the telephone calls from the early morning rewritemen on the *World-Telegram, Journal-American* and *New York Post* between 2 and 6 A.M. during the night.

Meanwhile, new men were being appointed. We had at least two press conferences, almost daily, in the morning and in the afternoon. Since I had attended many of Mayor Wagner's press conferences and watched his press secretaries, I knew how to set up these sessions and how to help the Mayor-elect conduct them. The announcements of appointments in December generally went well, but Lindsay had one major problem: Almost invariably, news of one appointment or another would leak out before the scheduled press conference. This was a source of considerable concern to the Mayor-elect, even though he, like the reporters and those of us working at the Roosevelt, had his own theories about where the leaks were coming from. Bob Price had run a highly successful campaign by fully utilizing the fine art of leaking stories, one here, another there, making sure every reporter got one exclusive, and there was little doubt that it was Price who was giving out many of the stories ahead of time. This did not make my job any easier at the outset. Finally, one day in mid-December, one newspaper carried a "dope" story about how Lindsay was considering "dumping" Vincent P. Broderick as Police commissioner because he (Broderick) was not in favor of the Civilian Review Board Lindsay had pledged to create in his campaign. Lindsay telephoned me from his suite—Room 861—as soon as he saw the newspaper.

"Woody, can you find out who leaked that story about Broderick? There's not a word of truth to it. Issue a denial immediately in my name, will you?"

I wasted no time in heading for Bob Price's office next to Lindsay's. I went in and told him of my conversation with Lindsay.

"Look here," Price said sternly. "Are you accusing me of leaking that story?"

"I'm not accusing you of anything. I just want to know if you have any idea who might have done it?"

"I don't have to tell you what I do. I don't have to tell Lindsay, either. I know what's best for him—I know what is better for him than he does. Now I don't want to talk about this any more." He turned his back and answered one of the three telephones that were ringing on his desk.

The next day I arranged to have lunch with the reporter who had written the story about Broderick. I told him what had happened and then explained to him that even though I knew better than to ask a newsman who his source was, the Mayor-elect wanted to know. I asked him point-blank who had given him the Broderick lead.

"Look," he said, "you know I can't tell you officially. But this much I can say. Your instincts are right. You're going to have trouble from that other fellow after you get to City Hall. That's why Harry O'Donnell didn't want to stay on with Lindsay as press secretary and that's why you're going to have a rough time." The reporter and I both knew we were talking about Bob Price.

This incident was a sign of more such trouble to come from within the organization. Another kind of problem was signaled by an entirely separate and unrelated incident at the Roosevelt. I was standing outside my office one day when Alex Benson, of the *World-Telegram's* City Hall staff, and a friend for more than nine years, came walking down the hallway. After we chatted a few minutes, he said, "I think you should know that it's my job to give you a hard time and that's exactly what I'm going to do." Somewhat surprised, I turned away and went back to my office. I knew he had meant what he'd said because Alex was a very intense person. It was a forceful reminder to me that when a reporter becomes a press secretary, he is treated quite differently by his friends and former colleagues.

Despite these discomforting signs, I still was optimistic about the future. By December 13, Lindsay had appointed both Deputy Mayors—Robert Price and Timothy W. Costello—and nine commissioners. These included Thomas P. F. Hoving for Parks, Robert Lowery for Fire, J. Lee Rankin as Corporation Counsel, Joel J. Tyler for Licenses, Richard Lewisohn for Purchase, Murray Drabkin as special tax consultant, Arnold Fraiman for Investigation and the reappointment of Traffic Commissioner Henry Barnes.

While the city waited anxiously for Lindsay to take office, the Mayor-elect was trying to take hold of the critical issues as quickly as possible. He held daily "Cabinet" meetings in his Roosevelt Hotel office. Looming in the background, meanwhile, was the threat of a transit strike by Michael J. Quill, the fiery leader of the tough Transport Workers Union. Of course, threatening New Year's Eve strikes was an every-other-year ritual by now and nobody seriously believed that Mayor Wagner, with or without Lindsay, would not work out a last-minute "deal" to pacify Quill and his 33,000 union followers—the men who run and maintain New York City's 239.87 route miles of subways.

Bob Price, by this time, had made it clear to Lindsay and to me that he wanted recommendations for appointments in the housing, civil rights and antipoverty fields to come through me. Price was handling almost all of the other appointments, interviewing dozens of people each day who could not get to Lindsay. Top Wagner appointees were seen almost daily in the corridor outside of Price's office, leading to speculation by newsmen that they might be reappointed. One of Wagner's top aides, Judah Gribetz, commissioner of Buildings, was among those who came to see Price. I was not present during their discussion, but I happened to be leaving the Roosevelt at the same time Gribetz finished his interview. As we stood talking on Madison Avenue outside the Roosevelt Hotel, I noticed that he was visibly upset. "Price certainly wasn't very receptive," Gribetz said. "He gave me a hard time. Frankly, I was surprised—especially since Lindsay has said he wants some Democrats in his Fusion Administration."[1] The decisions as to who would get a job and who would not rested primarily with Price, for all practical purposes, although it was Lindsay, of course, who held the press conferences and who appeared to be in charge. It was a pattern, I had come to realize after only a few days, that must have been established in the campaign.

At Price's request, I gave him a list of Negroes and Puerto Ricans who might qualify for top positions. I also made many recommendations, some in writing, about jobs in the housing field. One day, Price called me into his office. He told me Charles Moerdler wanted to be the next Buildings commissioner and that he had ruled out Gribetz. Moerdler, he said, had a reputation for being impetuous and for shooting from the hip. Yet, his knowledge of the housing problem was unquestioned and he was a very sharp prosecuting-type lawyer. Price turned to me without any formalities:

"Moerdler wants to be Buildings commissioner. Maybe we should make him deputy commissioner first. What do you think?"

"I think he'd make a good commissioner," I replied.

"Okay, but someone will have to keep an eye on him—make sure he behaves. He's your responsibility."

"From everything I've seen," I added, "he'll handle himself all right. He learned a great deal about the Buildings Department in the last—"

"Okay, okay, he's got the job," Price interrupted, waving me out of his office. "Now get out of here. I have a hundred people out in the hall who want to see me."

As I turned to leave, I realized that Price had meant no discourtesy to me. That was just the way he did business—with friend or foe alike. He was a strange, brilliant, restless person, talented but without a trace of grace.

I tried several times after that to talk to Price about the salary structure for the Mayor's press office staff. I needed to know what I could offer for the still unfilled post of assistant press secretary. Lindsay had made it clear the day I was announced at the Roosevelt that there was only one qualification he would put on my choice: He wanted the assistant press secretary to be a Negro. I agreed and, while attending to my press duties, began searching for a qualified candidate.

It soon became an open secret that Lindsay wanted a Negro in the number two press job. I was overwhelmed with letters, telephone calls and visits from black writers and reporters, some in the news business, some from public relations, most of whom I had met in my travels as a reporter in the Negro community. I interviewed everyone, and finally decided that Warren Gardner, a forty-two-year-old public relations man for Mobilization for Youth, an antipoverty project in Manhattan's lower East Side, would be the best choice. Gardner had been helpful to me when I had written stories about the project and I remembered him as a friendly, calm professional who would undoubtedly be able to handle the responsibilities that I would have to heap upon him. Price decided that he could "squeeze out" $15,000 for the job of assistant press secretary. Price was the one person who was to decide salaries of all of the Mayor's City Hall aides, so I made the offer to Gardner. After some thought, he accepted, somewhat reluctantly, because it did not involve any increase in pay for him. I didn't blame Gardner for feeling less than enthusiastic. Nevertheless, I promised him I would recommend an immediate raise for him during our first few months of office. A warm, pleasant person who was easy to get along with, he accepted this pledge in good spirit and, explaining he needed several weeks to clean up his affairs on the old job, agreed to join me at City Hall on or about January 1.

The sessions with Lindsay each day dealt mostly with problems we would face immediately upon taking office. We talked about everything—Barnes told the Mayor about his plans to raise meter charges, and Lindsay responded with an anecdote that brought a big smile to Barnes' face. "I saw Arthur Goldberg [then Ambassador to the United Nations] the other day," Lindsay began, "and I told him I'd have to do something about the diplomatic immunity on parking. I said I'd have to be a son-of-a-bitch on parking all over the city—particularly the Arab delegation!" Lowery said he was concerned with reorganizing the Fire Department and his labor problems; Fraiman reported he was searching for bright young lawyers to help him; and

Alonzo Yerby, a Negro professional who had been reappointed Hospitals commissioner by Lindsay, talked about the major construction and repair problems. Perhaps the most significant topic to arise during these meetings was the budget. Price said we would have to get ready for a 10 or 15 percent "across the board" budget cut in every city department. This would mean, he said, that every newly named commissioner should start examining his budget even before he takes office. We also discussed the need to publicize our new programs through the media, with particular emphasis on increased use of television. Lindsay specifically asked me to start making arrangements for the TV and radio stations to have outlets in Gracie Mansion and City Hall. To accomplish this, he asked me to announce that Dave Garth, an independent television producer, would be serving as non-salaried special consultant to the Mayor. Garth had assisted Lindsay during the campaign. Other commissioners-designate raised additional problems. Tom Hoving reported he had met with Robert Moses and learned that a Parks Department commissioner had little power to appoint aides; most of the jobs in the department were filled by Civil Service. "About all I had left," complained the effusive Hoving, "is the power to appoint life guards and I can't base my structure on that!"

The *New York Times* ran daily editorials on city subjects, beginning around December 20. These added additional pressure to the Lindsay staff to launch some programs quickly that would capture the imagination of the public. Lindsay pushed his Task Forces, which had been working since shortly after Election Day, to come up with new ideas for housing, education, anti-poverty and several of the other key areas. He drove himself day and night, meeting with Norman Cousins, editor of *Saturday Review* magazine, on air pollution; with James V. Bennett, a former Federal director of the Bureau of the Prisons in Washington, D.C., on corrections; and with groups of other city leaders who felt, for the first time, that they might be getting a share of City Hall.

On December 23, the leaders of the National Committee Against Discrimination in Housing, a nationwide housing group, arrived in Lindsay's suite at the hotel. They were one of the dozens of civic, religious, business and political organizations that wanted "just a few minutes" with the Mayor-elect. George R. Metcalf, a former New York State senator, and Algernon D. Black, a leader of the Ethical Culture Society, headed the small contingent. They asked the Mayor-elect to take swift action in three areas: (1) rebuild the ghettos of the city, (2) build low-income housing outside of the ghettos, and (3) issue a policy statement on integration throughout the city. Lindsay asked Metcalf for a full memorandum, emphasizing what he (Metcalf) wanted to do "right away" and stating how much it would cost. Lindsay then turned to Metcalf and his colleagues and told them he wanted their support in what he would be trying to do in reforming the city. It was a technique he developed and refined as each group passed through his Roosevelt Hotel office.

Al Black, a sensitive, idealistic man who had fought for good causes his entire lifetime, asked the Mayor-elect if he had chosen a "theme" for his Administration—like John F. Kennedy's New Frontier, or Franklin D. Roosevelt's New Deal. Black suggested the term "Proud City" as a fitting theme for the Lindsay Administration.

Lindsay listened attentively. When he heard the suggestion, "Proud City," he said quietly: "That has a nice ring to it. It's a good image. I like it. Let's think about it." After this group left, I discussed the whole question of a theme for the new Administration. For the first time since I had joined him at the Roosevelt on December 1, Lindsay unwound a little and began to talk:

"This is a theme," he said, "that might catch on—The Proud City. Can Do. That's it—we want to get across the idea that there's nothing you can't do if you put your mind to it. People should be able to say about New Yorkers: 'They have such pride!' For a long time, New Yorkers haven't been proud. We need to have a widespread feeling that they can do the job and I can do the job—government can do the job."

"Do you mean people should have pride in New York as most Americans take pride in Washington, D.C.?" I asked.

"There's a great sense of pride in the center of national government. Tourists are always pleased by their visits. Government is respected there. There is a great feeling of history."

"Do you want our theme to be nationwide?"

"I think so. This is going to be the year of the city. It's foolish to say you can't do things. Of course, there are problems —the big one of communications in a city like New York. Our programs and policies, our local government must not be remote the way it has been for decades."

"And where will the sense of pride come from?"

"It will come from trying," Lindsay replied, "and I think that will lead to accomplishment. The political machinery must be prepared to try. We won't have the cooperation of organized power groups, just Joe Doaks, the consumer. We can clean up a block, several streets. We can make it possible to ride the subway and feel comfortable in it. We can make it possible to build enough houses that people can afford and that are open to every race."

"Why is this theme so important?" I asked.

"It's important to shoot for a Proud City—to aim for it. It gives people a sense of accomplishment, a feeling that they are going somewhere. You can feel a sense about the holiday season. People extend themselves a little extra. They make allowances. The way to bring this about is to give every New Yorker a sense of participation. That's why I have asked every commissioner I appoint not to regard his own department as the limit of his involvement. I want them to have a sense of excellence in everything they do. This is a goal which we can have in every aspect of city life—in the poverty program, which has lost sight of goals—in the schools, where our purpose must be to produce character and a sense of 'can do.' We must have it throughout the fabric of city life. I believe that. If we don't we won't succeed."

The next day, December 24, we were both brought back to more immediate practical matters at the daily meeting of commissioners. A budget crisis of fantastic proportions was shaping up, according to Murray Drabkin. It looked as if we would have to ask the State Legislature for a city income tax—the first one in the history of New York City. The meeting was one of the most hectic I had attended since joining Lindsay. Lowery was concerned about the alarming rise in the number of ghetto fires; Yerby said the hospital situation was bad; Lindsay and Price urged all those present to make plans to testify in behalf

of the city at legislative hearings in Albany in January; appointments to the Criminal and Civil Courts had to be made and a
new system for reviewing candidates installed; air pollution was
becoming a menace and something had to be done; the Department of Correction needed more money; Moerdler wanted to
launch a program immediately after taking office to permit
tenants to withhold rents in buildings without essential services;
the Mayor-elect wanted a report from me as soon as we took
office about where we could "trim the fat" in public relations
personnel.

I was part of a small, tightly-knit group that was already
making major plans for New York's revival, but this policy-
making team was growing. We issued press releases in late
December announcing appointments that included: Frank C.
Arricale as director of the New York City Youth Board; and
Roy M. Goodman, director of finance; Frederic S. Nathan and
Norman Redlich to join J. Lee Rankin as first assistant corpora-
tion counsel and executive assistant, respectively; and Herbert
B. Halberg, as first deputy Marine and Aviation commissioner to
Leo Brown, a Liberal Party stalwart who would remain as
commissioner. A task force on the Judiciary to review qualifica-
tions of candidates for the bench was appointed, headed by
Judge Samuel I. Rosenman. Frederic S. Berman, a Democrat,
and a former state senator, was named city rent and rehabilita-
tion administrator; Donald H. Elliott, counsel to the Mayor;
Joseph F. Periconi, commissioner of Sanitation; Royal S. Radin,
commissioner of Relocation; and Louis A. Craco, to head Task
Forces on reorganization of city government. Finally, in the
waning days of 1965, Lindsay named Constantine Sidamon-
Eristoff, Barry Gottehrer, Jay R. Kriegel, Sidney Davidoff, John
I. Ortiz, Donald F. Shaughnessy, Robert M. Blum, James W.
Smith, James R. Carberry and Werner Kramarsky as assistants to
the Mayor. And on December 30, Warren Gardner was officially
named assistant press secretary and Edie Radley administrative
assistant to the press secretary.

Also on December 30, Lindsay held an important meeting
with black leaders at the Roosevelt. The group was known as
the United Council of Harlem Organizations, a federation of
Negro civic, business and civil rights groups. About fifteen black

spokesmen jammed into the Mayor-elect's small hotel suite. Each sounded off; several demanded that Lindsay promise to do a lot more for the blacks in New York than his predecessors had done.

Among the men who came to the Roosevelt were J. Alexander Allen, of the Urban League of Greater New York; James Lawson, head of a militant black organization; Basil Paterson, a Harlem attorney; Percy Sutton, borough president of Manhattan; Hulan Jack, a former Manhattan borough president; and Arnold Johnson, a Harlem business leader. They wanted Lindsay, after he took office, to make it easier for Negroes to become policemen and to increase the number of Negroes in the Police Department; to put Negro police captains in command positions; to issue an executive order implementing his campaign pledge to guarantee the black man a better chance. The Negroes' complaints were mostly about the Police Department—their arguments coming only eighteen months after the Harlem riots of 1964 when the police turned back Negro masses in Harlem by firing thousands of rounds of ammunition into the air. They asked for a Civilian Review Board completely independent of the Police Department. The Council also urged Negro participation in all levels of government, the rebuilding of Harlem, educational improvements there and in other Negro areas, strengthening of the City Commission on Human Rights and encouragement of Negro business enterprises.

Lindsay sat back and listened carefully to each man who spoke. And, as in other situations like this when he was pressed, he tended to resist—politely but firmly. He chose his words carefully when he began to speak: "I have listened to what you have all said. Some of this will be done, but we must have a Police commissioner who agrees with it. Your goals are reasonable. You know that I have already proposed a Review Board with both police and civilians—more civilians than police. But we can't do it in two weeks. We can make a beginning." Then, unexpectedly and bluntly, he added: "Meanwhile, I will need your help—I may have to ask for a tax program to help pay for some of the things you want. You help me get that tax program passed and we'll have the money to improve the ghettos and hire more cops."

One visitor asked Lindsay: "Can Negroes sponsor housing?"
"Why not?" Lindsay replied.

"Then you are in favor of our proposals?"

"I agree in principle with all of your requests," Lindsay
said. "I hope to make a beginning as soon as I get into office.
We will be in touch with the representatives of this Council
on a regular basis. As for appointments, I have already appointed
three Negroes and I intend to appoint more. But my appointments will be based on merit, on experience and on talent—
not on race. I am sure you will all agree."

He then told the group to remain in touch with the aides
whom he had selected to attend this meeting: James W. Smith,
a Negro, was slated to become an assistant to the Mayor; Richard
Rosen, another mayoral assistant; and myself. The group nodded
in agreement and left quietly, some thanking the Mayor for
his frankness, others somewhat disappointed, but all—I felt
certain—impressed with the fact that Lindsay was going to try
to be a new and different kind of Mayor from anyone the
black community had known before.

During our last few weeks at the Roosevelt, I had grown
more and more aware of the competition between a number of
young Lindsay aides who had worked either for him or Price
in the campaign. I discovered two separate, and at times, almost
warring camps: "Price people" and "Lindsay people." One
campaign worker who fit neither description and, therefore,
was not chosen for a top spot was William F. Haddad, the ex-
New York Post and ex-*Herald Tribune* reporter who had twice
run unsuccessfully in the Democratic primary for Congress in
lower Manhattan, and who had served as an aide in Robert
Kennedy's successful 1964 Senate campaign. He told me he
wanted to head up Lindsay's antipoverty program, and he had,
in fact, arranged for Lindsay to appear at a series of public
forums in poor neighborhoods throughout the whole month of
December to hear complaints from the public. The hearings
were a tremendous success; Lindsay was mobbed wherever he
went. Still, Lindsay rejected Haddad's request for a top post and
Haddad subsequently dropped out of sight after the New Year.
Among Lindsay's reasons, I learned later, was that he did not
feel he could put complete trust in a man who had been touted

as a close ally of Robert Kennedy's. Lindsay left little doubt to those of us who knew him at the outset of his Administration that he viewed himself—as did the press—as a rival of Kennedy's. As writer William V. Shannon said on December 28 in an article entitled "Lindsay, Kennedy, and the Power Struggle in New York" in *Harper's* magazine: "There will be a direct confrontation between the brightest young stars of both parties—44-year-old Lindsay and 40-year-old Kennedy. It might come in the gubernatorial race of 1970. Or, since both men would like to be President and have a reasonably good chance of making it, their decisive encounter may not take place until November, 1972. Lindsay and the Republicans clearly bested Kennedy and the Democrats in the first round of their struggle for national power."

One of the tasks Lindsay had assigned to me on the day I was named press secretary was to "coordinate the system of making information public in all city agencies." This meant, he told me during the month of December, he wanted a thorough review of all city public relations personnel and some recommendations on who should be retained in the new Administration. On the surface, this seemed like a reasonable project. I had dealt with many of the public relations men in city departments and, with a few exceptions, I had not found them particularly well informed or talented. Still, I approached this task of making judgments about this group of men and women with some concern. Some of them expressed fear when they learned of my assignment. Several came into my office in the Roosevelt Hotel and told me stories of personal family hardships that had put them in positions too difficult to think of changing jobs. After a few of these visits, I saw how difficult it would be to make a judgment on whether or not the public relations personnel should remain on their jobs.

Nevertheless, I proceeded to call on the city's Personnel Department, and I formally requested a survey be taken of names, salaries, job titles and duties of all public relations, community relations people and photographers in city government. Bob Price asked me several times during that month of December how the "survey" was going. I replied that I had started it, but that I would not be able to complete it until we were in office. By this time, there was considerable interest among the press in the survey, too. The *New York Times* carried a story headlined: LINDSAY TO REVISE PUBLIC RELATIONS. The subhead read: Commissioners Must Clear Major Press Discussions. The story quoted me explaining that this meant commissioners would be free to talk to the press, but they would let the Mayor know what they planned to announce on "major matters." The *Times* story also quoted me as saying "ample notice" would be given those relieved of duties so they could find other jobs outside of city government. Salaries of the top Lindsay aides was another recurrent question in those weeks and days before we took office, but I was unable to give the answers because there were none: Price had not yet decided who was to receive what among Lindsay's top City Hall aides.

On December 25—Christmas Day—I had lunch with Maurice (Mickey) Carroll of the *New York Post*. He asked me to detail as much as possible my plans to cut back the public relations staff. Thinking that such a story would serve as a warning to many of those people who would have to receive their pink slips soon, I gave out my early findings in the preliminary survey I had made with the Personnel Department. I told Carroll I had found there were more than 200 persons on the city payroll in public and community relations jobs, including clerks and typists whose annual salary totalled $1.5 million. Since I was not anxious to take full responsibility for the firings that then seemed inevitable, I told Carroll that I would consult with Bob Price before cutting back. Thus, Carroll wrote on December 26 under a headline: LINDSAY READY TO SLASH THE MUNICIPAL PR STAFF: "Price, the Mayor-elect's closest adviser, will have the final word on who stays and who goes in press relations as, it appears, he has in all other aspects of the administration-to-be."

Carroll's story also pointed out that I was ordered upon my appointment by Lindsay to study how municipal information policies could be coordinated. "It is that study which revealed the unsuspected size of the public relations operation in government," Carroll continued. "Klein will report to Price next week and then, he says, he will launch a supplementary study of the numerous publications by city departments."

Actually, my preliminary survey had turned up more information than I thought it would. I was surprised at the number of people in public information and I was particularly amazed at the high salaries—many were in the $15,000 to $20,000 brackets and several went as high as $23,000. Generally, the highest salary in government during the Wagner years for any public official— with the exception of the Mayor and two Deputy Mayors— was $25,000 for commissioners; only a few city officials were paid more. I began to scrutinize each department or agency, the number of public relations personnel, individual names and salaries and Civil Service classification. I became aware, for example, of the fact that there were four separate and distinct categories: Unclassified: people who could be hired or fired at the Mayor's pleasure; Exempt: the same as Unclassified except that veterans could not be fired, except for cause; Competitive: people appointed from a Civil Service list after they have taken a Civil Service competitive examination—these could not be fired, but their jobs could be abolished; and Non-competitive: those who met Civil Service requirements but who could be hired without taking an exam and could be fired, except if they were veterans.

About this time, I was told by Price one day that Lindsay wanted to revamp WNYC, the city's municipal radio station. He said Lindsay had asked Richard D. Heffner, professor of communications and public policy at Rutgers University, to make a study. Heffner, a well-known television executive, was president of his own communications consulting firm and he had been a CBS editorial consultant and general manager of Channel 13 from 1961 to 1963. I saw no problem and promptly released the information to the press. The news release pointed out that Heffner's findings would be used to help reorganize and coordinate all of the city's public information and communications services.

The whole subject of communications was one which I discussed several times with Lindsay before we took office. He talked about using WNYC as a means of regular broadcasts to the people of the city, much in the same way that La Guardia once did. He wanted "live" television press conferences from City Hall, similar to the ones which John F. Kennedy held nationwide when he first took office. And Lindsay wanted new and modern equipment installed in the "Blue Room" at City Hall where mayors had traditionally held press conferences. He wanted to set up proper lines for radio and TV reporters. I agreed to look into the whole subject of revamping facilities for the electronic press in order to give him an opportunity to communicate regularly with the people of the city.

I was so enthusiastic about such a plan that I "leaked" a story to Marvin Sleeper of the *Journal-American*, one of the veteran City Hall newsmen. His paper carried a small story with the headline: LINDSAY TO TAKE HIS CASE TO PUBLIC—A LA FIORELLO. The story quoted me as saying that broader use of WNYC was part of the Mayor's plan to project the image of New York "as a proud city" and to change the people's attitude "from despair, hostility and pessimism to one of participation."

Meanwhile, in the background, looming up as a possible problem—but one which we did not really believe would occur —was the threat of a transit strike. I was asked many times by the press what we were doing about the threat, and time after time, in response to questions, I would tell reporters: "The Mayor-elect is in touch with the Wagner Administration and both sides in the dispute." I was uneasy, however, because I knew that, as a matter of fact, no negotiations had taken place since the day I joined Lindsay at the Roosevelt. On Sunday, December 12, the Mayor-elect discussed the contract demands with the three-man mediation panel he and Mayor Wagner had jointly selected three days earlier. Lindsay's ninety-minute meeting with the mediation board—which took place in his Congressional office at 30 West 44th Street—was his first participation in discussion on how to resolve the contract dispute. I accompanied him to his office where, for the first time, I met Nathan Feinsinger, the mediation board chairman, and Sylvester Garrett, both of whom had traveled long distances to help mediate the dispute. Feinsinger, who walked on crutches due to a hip ailment, was a professor of law at the University of Wisconsin at Madison and arbitrator of the contract between General Motors and the United Auto Workers Union. Garrett, a Pittsburgh resident, was permanent arbitrator between the

United Steelworkers Union and the United States Steel Corporation. The third member of the panel, New Yorker Theodore W. Kheel, was arbitrator of previous contracts between the Transit Authority and the 33,000-member Transport Workers Union.

After a congenial meeting, Lindsay stepped out into the narrow main floor corridor and announced to the awaiting reporters: "I have informed the mediators that I would like for them to keep me informed on all developments. I will receive their advice and suggestions and be kept up to date. I am sure Mayor Wagner will do the same." He said he thought the meeting with the mediation panel represented a "good beginning."

Following Lindsay, Feinsinger, sitting at a makeshift table in the hallway, told the reporters in a wry, offhand manner: "I have been designated chairman because of my age and my infirmities. We are old friends," he continued, pointing to Garrett and Kheel who flanked him. "We hope to achieve a reasonable settlement and before the strike deadline. We would like to get the pressure off and avert a cliffhanger. If everyone is normally reasonable, I think we'll get along all right."

Although this was Lindsay's first direct involvement in the talks, he still tried to remain aloof from the day-to-day negotiating. He had said several times—and again on this occasion—that he thought this was a matter that could best be worked out by the transit agency and the union, with the help of the mediators. It was obvious to me—and to the press—that neither the new Mayor nor the old Mayor wanted to be blamed for a strike, if there was to be one. Actually, I was not worried about such a possibility because the TWU had never struck the city's transit system in twenty-eight years of contract bargaining, despite Mike Quill's biennial threats and antics. This time, of course, Quill had said a new city Administration was taking over "in a maze of confusion," but few people took this rhetoric seriously.

On Tuesday, December 14, Lindsay announced that he intended to set up a permanent Mayor's Council on Transportation. He appointed Roswell B. Perkins, a former assistant secretary of the Department of Health, Education, and Welfare, to devise a plan to integrate the city's transportation system. In the meantime, Feinsinger had instructed both sides in the transit dispute to be prepared for full-scale contract talks and to submit their position papers. It appeared to me, a newcomer to politics and labor relations, that Lindsay was taking adequate precautions against a possible strike.

On Tuesday, December 21, Mayor Wagner, apparently somewhat concerned about lack of progress in the talks, went to the Americana Hotel himself and met with the mediation panel. "I told them it would be intolerable to have a strike," he reported after a ten-minute meeting with the negotiators and the mediation panel. "I urged them to speed up their talks," he added. It was Mayor Wagner's first direct participation in the negotiations since the three-man mediation panel had been named. The story in the *Times* the next day reported that he was asked if he thought Mayor-elect Lindsay should personally enter the talks at this time. "I don't know that that's necessary," was his reply. "I'm sure he'll come at the proper time. I have the responsibility at present because I'm still the Mayor." At the same time Mayor Wagner was asserting himself in the transit talks, he was also critical of Lindsay's attempt to postpone any actions by the Board of Estimate until after January 1. "I do not intend to see government paralyzed merely because of an indication that the next Administration would like the chance to make the decisions themselves," Wagner said. It was the first sign of acrimony between the outgoing and incoming Administrations I had seen.

Four days later—it was Saturday and Christmas—I realized there was genuine unrest among the mediation panel. Dr. Feinsinger was at his home in Aspen, Colorado, to celebrate the holidays when the news broke that the parleys at the Americana had become badly stalled. He telephoned Lindsay that he would cut his vacation short and he asked the Mayor-elect to meet with the mediators and both parties at the Americana on Monday, December 27.

On that Monday morning, I awakened to read on page one of the *Times* that "eight thousand shouting transit workers voted unanimously yesterday to strike the city's subways and buses at 5 A.M. the following Saturday if they did not have a satisfactory new contract." As I read down into the story early that morning, I became aware for the first time that Mike Quill's "charade" might be something more serious. Mayor Wagner would be leaving office on January 1. Joseph E. O'Grady, the Transit Authority chairman, had announced he planned to retire shortly after January 1. Quill was complaining publicly about "meddlers" hindering a contract settlement. He named the *New York Times* for one, which, he said, was giving advice to Lindsay against the interest of the union.[2] Quill was quoted as saying his union "is closer to a strike than any time in our history. O'Grady, an experienced man, is getting out; Mayor Wagner, experienced in mediation, is getting out; John Lindsay is coming in with new faces we are not keen about." Meanwhile, the Transit Authority had made it clear it already faced a $43 million deficit in the fiscal year ending June 30, 1966, and it estimated Quill's demand for a four-day, thirty-two-hour week, and 30 percent wage increase and other contract improvements at about $680 million in a two-year contract. The previous contract in 1963 had been settled for $39 million.

A little shaken by these developments, I accompanied Lindsay to the Americana for a "fact-finding" meeting with the Transit Authority and the union leadership on December 27. I felt somehow reassured that once Lindsay stepped into the negotiations everything would be worked out quickly. Quill was making headlines, I thought to myself, but he had made those same threats many times before. It was all part of the cat-and-mouse game, I thought, and Quill was entitled to his moment in the sun. He had to prove to his men that he was as tough, colorful and demanding as ever.

At the meeting with the members of the Transit Authority in a fourth-floor suite at the Americana Hotel, I heard that the Transit Authority was hoping for a settlement of no more than a 3.2 percent raise—the national labor-management guidelines figure. In dollars and cents, such a settlement would cost the city about $35 to $40 million over two years. The Transit Authority chairman, Joseph O'Grady, flatly declared: "The settlement should be 3.2 percent. It's within the framework of Presidential guidelines. That's all there is to it."

Lindsay replied: "Yes, that's fair and reasonable. But Mike is going for a bundle. He's asking for $45 to $50 million over two years." After a short discussion, the other Transit Authority members—Daniel T. Scannell and John J. Gilhooley—agreed with O'Grady that a $35 to $40 million settlement would be a decent package for the employees and the public. They agreed it should all be in wages, no pension increases and that there should be no reduction in the work week. That left one un-answered question: How would the Transit Authority raise $35 or $40 million?

State law required that the Transit Authority pay its operating expenses out of its own revenues, not from city subsidy. One way to raise revenue, of course, would be to raise the fare on buses and subways, a politically dangerous move that had been resisted year after year. Now, clearly, if the 15-cent fare were to be preserved, the law would have to be changed or circumvented. The Transit Authority operated not only all city-owned buses and subways, but also buses of the huge Manhattan and Bronx Surface Transit Operating Authority (MABSTOA). This line too would need help if it was to hold the fare at 15 cents, and still meet the cost of a new contract with Quill's union. Moreover, another union, representing employees of the city's small private bus lines, were awaiting a signal from Quill before pressing their demands.

Gilhooley wanted some of the necessary money to come from a joint treasury that would result from an amalgamation of all city transportation agencies, including the Robert Moses-dominated Triborough Bridge and Tunnel Authority, a profit-making enter-prise. "We can preserve the fare by moving rapidly to amalgamate all these agencies," he said. "We can put it through this session of the Legislature—with the maximum cooperation of Albany—by the latest April 1." Someone else reminded Lindsay that in his transportation white paper he had suggested using the city's gasoline tax and license fees for the purpose of aiding mass transportation. But this, too, would require state legislation. Then the question of a union lawsuit came up, if the Transit Authority should decide to wait until the Legislature passed the necessary law to combine all city transportation departments. The more we discussed the problem, the more tangled it seemed.

Lindsay then met privately with Quill and a few of Quill's aides. I was not in the room. He took only Bob Price inside with him. After meeting with Quill, and with the panel of mediators,

Lindsay seemed to suddenly grow tense. To newsmen, he would only say that he expected both sides to negotiate what he called a "fair, reasonable and equitable settlement. I am neither optimistic nor pessimistic about a settlement at this point," he told them. "I am a realist. I am not an expert in labor matters. There are involved human problems here," he continued. On the touchy problem of preserving the 15-cent fare, in answer to a reporter's question, he commented: "I strongly hope and deeply feel that the fare ought to be preserved in these negotiations. I believe it will be kept." On the way out of the hotel, Lindsay posed—for a moment—so photographers could take pictures of him alongside Quill. Lindsay looked a little tired and Quill was pale and thin. The union chief seemed to walk with some difficulty, leaning heavily on a cane.

As I left the Americana with Lindsay, I noticed that his mood had become somber. For the first time, he seemed troubled about what lay ahead in the transit crisis. He jumped into the back of the waiting limousine outside and sat for several minutes looking out the window. "This is going to be a bitch," he said, after a long pause.

The next day, December 28, at the Roosevelt, Lindsay and Price asked for reports from all appointees about what they planned to do in the event of a transit strike. James B. Kelley, the outgoing deputy city administrator, said Mayor Wagner's Emergency Control Board had last met on December 9. Lindsay then instructed me to announce that he had formed his own Committee on Transit and that the following people should be on the list: Deputy Mayor-City Administrator Costello; Police Commissioner Broderick; Fire Commissioner Lowery; Corporation Counsel Rankin; Transportation Coordinator Palmer; Traffic Commissioner Barnes; Parks Commissioner Hoving; Sanitation Commissioner Periconi; and myself.

We discussed possible measures that could be taken in case the union struck. It was suggested that doctors could ride with radio police cars to respond to emergency calls. Other ideas included: staggering work hours for city personnel and reassigning city personnel to areas near their residences. Lindsay said he wanted WNYC to prepare and send out information to the general public and an emergency telephone number (999-1234) was selected for the public to call to obtain strike information. He said private industry could be encouraged to stagger work hours, too, and the Board of Education could stagger classes in order to avoid heavy concentrated automobile traffic. Lindsay told Barnes to insist publicly that all "non-essential" driving be avoided and that every car that was on the road "be filled up." Someone suggested that people could charter buses in large groups to and from work. And, he added, perhaps the schools should even be closed for the duration of the emergency, if there was one. The meeting seemed almost unreal. We were trying to prepare ourselves for a crisis with which none of us had any previous experience. After the meeting, I released the following:

STATEMENT BY MAYOR-ELECT JOHN V. LINDSAY: I met with my emergency committee to apprise myself of the preparations underway in the event of a transit strike. We discussed plans already under consideration and we arranged to work out more details. I have instructed Tim Costello to report back in 24 hours with additional information about steps we could take. I wish to stress the action should in no way be construed as meaning I expect a strike. This was purely a routine, precautionary step.

Meanwhile, it had been reported that the Transit Authority was planning to go to Court to seek an injunction—as it did in 1963—to bar the strike if an agreement was not reached soon. By now, I was beginning to believe that there might, indeed, be a transit strike. Still, it did not seem to me that it could last very long. New Year's Eve was only two nights away and I felt that nobody—including the bus and subway men—really wanted a strike. Nevertheless, the atmosphere at the Roosevelt became increasingly intense. The December 29 meeting of Lindsay's "Committee on Transit" turned out to be a working session at which specific steps were agreed upon in the event of a walkout. "I want to assure New Yorkers," Lindsay told us grimly, "that provisions have been taken by the city and all of its departments to handle the situation. I want city government cut back to essential agencies. I want to be certain that only essential industries send their people to work—that would include food, fuel, medical, banks, communications and perhaps one or two others." Lindsay said he planned to ask "essential industries" to send as few people into work as possible—about 50 percent of all personnel. He said he also planned to request taxi companies to cruise along bus routes and to arrange for private car owners to use large parks for parking areas. And he would urge all people who normally drove into the city to use commuter rail and bus lines, instead.

On December 30, a *Times* editorial pointed up what most of us close to the negotiations already knew: There would be a strike if the only alternative was giving in to Quill's demands.[3] Two more meetings of the Committee on Transit ironed out more details of what we would do, and ask the citizens of New York to do. It was decided that an "Emergency Control Center" with Tim Costello in charge would be set up at 60 Center Street, where the City of New York had already had a vast communications system in operation. Lindsay then asked me to release another statement to the press outlining the procedures we would ask the public to follow if there was a strike. He was careful to preface the release with the following underlined cautionary note: "The following announcement should not be taken in any way to indicate that I believe there will be a strike. It is my belief that a fair agreement should be reached and thus, that the public interest will be served. Nevertheless, I see no alternative but to take this preliminary step and I do so after consulting with Dr. Nathan Feinsinger, chairman of the distinguished panel of mediators in the transit negotiations." I was growing quite concerned about the possible consequences of a citywide transit strike.

At the same time, I was happily anticipating the Inaugural Ball, a major social event which was set to be held at the Americana Hotel, the same site as the transit negotiations, on the evening of Saturday, January 1. I was busy getting copies of Lindsay's inaugural speech[4] ready for distribution to all radio, TV stations, newspapers and magazines. He was scheduled to be sworn in officially on Saturday morning at 10 A.M. in a formal ceremony in front of City Hall.

Overall, I felt gratified that Lindsay had been able to cope with so many unexpected events in this period before assuming office. He had made a number of good appointments, gained a start on his plan to reorganize city government, met with important civic groups, and most importantly, I thought, he was going into office with a reservoir of good will among the press in the city. Despite the rash of "leaks" in the early weeks of December, the Mayor's personal relations with newsmen remained good. As Debs Myers, a former press secretary to Mayor Wagner, told a reporter in the closing days of December: "John Lindsay is the only man I've ever heard of who is already the greatest Mayor in history before he takes office."

With one more day to go, I felt the excitement of moving into City Hall. Less than two months before, during the famous blackout of 1965, I had spent the night at City Hall as a WCBS television reporter interviewing Mayor Wagner and waiting for the crisis to be over. Much of that waiting time had been spent in the office of Paul R. Bragdon, then press secretary, the office that was to be mine in twenty-four hours.

As the suspense heightened, the two major transit unions walked out of the negotiations at the Americana, charging that the Transit Authority had failed to even make an opening offer. The union spokesman said they would not return until Lindsay joined the talks on a continuing basis. "If he doesn't do this," Mike Quill was quoted as saying, "the whole thing will be decided on the streets." Quill said Lindsay had acted "like a babe in the woods." He demanded that the Mayor put in a full eight-hour day at the bargaining table. "It's now his baby," Quill added. Lindsay responded to Quill's ultimatum with a controlled statement that he would meet with the mediation panel on the morning of Friday, December 31, and that he would decide then on further steps he might take.

Then, in a dramatic gesture on television Thursday night, December 30, Quill tore up the court papers that had been served on him during the day. The Transit Authority had obtained a "show cause" order in State Supreme Court earlier in the day calling upon Quill and other officers of the union to explain why they should not be enjoined from striking the subway and bus lines. Dr. Feinsinger had asked both parties to start compromising, stating in particular that the Transit Authority could not refuse to make a money offer. Meanwhile, Mayor Wagner removed himself from the strike controversy and boarded a plane for Mexico City, saying: "From now on, it's the responsibility of the Transit Authority, the mediators, the unions and the Mayor-elect."

On the last day, Friday, December 31, the mediators continued to try and get the union leaders to reduce their demands and to get the Transit Authority to make a formal offer. But both sides held off making any commitments, apparently waiting for Lindsay to reach the Americana and tell them how much money would be available for a labor settlement. Earlier that day, Lindsay had been at the Americana, but only for the purpose of conferring with the mediators. He had first sat down at a joint meeting of the Transit Authority and the two unions at 12:38 P.M. At the outset of this meeting, the Mayor-elect, looking strained but stern, had urged both parties to "settle the dispute in the public interest. The union has waited until the 11th hour."

Quill's lips tightened. "You wanted the job and you're here for the duration," he had snapped in reply. "Why don't you grow up and stop being a juvenile. That's a lie that we waited until the last hour. We still haven't got a legitimate offer from the Transit Authority. I say you are telling us a deliberate lie."

About an hour after it started, Quill had left the meeting to hold a hallway press conference during which he heaped abuse on Lindsay. He said he had left the session only after cautioning Dr. Feinsinger not to let "that pipsqueak Lindsay" leave the building.

After Quill had stormed out of his meeting, Lindsay had held private talks with the Transit Authority and with the mediators. We all had lunch together in our new suite on the forty-ninth floor. At 3:30 P.M. a much calmer Quill and the negotiators for both the Transport Workers Union and the Amalgamated Transit Union joined Lindsay and the mediators in our suite. At this session, Dr. Feinsinger urged Quill to reduce his demands, which the Transit Authority had estimated would cost $680 million. Quill refused to lower his demands and the session broke up quickly. At 5:10 P.M., Lindsay left the Americana to go to City Hall where he was officially sworn in by Supreme Court Justice William C. Hecht, Jr., in a private ceremony at 6:04 P.M. in the presence of Mrs. Lindsay, the Lindsay children and a few close friends. Lindsay wore a dark, pinstripe suit and blue tie with a diagonal green stripe. Mary, who stood by his side as the oath was administered, wore an apple-green, silk cocktail dress adorned with a string of pearls. The ceremony, which took only six minutes, went smoothly. I told the reporters the Mayor would not answer questions about the transit strike until he returned to the Americana later in the evening. They accepted my request— grudgingly. Shortly after Lindsay was sworn in, at 7:45 P.M., State Supreme Court Justice George Tilzer temporarily enjoined the unions from striking.[5]

At 9 P.M., Quill emerged from what he called a final meeting of his 1,000-member committee in the Americana. Angry once again, he warned: "Only a miracle can bring about a settlement tonight, and I personally don't believe in miracles." He also repeated his intention to defy the court injunction, which he had already publicly torn up. "If they want the body in jail," he shouted in his brogue to newsmen, "they can have it. We have five teams to carry on the strike." Asked by a newsman whether he disliked John Lindsay and was, therefore, going to carry out his threat of a strike, Quill replied: "I have no dislike for him. But I don't think he knows what it's all about. In our talks with him, he sits and stares and looks over my head."

After Lindsay was sworn in, I had left City Hall for home and a quick dinner with my family before leaving for the Americana. While at home, I thought of the events of the past six months— of the campaign, Lindsay's victory, the plans for reform, my appointment and the worldwide interest in the man who at midnight would become the 103rd Mayor of the City of New York. Despite the impending transit strike and some of the internal political problems I had discovered at the Roosevelt since December 1, I still felt optimistic about the upcoming year. It would, I thought, be the year of the city, as Lindsay had once said. It would be the beginning of a major renaissance in municipal government—a time when all New Yorkers would join in to uplift their city. As I looked forward to our bargaining session with Quill later that evening—New Year's Eve—at the Americana, I was hopeful that an agreement would be reached and that we would begin the next day to make New York a Proud City.

3 *"This is a city which is on its knees."*

"You," shouted Michael J. Quill, pointing his finger at the new Mayor of New York, "are nothing but a juvenile, a lightweight, and a pipsqueak. You have to grow up. You don't know anything about the working class. You don't know anything about labor unions."

Quill was standing in Albert Hall, a large curtained, secluded room in the basement of the Americana Hotel. As his voice bellowed throughout the room where negotiations were taking place, he leaned on a black cane. His face was bright red. Watching him intently and sitting directly opposite were the three members of the Transit Authority. Lindsay, the transit mediation panel, Bob Price and I sat at a small table between the two sides with our backs against the curtain.

As Quill delivered his vitriolic attack, Lindsay's face paled. I leaned over and whispered, "Take it easy. Keep your cool." His jaw tightened and began to twitch slightly. When Quill finished and sat down, Lindsay slowly rose.

"I don't mind your words about me personally," he responded. "You are entitled to your own opinion. But I will not have you addressing the office of the Mayor that way. It is an affront to the people of the City of New York."

I glanced down at my watch. It was two minutes past midnight. Lindsay was now officially Mayor of New York. I leaned forward, excited. Lindsay's voice rose.

"Mr. Quill, distinguished New Yorkers," he continued, looking at the crowd of union workers sitting behind Quill, "I call upon you and all of your members not to walk out on your city. This is a city which is on its knees. We have obligations. You have an obligation to your members. I have an obligation to eight million people. A strike will create great personal hardships for everyone. It will have a disastrous effect on the city's major life functions. I am inheriting a bankrupt city with a multitude of problems. I therefore call upon you in the public interest to respect the city in which you live and all of its eight million inhabitants. I am asking you to extend this contract long enough for me to pull the show together. I am asking you to come to my suite of rooms and spend the night negotiating this matter. We have an obligation to stretch ourselves." Lindsay sat down. After a pause, Quill replied:

"We do not agree with you that the city is bankrupt. We do not think that the city is as bad as you say it is. I would urge you to stop campaigning. The election is over, Mr. Lindsley [sic]. I now have before me your offer of a $25 million wage package. I am not going to turn it down here. Although I can tell you I intend to recommend that it be turned down. We are not going to stay here all night. This is lunacy."

Then, without any apparent notice, Quill stood up and declared: "It is after midnight. And I tell you as the Mayor of New York that there is a transit strike. As far as I'm concerned, the strike is as good as on." Then Quill abruptly left the room.

Up to the moment Quill walked out, I had believed that despite the bitterness and histrionics, a strike could be avoided. Lindsay sat quietly for a full minute after Quill walked out. He appeared stunned. So did the mediators who, I felt, should have done something to have avoided such a final move by Quill when there were still nearly five hours left in which to bargain. The strike deadline had previously been set by the union for 5 A.M.

Earlier in the evening, even when the negotiations were going slowly, I had still felt confident that a strike would be avoided. At about 8 P.M. the Transit Authority had informed the mediators it was prepared to offer a 3.2 percent increase in wages and fringe benefits, totaling about $25 million for a two-year contract. Full-scale negotiations had gotten underway about 10 P.M. when O'Grady told Quill that he had given the mediators a "fair, equitable and substantial" offer, but that he would not present it to the union until the union reduced its contract demands. The union then had retired to caucus and ten minutes later, returned. Quill had asked the Transit Authority for the "dollar evaluation" of the offer.

"We won't tell you until you reduce your demands," O'Grady had replied.

"This sounds like 'What's My Line?' " Quill had snapped back. "We won't play a hiding game. We'll only bargain until midnight."

At this point, Lindsay had asked the mediators for another break in order to meet with the Transit Authority members, who appeared to be unwilling to make their offer public. We left the room and went next door to an adjoining conference room on the same floor. We were sitting at a round table—the three Transit Authority members, the mediators, the Mayor and myself.

I remember leaning over to Lindsay and saying, "They have to make a public offer, John. If there is no Transit Authority offer, there will definitely be a strike. It's that simple." Although I knew little about labor negotiating, I believed that unless the Transit Authority put an offer on the table, the whole thing would collapse. The Mayor responded to my suggestion:

"We have to have your offer," Lindsay said aloud, turning to O'Grady. "We have no alternative."

After a short conference with his two colleagues, O'Grady agreed to make public his $25 million offer. When we returned to the big room and O'Grady finally named the figure of $25 million, there was an outbreak of derisive laughter from Quill and the other union negotiators. Quill then launched his attack on the Mayor, and Lindsay replied with his appeal—only to have Quill get up and walk out. We remained at the Americana long enough to hold a brief press conference at about 1 A.M. I wrote out a statement which I handed to Lindsay to read to the entourage of awaiting newsmen:

As you may know by now, negotiations between the Transport Workers Union and the Transit Authority have broken down. It appears certain there will be a subway strike beginning at 5:00 A.M. this morning. It is my hope that this dispute can still be speedily resolved and normal transit service soon restored. I have urged all parties to the negotiations to continue vigorous efforts toward achieving a prompt and reasonable settlement to get on with the job of constructive collective bargaining. I must also ask the public's cooperation in surmounting the hardships that will now be imposed.

A day later, one newspaper account of this night at the negotiating tables in the Americana quoted one unnamed person who took part in the talks describing the atmosphere as follows:

It was down with the English Protestant! Up with the Irish! Obviously, the new aristocratic 44-year-old Yale-educated Mayor, whose ancestors came from the Isle of Wight, was viewed as no match by some who attended the session for the crusty, rough-speaking 60-year-old Transit Workers Union president from Ireland's County Kerry!

Or, as columnist Jimmy Breslin, writing for the *Herald Tribune,* put it:

Mike Quill is a man of the past. John Lindsay standing in front of him, was young and tall and thin with hair falling down onto his forehead. His speech is out of Yale and the theatre district. Lindsay is a man of tomorrow, when there would be a chance to try to become President of the United States. John Lindsay looked at Quill and he saw the past. And Mike Quill looked at John Lindsay and he saw the Church of England.

We arrived at City Hall at 1:40 A.M. on that first morning in January, 1966. The scene was chaotic. Everywhere I looked people were running around, unpacking cartons, trying out unfamiliar telephones, looking for office supplies—notebooks, pencils, mimeograph machines and paper, erasers, pens. As it turned out, the previous occupants had thoroughly cleaned out their offices and there was very little to be found on the shelves or in desk drawers.

I entered the press secretary's office, a large, elegant old room with two wall windows facing City Hall Plaza. It had previously been occupied by Paul Bragdon, who was Mayor Wagner's last "executive secretary" and acting press secretary after Debs Myers and Leslie Slote had left politics a few months earlier. There was a handsome red mahogany desk—modeled after an original of the Mayor's desk, which was itself a replica of the writing table George Washington used in the nation's first capital a few blocks to the south of City Hall. On top of the desk I found a small blue-and-white-covered paperback. It was a copy of Machiavelli's *The Prince*. A piece of paper had been inserted in it. I opened to the page and a passage of it caught my eye: "There is nothing more difficult to take in hand, more precarious to conduct, or more uncertain in its success, than to take the lead in the introduction of a new order of things." In the Mayor's office, a more pointed message had been left by one of our Democratic predecessors: a picture of General Douglas MacArthur, inscribed with his famed vow: "I shall return."

Shortly after 2 A.M., with all the TV and radio cameras already set up in the 32-by-28-foot Blue Room across the hall from the Mayor's office, Lindsay held his first full-scale press conference. He began: "Fellow New Yorkers: First of all, may I wish you a happy 1966." He told his viewers it appeared "certain" there would be a subway strike beginning at 5 A.M. and that all city departments had been ordered to put emergency plans into operation. He told his New Year's Eve audience that, should the strike continue to Monday, only 25 percent of those who normally travel into Manhattan would be able to do so. Therefore, he said, he was restricting all "non-essential" auto travel into the city—people engaged in the "critical activities" of providing food, fuel or medical services; or who are requested to come in by their employers because they were "essential" and individuals who would suffer "unusual and severe economic hardship" if they stayed away. He asked New Yorkers for their cooperation and said he hoped all hardships would be held to a minimum. It was a brief but sober announcement and most of us just accepted it as routine. I was distressed that the strike was now a certainty, but I felt it would not last more than a day or two.

My first hours as press secretary at City Hall were occupied trying to figure out how the telephones on my desk worked. I began to receive press calls almost the moment I walked into the office. *The Times, Herald Tribune, Daily News, World-Telegram, Journal-American* and *Post* each had at least one reporter at City Hall in the middle of the night to cover Lindsay's first hours as Mayor. The electronic press—radio and television—sent twenty-five to thirty more correspondents and crews, and there were more than a half dozen magazine and foreign press representatives, too—a press corps totaling about fifty people. During the night, Lindsay took a two hour and fifteen minute nap, sleeping on a couch in the small gymnasium in the City Hall basement beneath his office. The rest of us found some cots and moved them into our offices. I slept for about two hours on a cot in my office, taking turns with Warren Gardner. Although there were no new developments in the strike all night, the newsmen remained until morning. About 2 A.M., I was sworn in as press secretary by Bob Price during an informal ceremony, along with a group of commissioners on duty. We all crowded into the new Deputy Mayor's office and participated in a brief ceremony. I was officially sworn in as "Elihu B. Klein"—my real name—and with the official title of "Director of Communications," which Price had suggested I use.

At about 6 A.M., I went inside to tell the Mayor that the press wanted some comments from him about his next step in the strike.

"You mean to say the press is still here?" he said, incredulously.

"Yes, and they are likely to remain with us for a long time," I replied. Shortly after 6 A.M., a group of fresh new faces greeted me in the press office from the news media—the day shifts from the newspapers, radio and television stations. They came into my office, in groups of twos and threes, asking to speak to the new Mayor. I told them their colleagues during the night shift had talked with him, but they wanted their own stories—their own quotes. They had been sent to "The Hall" to do a job and they wanted to do it—no matter how little sleep anybody else had, including the new Mayor. For the first time, I grew impatient because nothing at all had happened during the night relating to the strike. Nevertheless, in order to pacify the new shift I asked the Mayor to hold another press conference, and he obliged. The questions dealt mostly with what he had eaten, whom he had talked to, how he liked being Mayor—the usual human-interest type questions. Finally, when asked what his plans were, Lindsay replied: "I'm going up to the Roosevelt Hotel to shave and shower, have some cornflakes, see my children and kiss my wife." The newsmen laughed—and finally let him go. I went home, too.

About 10 A.M., I was back at my desk in City Hall, receiving telephone calls, readying for another press conference in the Blue Room at the southwest end of the building, the same room in which Lindsay had been sworn in some sixteen hours before. He called me on our interoffice phone and told me he was going to announce to the public various steps which he had worked out with four key commissioners, each of whom would attend the press conference with him. They were: Henry Barnes, Traffic; Vince Broderick, Police; Bob Lowery, Fire; and Alonzo Yerby, Hospitals.

I went into the Blue Room where a large crowd of newsmen awaited the new Mayor. The chairs needed straightening so I lined them up properly. I asked the TV crews to remove some of their equipment so the "written press" could be seated. The room was so crowded by the time I brought the Mayor in, he could hardly get through the mob of newsmen to the desk in the Blue Room on which a cluster of microphones was perched. At about 11 A.M. he began his news conference by reading a statement that had been hastily compiled a little earlier with the help of Tim Costello and others.

Lindsay reported that traffic was light, but he expected it to get heavier as the day wore on. Therefore, he announced he was cancelling the plans for the five borough receptions that had been scheduled in connection with inaugural ceremonies from noon to 5 P.M. What was to have been the city's showiest inaugural since George Washington was sworn in as President in New York in 1789 was reduced to an outdoor inaugural speech at City Hall Plaza at 7 P.M. Following this, the Inaugural Ball at the Americana Hotel was to take place.

As for the strike, Lindsay said, "I remain committed to the principle that the public interest must be served." He ordered public schools closed and then he listed traffic regulations, in the event the strike continued through Monday. He urged New Yorkers to stay home, if possible, or to get to work before 8 A.M.

He said only "essential" industries should continue during the strike. "This unfortunate disruption of our city's vital transit services will, in the best of circumstances, impose untold hardships on New Yorkers and I can only hope that this hardship will be held to the absolute minimum," he continued. "I feel confident that as New Yorkers who are proud of our city, you and I together will be able to endure this critical emergency, and again I wish all of you a happy New Year and I look forward to working for you and with you for the betterment of our city."

After the press conference was over, I accompanied Lindsay back into his inner office in the northwest wing of the building. He seemed buoyant and in good spirits.

"How did I do?" he asked.

"Very well," I replied. "You're doing the best you can under the circumstances."

"You have to be tough," Lindsay said, talking more to himself than to any of the aides who were gathered around him.

It was a wild, virtually uncontrollable scene on the first official day in office. Lindsay's small 20-by-22-foot office, decorated in a motif typical of the post-Revolutionary period, was jammed with young aides, secretaries, would-be advisers from outside of government, and, at times, members of the press. I found it impossible to talk to Lindsay for more than thirty seconds without being interrupted. I could not find out what he really thought about the strike, nor could I determine what his plans were. As a result, I could not answer all of the questions from the press. To get their answers, reporters would buttonhole the Mayor as he walked in and out of his office. The press jammed the hallway between the Mayor's office and the Blue Room next door. It was impossible for the Mayor to leave his office without being almost accosted by a dozen TV cameramen and a mob of reporters. Asked by one reporter whether he would attend any of the bargaining sessions at the Americana that day, the Mayor replied firmly: "I shall not go there today. I shall be right here at City Hall running the city. If my physical presence is necessary and it is requested by the mediators, then I will order all the parties to City Hall." Later in the day, when told of Lindsay's comment, Quill responded: "We would refuse to go to City Hall. No counter proposal will be made to the peanuts package. Negotiations are so loused up now that only time will loosen it up."

I spent much of the afternoon informing the press corps in Room 9—the City Hall press room—who was visiting Lindsay and trying to find out what decisions had been made. It was still difficult to get Lindsay to sit still long enough to summarize for me what he had been discussing. Many of his aides also seemed to block entry to his office by jamming the inner office and just hanging around waiting to tell him what each thought he should do. He conferred with Vince Broderick at some length in the afternoon, giving rise to speculation that the Police Department was going to lay down some firm regulations about parking and driving. But neither the Mayor nor Broderick was very communicative after their meeting. And so the afternoon wore on without much happening. It was a decided anticlimax after the suspense of the night before. The only important activity was within Lindsay's office, where he was busy rewriting his speech because, as he had said at the time, it "did not quite catch the spirit" of the hour. After he had finished putting his pencil to it, I marked it, "For release on delivery, 7 P.M., Saturday, January 1, 1966," read it over carefully and gave it to a secretary to be run off on the mimeograph machine. (See Appendix, pages 304–307).

As a result of the events of the previous twenty-four hours— and a *Times* editorial in the morning—the Mayor placed an insert into the speech about the strike. The *Times* had said, editorially: "The immediate need is for a demonstration by Mr. Lindsay that the city will not capitulate by granting wage increases and other concessions beyond those justified by economic reality. The recommendations of the three expert mediators . . . represent the only dependable guidelines to a fair settlement. Anything more would be appeasement." Accordingly, Lindsay inserted the following passage into his speech:

"As I speak, our city is crippled by a strike against the bus and subway system. It is an unlawful strike against the public interest, called even before the collective bargaining process had run its course. It is an act of defiance against eight million people. I shall not permit the public interest to be flaunted, no matter how severe the stress. The oath of office I have just taken requires me to uphold the law of the land. That I shall do—in the name of those eight million people. I say to the parties to this dispute that theirs is the immediate responsibility for arriving at a swift and equitable settlement and I insist that they discharge that responsibility."

The main body of the speech itself was a blueprint for the changes Lindsay hoped to bring about.[1] He emphasized the "Proud City" theme: "My hope," he said, "is that the highest levels of this Administration will establish a moral and ethical tone which will pervade every department and agency with an unshakable respect for decency and honesty. In this way we shall lay the foundation for the Proud City. My vision of the Proud City encompasses far more than self-esteem; the phrase describes the kind of city we hope to achieve for ourselves and our sons and daughters—a city in which each individual can fulfill himself in dignity and freedom."

As Lindsay spoke from a flag-decked stand to an audience of more than 2,500 people in flood-lit City Hall Plaza, I stood on the top steps behind him and looked at the crowd. There was warm applause seven times throughout the ten-minute speech from the onlookers, many of whom were in formal dress in preparation for the Inaugural Ball at the Americana which was to follow. It was an unusual night in many respects. The temperature outside was springlike, in the upper fifties, and most of the commissioners being sworn in, as well as the Mayor, did not wear a topcoat. When Lindsay finished, the audience cheered and clapped. After thirty-five seconds the applause was still thunderous, but Bennett Cerf, who was serving as master of ceremonies, shut it off with a wave of his hands in order to keep the program on schedule.

On Saturday night, January 1, 1966, my wife and I, in formal dress, went up to the Americana Hotel. It was somewhat ironic, I thought, as we entered the hotel, that only twenty-four hours before I had gone to the same place with Lindsay and sat by his side while the transit strike had begun. The Inaugural Ball was a crowded, joyful affair. Audrey and I spent most of the evening in a private box overlooking the dance floor with the Lindsays. Despite the strike, the atmosphere was altogether happy.

Lindsay had many visitors wishing him well during the evening. The picture that made a lasting impression on me was Sammy Davis, Jr.'s entrance: Davis, an old friend of Lindsay's, literally jumped a foot off the floor and into Lindsay's outstretched arms as the two men exchanged bear hugs. It was a marvelous demonstration of affection—Davis, about five feet two inches, in the arms of the six foot four inch Lindsay. The whole evening temporarily took some of the pressure off a situation that had left all of us tense and fatigued. The new Mayor even managed a quip about the awesome strike: "I've been in office less than a day," he told the crowd in the ballroom, "and I've already solved the problem of crime in the subways."

The next day—Sunday, January 2—there was some movement in the negotiations. Quill reduced his demands from $680 million to a package estimated at $180 million. But O'Grady commented at the Americana after both sides completed their first joint bargaining session since the strike began at midnight Friday: "We don't regard it as a counter-proposal made in good faith." The joint session started at 5:30 P.M. Sunday and ran until 1 A.M. Monday when Kheel emerged to tell reporters that the strike would not be settled in time for the beginning of the business week. All he could give was a "dismal report." At 11 A.M. on Sunday, Lindsay had left the Roosevelt Hotel and set out for City Hall—walking. Wearing a black topcoat but hatless in the forty-degree weather, Lindsay strode from the Roosevelt to his office in fifty-five minutes—a distance of seventy blocks or a little more than three miles. When Lindsay got to his office, he conferred with Don Elliott, his counsel, about the reappointment of some Criminal Court judges, scheduled a few hours later. He also talked with Dr. Feinsinger on the telephone and he asked Tim Costello to call an emergency meeting at City Hall of all commissioners whose departments were involved in the strike operations.

At 1:30 P.M. he called me and told me he wanted to look at the Civil Defense headquarters nearby where the city's emergency communications center had been set up. We left at 1:40 P.M. in the rain for the center—a five-minute walk. He walked so fast that Tim Costello, Sy Siegel, head of WNYC, the city's radio station, and I had trouble keeping up with him. So did a majority of the reporters and photographers, who were busy scribbling notes or snapping pictures. The Civil Defense headquarters, I was surprised to find out, was a large basement room with rows of cubicles where staff personnel were answering telephones. We walked up and down the aisles, listening to conversations between New Yorkers and the clerks taking messages. Lindsay took a telephone from one of the men, John Roche, and began talking to a caller named John Friedman, of Queens, a garment district worker, who was anxious about reporting to his job the next day. He had heard Lindsay appeal to all New Yorkers to stay home unless they were "essential."

"Hello, Mr. Friedman, this is John Lindsay," the Mayor said to the startled caller. "Look, I have asked all employers to try and let their employees stay home until the emergency is over. I am sure your boss will understand if you do not come to work tomorrow. So stay home and help ease the congestion, will you?"

As I stood by Lindsay's side, listening to this conversation, I imagined what John Friedman of Queens must be thinking. He had just talked to the new Mayor of New York—but was that enough to satisfy his boss?

After our visit to the Civil Defense center, we returned to City Hall and, for the first time, Lindsay decided he wanted to talk to the reporters on their home grounds—in Room 9. I thought it was a good idea and I encouraged him to walk right into the room.

The reporters were pleased to learn that Lindsay was a "regular guy." He sat on the edge of one of the battered, old desks in the press room and answered all of their questions. I was delighted. Maurice (Mickey) Carroll of the *Post* asked me if this was going to be a "regular thing." I replied: "Why not? The Mayor wants to establish direct contact with the press and what better way is there than coming to the press room?" I realized as I answered the question, that I was engaging in some wishful thinking, because I knew that Lindsay really wanted to remain aloof and did not want to mingle with the press. Only hours after we had arrived in City Hall, the Mayor began asking me to "keep the press away from my office."

Lindsay went from his Room 9 talk to an official swearing-in of nine Criminal Court judges upstairs in the Board of Estimate

Chambers. Then he told me he wanted to hold another press conference in the Blue Room. I had the room set up for the conference and, in a little while, Lindsay was seated at a table with the cluster of microphones in front of him. It had been less than twenty-four hours since he had taken the oath of office as Mayor in this same room. The flowers on the mantlepiece behind him, remnants of the swearing-in ceremony, were still there, but faded and wilted. Despite the lack of sleep, Lindsay appeared even more vigorous than he had the night before.

In a carefully prepared appeal to New Yorkers on that Sunday, the Mayor asked all "non-essential" workers to voluntarily keep their cars off the streets in order to assure the continuance of essential services—police and fire protection, the movement of ambulances, the shipments of food and fuel. He appealed to every New Yorker to be "reasonable" and to judge for himself whether or not he should report to work the next morning. "It's very difficult for a man, when he's shaving in the morning, to look at himself and say, 'I'm not really essential to my job.' Most people prefer not to do that. Most people have great pride and think that they're essential to their work, and they are. But bear in mind this, that there's a higher priority of essentiality, and that is helping the City of New York and helping the Traffic commissioner and the Police and the Fire departments by making up your mind that the shop can do without you today."

Meanwhile, reports of another attack from Mike Quill were circulating around City Hall, lending support to the growing feeling that the strike might not be as short as we had anticipated. Quill, on a local television interview program Sunday morning, had said he was prepared to "rot in jail" if he was arrested. He said he was not afraid of the courts. "I was born," he added, "in the injunction age." He urged New Yorkers to defy Lindsay's travel ban: "Working people can't afford to stay home," he said. He also blamed the stalemate on rivalry between Lindsay and Rockefeller, who, he said, "are locked in a death struggle for the White House." Calling Lindsay "a boy in short pants" and an "apprentice" in labor relations, Quill continued his personal attack on the Mayor. "He's promised the sun, moon and stars," Quill said. "He told us that if we want to be good Americans, we shouldn't strike. The hell with that. Labor unions made America.

I told Mr. Lindsay, 'You'd be down in some Hooverville shack if it weren't for the labor unions.' "

I discussed Quill's attacks with the Mayor and several other mayoral aides. The general feeling was that the Mayor should not engage in a name-calling contest, but that he should not ignore the attacks either. He should reply with restrained dignity. Thus, when the newsmen brought up the subject, Lindsay fielded questions like these:

Q. Mr. Mayor, Mr. Quill was quite vituperous concerning you today. He said various things, called you various names. What's your reaction to that?

A. I never mind being called names as a personal matter, but anybody who's dealing in the public arena like Mr. Quill has an obligation to treat the office of Mayor with respect.

Q. Do you think he's fulfilling that obligation?

A. Well, that's up to the public, I think, to judge. Sometimes it's best to let men be subject to the highest court—the judgment of the people—and the judgment of the people will ultimately prevail here on the behavior of the parties to this dispute.[2]

The next morning, Monday, January 3, I arrived at City Hall at 6 A.M., in time to help in the preparation of a statement on existing traffic conditions throughout the city. Tim Costello set up a "command post" in an office near Lindsay's and all incoming information was fed into his office. The atmosphere was tense, but everyone from the Mayor down was buoyed by the conviction that we were handling the situation correctly. The *Times* editorial that morning had thundered:

Mayor Lindsay, confronted with this grim crisis in the first minutes of an administration committed to fight for a better city, has comported himself with dignity, courage and resolution. His conduct thus far encourages confidence that the Quill demand for extortionate benefits as the price for peace on the subways and buses will be met in the spirit of Mr. Lindsay's inaugural address: "That the public interest must prevail over special interest, the good of the community over the desires of any group."

Lindsay, who once again had walked from the Roosevelt Hotel to City Hall—this time in only forty-five minutes—arrived about 6:45 A.M. He had started his walk accompanied by more than thirty reporters, but by the time he arrived there were only twenty. "It was good for us," I heard the Mayor tell the reporters who stuck with him until he reached the front steps of City Hall. "It brought the blood surging. Good for the circulation."

I had been preparing for a 7 A.M. press conference, but I did not know that Lindsay had a surprise in store for many New Yorkers travelling by car at that hour. With the report on traffic conditions in front of him, he said on radio: "If you're on your way to Manhattan in your car at this time, turn around and go home. Turn off the highways and head back to where you came from. Don't head for Manhattan by car—because you won't make it." His warning was blunt and to the point.

The press corps at City Hall had grown in size over the weekend and by Monday morning it was immense. I counted nearly 100 men and women reporters, cameramen, photographers, TV crews and messengers. They came in shifts, of course, some from midnight until 8 A.M., others replacing tired night shift reporters at 9 or 10 in the morning. The six morning and afternoon newspapers each had at least two—and as many as six—reporters on duty at once. The radio newsmen, anxious to give their listeners hourly bulletins, walked in and out of my office all day and night, asking for some comment from the Mayor, which I, in turn, gave them as his spokesman. There wasn't much new each time, but I tried to vary my statements in the hope that every station would get something different. There were other newsmen, too—magazine writers, members of the foreign press—who wanted to talk to the Mayor, particularly since he was not talking to the press much except for the formal, overcrowded mass press conferences two or three times a day in which he made announcements to the general public.

The feeling of continuous pressure began to mount on that first full day of the strike on Monday. I had slept for no more than a total of nine hours during the previous three days and nights. When I wasn't in my office at City Hall, my telephone at home was constantly ringing, especially between midnight and 6 A.M., when the afternoon newspapers were looking for "second-day" leads, a means of updating the news which the morning papers had already printed. These middle-of-the-night telephone calls started out at the rate of about one every hour. I soon reached the point where I learned to doze off with my hand on the telephone receiver next to my bed, so my wife and daughter would not be awakened every time it rang. This kept me in a state of extreme tension, however. I soon found I was unable to really relax at any time, anywhere.

After the televised press conference Monday morning, the Mayor called me on the black telephone on my desk which served as our direct line to each other. I went to his office.

"I can't get any work done with the press wandering in and out of my office all day and night," he told me. "I want you to shut off this end of the hallway. The Mayor should be entitled to some privacy. I don't understand why they can't stay in Room 9 until I have something to say. Close the glass doors outside of this wing of City Hall and get rid of the press."

I began to protest quietly. "But you can't just throw the press out, John. They have a right to be here. They want to know what's going on."

"Look," he interrupted. "They're just a bunch of God damn animals. Why the hell should I have to put up with all of their shenanigans, anyway? I'm the Mayor and if I want them out of my office, out they go. Now tell them that."

"What about the bathroom at this end of the Hall?" I blurted out. "What if they want to use that?"

"It's off-limits. Let them go downstairs. They have a head downstairs. And we've set up a special room for radio and TV down there, too."

What Lindsay did not realize was that the electronic press had set up near-permanent lines in the Blue Room—which was on the Mayor's side of the glass doors. Many of the cameras were connected by heavy lines running out of the window to battery-powered trucks outside so that his press conferences could immediately be televised "live" from the Blue Room. The men wanted access to this equipment in the Blue Room. And I knew the newspaper reporters, long accustomed to wandering casually in and out of the Mayor's wing when Bob Wagner occupied it, would not be happy if they were told it was off-limits. Nevertheless, I chose not to argue with Lindsay, who, I thought to myself, needed some rest and was, after all, entitled to some peace at his end of City Hall. So I asked a plainclothesman on duty at the front gate to the Mayor's wing to close the glass doors.

No sooner had this been done when I began to get telephone calls from the city desks of several newspapers. One *Herald Tribune* editor said he understood that I had "thrown the reporters" out of the Mayor's office and he demanded to know why. I replied that it was the Mayor's desire to restore some calm and quiet to his end of the hall so that he could carry on the business of his office.

"The business of the Mayor is the business of the press," the editor reminded me. "You'd better tell Lindsay that he's Mayor now and everything he does—what he eats for breakfast and who he talks to on the telephone—everything he does is public information. He wanted to be Mayor. Now he's got to act like a Mayor."

I knew the *Herald Tribune* editor was right. So I relayed the message to Lindsay.

"What the hell do those hyenas think I am, anyway?" was his response. "I'm not going to live in a fish bowl and that's all there is to it. Now are you going to do your job and keep them out of here or do I have to do it myself?"

Fearing what might happen if the Mayor himself went out into the hallway to evict the newsmen, I agreed to enforce his ban. I found a hostile group of reporters awaiting me when I returned to the hallway. One television reporter refused to move as I tried to make my way out of the crowd. We exchanged some harsh words and as the discussion became heated, we began to push and shove each other. I realized instantly that I should not have made a stand at that point. But the damage had been done. After apologizing to the reporter, I made my way to my office across the hallway. The newsmen slowly left the Mayor's office and, as the doors closed behind them, several muttered something about "throwing us out" and "getting sick of this kind of treatment."

I was squarely in the middle between Lindsay and the reporters. To my own detriment—and to his—I had chosen to confront the press instead of the Mayor. And to make matters worse, the situation provided an opportunity for Democrats at the other end of the Hall to have some fun at Lindsay's expense. When he heard that the press had been barred from the men's room in the Mayor's wing of the building, the urbane Paul Bragdon, who was then executive assistant to the City Council President, announced, "The press is free to use our humble facilities."

But the Mayor was caught up in more urgent matters. Hardly had the commotion of this incident subsided, when he called again on the telephone.

"Woody, I want to take a trip with Broderick around the city to see what it's like. Maybe we can line up a second copter for the press. You figure out who should go. Okay?"

"When do you want to leave?"

"As soon as possible. Let's get going," he said, with a sense of urgency in his voice.

"Fine," I said. "You'll have to take one reporter and a photographer."

"You're the press secretary. You handle it." He suddenly hung up.

I made arrangements for a wire service reporter and a photographer to represent Room 9 on a "pool" basis. They would share what they saw and wrote with all of the other newsmen as soon as they got back from a flight in a second helicopter which would tail the one in which the Mayor and Broderick rode.

During the one hour and twenty-three minute, 110-mile flight in dismal gray sky, the Mayor and his party viewed the traffic snarls in four boroughs from about 200 feet. While in the helicopter, Lindsay broadcasted, by means of the municipal radio station, WNYC, some of his observations. Upon his return to City Hall, he seemed invigorated and in a much better mood. His behavior, I began to realize, depended to some extent on his public performance. If he thought he was doing well—giving off an image of the active, vigorous Mayor who cared—then he was inevitably pleased, in a good mood. If he was publicly criticized or under fire, he became tense, unhappy, apt to clam up and say little to aides around him. He held a second televised "live" press conference just as soon as he returned from the helicopter flight and reported that the city was "in good shape, thanks to the cooperation of eight million New Yorkers." Before the afternoon was over, Lindsay asked me to schedule a third "live" show for the press and the public from the Blue Room. It went off smoothly about 5 P.M. Lindsay asked the public to remain at home again on Tuesday, and he urged truck owners and store owners to use the evening and night hours for deliveries. Again, the press—especially the radio and TV reporters—crushed into the Blue Room, causing some tempers to become frayed. The competition for space near the Mayor between the "written" press—the newspapermen—and the "electronic" press—radio and TV—had been building up for three days and now it nearly exploded. Reporters began to push and shove and elbow their way to the front of the room so they could be a few feet closer to Lindsay.

Several times during the day, Monday, the press asked me for a comment from the Mayor on the pending contempt citation against Quill. He was scheduled to appear before Judge Abraham N. Geller later in the afternoon. Lindsay instructed me to issue only a "No comment" when this issue arose. He said he did not want to comment on anything the court was doing. At one point, I went into Lindsay's office and asked him if we weren't playing into Quill's hands by allowing him to go to jail. Lindsay paused for a moment and looked up at me:

"I don't want him in jail. The public doesn't want him in jail. It will be more difficult for us to bargain without him. But that's the law. And I'm not going to interfere with the law—or the courts. I have been asked by a couple of people to call Judge Geller, but I wouldn't do it. I have too much respect for the law."

At 9:35 P.M. Monday night, Judge Geller, having listened to nearly five hours of arguments on motions to punish Quill and five other officers of the Transit Workers Union and three leaders of the Amalgamated Transit Union for violating the Condon-Wadlin Act (which prohibited public employees from striking), turned in his verdict. He ordered Quill to jail by 11 A.M. the next morning (Tuesday) unless the men ended their walkout and returned to work. The Transit Authority's decision to seek a judgment against Quill had been firmly supported by J. Lee Rankin, Lindsay's much-respected city corporation counsel. Rankin, who had served as Solicitor General of the United States and as a key member of the Warren Commission, was on hand in court to advise the Transit Authority lawyers. "It's always a problem that you might make the man a martyr," Rankin said of Geller's decision Monday night. "But you have to ask the question whether the country can continue to exist if its laws are not enforced."

At 7:55 A.M. Tuesday, January 4, Lindsay gave another traffic report on live radio and television, again telling New Yorkers, "If you have left home and can possibly turn back, please do so." A little past noon, Quill was led away from the bargaining table in Albert Hall in the Americana to prison. Just before he entered the Civil Jail, he excoriated the State Supreme Court Justice who had ordered him to jail and he vowed to "rot" there before he would settle the strike on terms he considered unfavorable to his men. "The judge can drop dead in his black robes," he intoned, "and we would not call off the strike. We will defy the injunction and go to jail." Soon after he was arrested, however, he collapsed and was taken to Bellevue Hospital in "serious" condition. Some reports said he had a heart attack. He was immediately replaced at the bargaining table by Douglas L. MacMahon, a long-time associate of Quill's.

At 1:05 P.M., I released the following statement from my office:

The Mayor is pressing very hard to get this dispute on the right track in the public interest . . . that's why he's remaining at his desk. He is talking with the mediation panel on a continuous basis. He is using every expert at his disposal to bring the negotiations within proper dimensions. He is in session with the aides at this moment and is keeping fully informed. If there are any other announcements from this office I will keep you posted. We don't expect any further word for some time.

Later, Lindsay called me again on the black telephone. "Tell the press that I intend to step back into the negotiations tomorrow and that I will stay there until there is a settlement," he said. "Put all other rumors to rest. Tell them there has not been any new offer by the Transit Authority. I've heard this one all day." I carried out the Mayor's request by walking down to Room 9 and telling the newsmen there. By 4 P.M., the Mayor wanted another traffic alert put out. So I typed out a statement and read it myself on radio and TV. It said:

Traffic today was heavy, but again the city worked. Car pooling was much more effective today than yesterday. Half the cars today carried 3 to 6 people. Yesterday only 10% did. A great improvement. Many more workers were able to get to their jobs today—employment was better. Traffic into New York today was 50% greater than yesterday. Based on more cars in town, and last night's experience, the Mayor concludes that the principal problem tonight is getting out of Manhattan. If everyone tries to leave at 5 o'clock, everyone will be delayed for hours. The Mayor makes this suggestion for tonight: If you use a car, stay in town for a bite to eat and perhaps a movie or a show or some other entertainment. Start for home after 8:30 P.M. You will probably arrive home quicker this way. If you ride a commuter train, plan to catch your regular scheduled train, or a later one. The Mayor has made suggestions for tomorrow: Tomorrow is Matinee Day—if you come for the matinee—don't plan to leave the City before 8:30 P.M. and I say to all of you: Don't bring more cars into the City. Don't relax your cooperation. Continue group riding. Continue walking.

Less than an hour later, Lindsay called me again and asked me to put out another statement about Quill's condition. At 5:15 P.M. I released the following statement:

I have been in close contact with medical officials to check on Mr. Quill's condition. I have directed that everything be done to make him comfortable and to see to it that he gets every assistance. At my direction, the Mediation Panel came to see me at City Hall and I have the following report:

1) The Panel is proceeding immediately on the assumption that the newly authorized representation of the Union has clear authority as publicly stated by Mr. Quill and is prepared to negotiate and reach an agreement;

2) The Panel under Dr. Feinsinger's direction is driving hard to reach an agreement;

3) The Panel has arranged a meeting at 5 o'clock originally with the newly authorized union representatives and immediately thereafter with the Commissioners and other representatives of the Transit Authority;

4) The Mediation Panel expects the parties to work all night, and longer if necessary. I'll be doing the same and am available to the Panel and all parties. I have cancelled all appointments.

On Wednesday morning, January 5, I rode up from City Hall to the Americana with Lindsay about 8:15 A.M. after he had held another live traffic advisory. Shortly after 9:30 A.M. the Mayor met with the mediators. I realized then there would be two groups of press to serve—the room full of newsmen, about fifty, at the hotel itself in a large ballroom, and those who remained at City Hall to cover developments there. For that reason, I asked Warren Gardner to take charge of the Mayor's press office at City Hall while I stayed with Lindsay at the Americana. I went downstairs to talk to the reporters who had already assembled cameras and chairs in front of a large speaker's platform. I started to tell them what little I knew of the day's plans when one TV reporter asked me to step out to the microphones and start over again so he could record my words on film.

"The Mayor has asked me to tell you that he is pressing hard for a settlement," I said a little more formally. "He has come to the Americana for a settlement and he will not leave until he gets one. He intends to stay for the duration." The reporters had many questions, but I was unable to answer them. I had no more information at my disposal.

Back upstairs in Suite 4931—a parlor and a bedroom which we had reserved since New Year's Eve—I telephoned City Hall about midmorning. Gardner told me the *World-Telegram* was carrying a front-page story attributed to "sources close to Lindsay" that said the Mayor would try for an "interim settlement" if he couldn't get a permanent one, and that he would ask the union to run the subways and buses while details were being worked out. I turned to the Mayor as soon as I heard this and told him about the story.

"First I have heard of it," he said, shaking his head in dismay. "Find out where it came from," he said, matter-of-factly, and then went into the next room. I telephoned Bob Price at City Hall and asked him if he had leaked the story. "You listen to me," he said angrily, "I will tell the press whatever I want, whenever I want to and I don't expect to be asked about it by you. I do whatever I want to. I know what's best for Lindsay—better than he does. That's all I am going to say about it. Now put Lindsay on." I did—and then left the room. It was the last I heard from either Lindsay or Price about the incident. Later in the day, about 3 P.M., I went downstairs again to meet the press and try to answer their questions. There were many on that Wednesday:

When is the Mayor coming down? Will there be a settlement

today? What about his plan for an interim settlement? Is he going to capitulate to the union's demands? Does the Mayor want Quill in jail? Could Quill be paroled so he can get back into the negotiations? Are there any new offers on the table? Are there any joint talks planned? Why can't we have a press conference with the Mayor? These were only a few of the questions I had fired at me as I entered the makeshift press room on the main floor of the hotel. The reporters gathered around me. I tried my best to answer their questions. "Ladies and gentlemen," I said, looking at many of the familiar faces, "The Mayor, the mediation panel and both parties are now meeting in joint sessions. The Mayor is pressing hard for a settlement. The Mayor has no immediate plans to leave the Americana. That's all I can tell you. There will be no other statements for now. I cannot tell at this time whether any parties to the negotiations will be down here—or how soon. I will keep you posted. I'll call down from upstairs."

Meanwhile, Justice Geller—at the request of the mediators—postponed for twenty-four hours a scheduled hearing to determine whether the unions should be fined for having called the strike in violation of the court injunction. Most of the reporters viewed this request from the mediators as an indication that they wanted to make a major effort toward an early settlement. There were reports that steps were being taken to put together a money package of about $40 million, about $6 million more than the 1964 settlement, but when I asked Lindsay about these reports, he just shrugged and said: "Just give them a 'No comment.' Why do they have to know every detail of what we're doing, anyway?" I tried to explain why the press was following the negotiations so closely, but before I got started he was on the telephone answering a call.

At 5:30, I went downstairs once again and gave another general report to the TV cameras. "There has been no change in the negotiations since my last report," I said. "The parties are still hard at work negotiating with the assistance of the Mayor and the mediation panel. All parties are talking seriously. The Mayor has not authorized me to make any further statements at this time or to answer any questions. I'll be back between 7:30 and 8—whether or not there are any developments."

The next day—Thursday, January 6—the Mayor held his

traffic press conference at 7:45 A.M. By now, this had become part of the normal routine starting the day. President Johnson, acting at Lindsay's request, sent Labor Secretary W. Willard Wirtz to City Hall to try and assist in breaking the deadlock. And in another new development, the Mayor hinted that the Transit Authority might be considering asking the court to free Quill.[3] Lindsay made his statement after conferring at City Hall with Harry Van Arsdale, Jr., president of the New York City Central Labor Council. Van Arsdale, a tough labor veteran, had been an intimate adviser of Mayor Wagner's, but had remained aloof from Lindsay up to now. Despite those hopeful signs, however, on Friday, January 7, any hope of a settlement faded when the Transit Authority asked the Supreme Court to assess the damages of the two striking unions at $322,000 a day and, at the same time, rejected a plea from top city labor officials to seek the release of Quill and eight other strike leaders.

On Saturday, January 8, Feinsinger and the Mayor seemed a little more optimistic. Both said they hoped to settle the strike over the weekend. Negotiations continued until 5 A.M. Sunday morning and resumed again at 8 A.M. Sunday afternoon, the Mayor announced to the press that he was summoning both sides to City Hall for what looked like an all-night session. Lindsay told newsmen, however, in his twelfth major press conference during the first week that his action was not "to be construed as indicating an agreement has been reached or is imminent." He looked very tired after only two-and-a-half hours sleep the night before, and as the evening wore on, he appeared to be on the verge of collapse. He had put in a total of 106 hours of work during his first week in office—83 at City Hall, another 23 on mayoral business away from City Hall—including a 17½-hour negotiating session at the Americana; and, in contrast, a total of only 50 hours at the Roosevelt with his family.

As a result, at 3 A.M. on Monday morning, January 10, he went downstairs to the gymnasium below his office and fell asleep on the couch there. Bob Price, meanwhile, kept the negotiations going with the union leaders, who, by this time, were sprawled out on the floor taking turns napping. As the night wore on, a

$50 million package took shape, but the union rejected it. With Lindsay asleep, however, Price stepped in and—much to the surprise of both the Transit Authority and the union—tossed out a $500-a-year supplementary pension benefit. Lindsay, returning to the bargaining session, then came up with a 15 percent wage offer that would achieve a $4.00 hourly wage by July, 1967. Nevertheless, at 6:15 A.M. Monday, Lindsay, distracted by fatigue, told me to ask the press to come to the Blue Room. With a disappointed look on his face, the Mayor told the reporters: "We have recessed until sometime after noon." Thus what had looked like a certain settlement seemed to evaporate in front of our eyes. I was a little confused by the failure to reach an accord. Price had stepped in, wheeled and dealed, moving between offices, whispering to various union and Transit Authority representatives—and yet, we had failed to reach a settlement. I was amazed by his ability to manipulate people; if he had not been able to wrap it up by morning, no one could, I thought. And so we adjourned after a night that seemed to last forever. I had spent much of the night moving back and forth between the Mayor's offices and the press corps—who by now were learning to sleep in Room 9 or in the corridors, with the understanding that I would awaken them if there was any news.

A noontime rally of the union near City Hall followed on Monday. And MacMahon, who had privately expressed some optimism during the night, told some 10,000 cheering union members: "I've never met such amateurs in all my life. I tell you it was a sad day when Bob Wagner left this town. This guy [Lindsay] doesn't know what the hell he is doing." Several union members held signs; attached to one was the straw-stuffed body of a man hanging from a rope.

When Lindsay learned of the demonstration and MacMahon's remarks, he was furious. I have rarely seen him as angry—his face was expressionless, his jaws taut, his hands nervously twirling a pencil between them. Still he kept his sense of humor. He telephoned his twin brother, Dave, to break the tension and told him, with a big laugh: "Hey, Dave, they just hung a guy in effigy outside of City Hall. He looks like you!"

Several more Lindsay aides walked into his office while he was on the telephone. He was a little more relaxed after talking to his brother, but he still wanted to take some firm action. Several aides urged him to issue a warning to the "power brokers" of New York that the city government would not capitulate to special interests. The Mayor nodded his head in agreement. Those who advocated the "hard line" were Barry Gottehrer, the former *New York Herald Tribune* reporter, and Dave Garth. Garth and Gottehrer wrote the script for the Mayor's 5:40 P.M. televised report to the people. I did not fully agree with the approach taken in the speech, because I did not believe it would help settle the strike any sooner. Nevertheless, I went along with it because it appealed to my sense of indignation about the way Quill was crippling the city.

Thus, Lindsay delivered the remarks that were to embroil him in controversy for weeks to come. He asserted that the city "will not capitulate before the lawless demands of a single group . . . it will not allow the power brokers in our city, or any special interest, to dictate to this city the terms under which it will exist in New York. The paramount issue confronting us today, the one that threatens the destiny of our government, is whether New York City can be intimidated. I say it cannot and will not, for I sought the office of Mayor to give this city leadership, not to betray its spirit in a time of crisis."[4] Lindsay then asked the mediators to follow one of three alternatives: (1) make recommendations on all terms of the settlement; (2) agree to a fact-finding commission which would recommend terms of a settlement; (3) get both parties to the dispute to accept any new procedures other than the ones the Mayor had recommended. Lindsay made a reference to his new theme at the end of his statement when he said: "Adversity is the test of strong men, and, I should add, the test of a Proud City."

During the next two days—Tuesday and Wednesday, January 11 and 12—both sides considered the Mayor's proposals and the mediators moved back and forth trying to hammer out an agreement on procedures. I remained at City Hall with the Mayor, hoping that the strike would soon be resolved. By that time, however, pressure for Lindsay to take some affirmative action to get the subways and buses rolling again began to mount from outside and from within. The city's major business associates joined in a public statement demanding that the transit logjam be broken, by use of the National Guard, if necessary. There was some discussion among Lindsay's aides in the Mayor's office about calling out the Guard, but the Mayor was cool to the suggestion. "That's the last resort," he said. "It'll mean violence."

At 12 noon Wednesday, January 12, the mediation panel reported to the Mayor that there was still no mutual agreement between the parties. At 12:45 P.M. the Mayor announced that he was requesting the panel to submit to him by 3 P.M. a written report containing the panel's views "as to the basis for a fair, equitable and responsible settlement." While we were waiting for Dr. Feinsinger's recommendations, I was sitting at my desk when Lindsay called me on the black telephone and said, "Bobby Kennedy's secretary called and said he may be coming in sometime this afternoon." "When is he coming?" I asked. "I don't know," Lindsay replied, "but let's clear the decks and be ready for him." Less than a half hour later—before I had a chance to tell the press—Kennedy walked up the front steps of City Hall heading for the Mayor's office. There was a great deal of excitement outside and Kennedy made his way through the press crowd into the Mayor's outer office. I walked in and joined him. I had spent a few hours with him the previous October when, as a television newsman, I interviewed him about East Harlem slums.

"Hello, Senator, it's good to see you again," I said reaching out to shake his hand.

"Hello, it's good to see you again," he replied softly. "Congratulations on your new job, Woody."

He sat down in the waiting room, flanked by two aides, Tom Johnston and Peter Edelman. After several minutes of silence, I said, quietly:

"I just want to tell you, Senator, in case I never get another opportunity, that I had a great deal of admiration and respect for your brother." I was not sure that this was the proper thing to be talking about at this time, but I felt compelled to tell him, anyway.

"Thank you," he replied simply, in a barely audible voice.

After we had been waiting for about ten minutes, Lindsay strode out of his inner office and greeted the Senator warmly.

"Hello, Bob. It's good to see you," the Mayor said, smiling and shaking Kennedy's hand.

"Hello, John," Kennedy replied, also smiling.

"Bring your two colleagues," Lindsay said. He motioned for me to follow him into his office, where Tim Costello was already waiting. Lindsay sat down behind his desk. Kennedy sat in a chair to the side of Lindsay's desk, his legs crossed, his right hand on his chin.

Kennedy spoke first. "Well, tell me what it's all about, John. How has it been going?" he asked, matter-of-factly.

Lindsay, seeming self-assured, got up from his desk and, pacing back and forth, began to explain what the problems were: He described the issues, the demands, and what he felt he could and could not do. He told Kennedy that he was convinced that Quill had struck because he needed to insure his own leadership of the union, which had a great number of Negroes in the rank and file who wanted a voice in the Irish-dominated organization. Lindsay said there was considerable pressure for new leadership from within and that Quill was virtually forced into a strike by some of his own men.

Lindsay talked for about fifteen minutes and, throughout, Kennedy did not move. He asked three questions: How much do you think you can give them? How much is a fair settlement? How much longer will it be before a settlement? The Mayor told him he thought there would be a settlement within a day or two—that both parties were close, but that both must still accept the recommendations of the mediators. And he told Kennedy he wanted to get some legislation passed after the strike was over to bring about better collective bargaining procedures in the City of New York in the future and he said he might need Kennedy's help in persuading the State Legislature. Kennedy nodded in agreement and said he would have one of his aides contact Lindsay's office.

As the meeting broke up, there was a brief conversation about what should be said to the press. I asked Kennedy if he wanted to speak first and he replied that it would be better if the Mayor opened the press conference. We walked out to the mob of waiting reporters in the Blue Room nearby and the Mayor told them that Kennedy had been "concerned and helpful. We had a fruitful discussion." Then, without any warning, Kennedy got up and called the strike "intolerable" and "catastrophic" and he urged "the union as well as the Authority to accept the findings of the mediation board. There's going to have to be give-and-take on both sides. That give-and-take must take place today. The strike really cannot go on for another day." Then he disclosed that he had sent a telegram to the Mayor two days before urging immediate action.

A ripple of excitement ran through the room. They sensed that Kennedy had come to City Hall to upstage John Lindsay, and, indeed, he had succeeded with this report of his sharp call to action. Kennedy's timing had been perfect. I was caught completely by surprise. Judging by his behavior inside the Mayor's office, he gave no clue that he intended to make such a strong statement to the press. As Kennedy left the press conference, the reporters sat motionless for a moment. He had apparently taken the press by surprise, too.

Kennedy then went down to the other end of City Hall to confer with City Council President Frank O'Connor. Again, he repeated to the press the fact that he had sent Lindsay a telegram two days before demanding that the Mayor do exactly what he was now doing—urge the mediation panel to come in with some recommendations. There was no doubt in my mind that Kennedy sensed a settlement and that he wanted to try and take the credit for it himself.

While Kennedy was holding a second press conference with O'Connor, Lindsay walked into my office with a quizzical look on his face and asked, "Is he gone yet?" I shook my head no. "He's a real operator, isn't he?" Lindsay remarked. "Let me know when he leaves." The Mayor turned and went back to his office.

About fifteen minutes later, I looked out of my window to the City Hall Plaza and saw Kennedy walking down the steps. I telephoned Lindsay and told him. He seemed preoccupied by Kennedy's presence and he must have been upset by the way the press conference had gone. "He really put it to us," Lindsay said slowly, and then hung up.

After the Senator left, the mediation panel turned in its report to the Mayor. It recommended a $43.4 million wage and benefit package over two years. Attached to Dr. Feinsinger's report was a second report entitled: "Analysis and Appraisal of Proposed Money Package in Light of the President's Guidelines." I was told not to release either document to the press immediately. The Mayor first wanted to make sure both sides agreed to the recommendations. However, the press, sensing a settlement was close at hand, became desperate for information. I later heard that one newsman had tried to get a City Hall aide to smuggle a copy of the panel's recommendations. The aide agreed, but was never able to get his hands on the document.

At 1:35 A.M. Thursday morning, January 13, MacMahon announced that the union negotiators had agreed to the mediator's formula and would recommend that the union executive board approve it. Two hours later, at about 3:30 A.M., the Transit Authority said it, too, would accept the recommendations, and at 6:25 A.M. MacMahon made it official by announcing that his board had approved it. Meanwhile, I sat at my desk all night, so fatigued that when I heard of the agreements, I could hardly believe the strike was over.

There were still some formalities, of course. Lindsay asked both parties to come to City Hall where he said he wanted to announce the settlement. The members of the mediation panel, haggard and glassy-eyed, soon arrived. Dr. Feinsinger was limping badly. He needed help in order to make it from his car to the Blue Room. The union negotiators looked equally bedraggled, unshaven and bleary-eyed. By the time we gathered everyone together in the Blue Room and ran off a press release with Lindsay's comments, it was nearly 8 A.M. Then, finally, thirteen days from the time we had arrived in City Hall, the Mayor stood up, his hands shaking slightly from fatigue, as he read his statement:

Fellow New Yorkers: Perhaps for the first time since I took office as Mayor, I have undeniably good news to report—New York's transit strike is over.

He estimated the cost of the contract at $43.4 million for the Transit Authority alone, or a total of about $52 million, including related authorities such as MABSTOA. The settlement, he said, had cost the city $1.5 billion in twelve days. Still, he sounded a note of optimism: "I believe," he said, "the successful resolution of the subway strike may signal the beginning of a fresh and rewarding era in labor-management relations in New York."

As I stood in the doorway of the Blue Room watching John Lindsay, I couldn't help but feel that if this was, indeed, the beginning of a "fresh and rewarding" era—it certainly did not feel like it. I had never felt so worn out—mentally and physically—in my entire life.

For John Lindsay, the strike had been a major confrontation with one of the city's most powerful forces—the labor "power brokers" who had for the previous twelve years been calling the shots with Bob Wagner at City Hall. Lindsay had tried to make one point during this strike and, in the aftermath of the chaos, he told me he thought he had succeeded. His purpose in holding out, he said, was to establish the precedent that he would not live by the "deal," but by genuine collective bargaining.

For me, the first thirteen days had been a confrontation of a different sort. I never dreamt when I accepted the post with Lindsay that it would turn out to be so incredibly difficult—particularly at the very outset. In addition to the transit crisis, I had handled other matters from my office, including the issuing of thirteen press releases on appointments, responding to telephone calls from other New York leaders anxious to line up the Mayor for speaking engagements, and listening to "advice" from many people on the phone who could not reach the Mayor. In addition, I had released the salaries of the top City Hall aides, including my own, and that brought some ribbing from the press. Price actually set the salary levels and, as it turned out, I was to receive $24,000 a year, more than any other mayoral assistant.

I had worked as hard as I knew how to earn this distinction, but in my zeal to respond to reporters' questions quickly I had also made a few mistakes which caused some uneasiness in Room 9. The tense atmosphere and the exhausting pace forced the newsmen to compete fiercely with each other, looking for "new angles" every few hours and always pressing for more information. This led to several incidents which, although minor, were reported in the papers and, in my own opinion, blown out of proportion.

In one instance, Lindsay had been walking to work and I had been in my office. When he arrived at City Hall, a reporter told me he had not walked all the way, but had received a lift from a man driving a late model car. I was asked if I knew the man's name. I did not, but said I would find out. A detective, who had accompanied the Mayor on his walk, told me the man was "a stranger," so I reported that fact to the press. Later in the morning, at a press conference, in answer to the same question, Lindsay revealed that "the stranger" was Sid Davidoff, his personal aide, who frequently drove the Mayor in his own car.

Another instance occurred one night midway through the strike when a newsman asked me if Lindsay was going out for supper. I telephoned the Mayor's secretary and she told me he was having a sandwich at his desk. Later in the evening, another reporter came to me and told me he had seen Lindsay at a local restaurant. I checked and found out that Lindsay had, indeed, eaten dinner at his desk, but he had left with his twin brother, David, afterwards through the basement-level exit of City Hall to have a drink at Whyte's Restaurant. The press reported the story as if my office had purposely misinformed the first reporter.

Still another incident cropped up in the papers after I disclosed to newsmen that Sid Davidoff was negotiating with the Ford Motor Company for a car which the Mayor would use free of charge in order to save the city the cost of a large new city limousine. However, after a *New York Times* editorial criticized the Mayor for accepting such a gift, I was instructed by Lindsay to tell the press that he had decided to lease the car, instead. The second round of stories about the car was reported in such a way as to imply—once again—that my office was inaccurate the first time.

As a result, I grew more cautious in the office about answering press inquiries on-the-spot. And, at home, I tried a different approach—I instructed my two-and-a-half-year-old daughter Wendy, to answer all telephone calls with a pert "No comment."

4 *"Who are the power brokers? They know who they are!"*

JUST AS WE BEGAN to settle down in the aftermath of the strike, we received word that President Johnson, in an unexpected move, had held a press conference in Washington in which he had attacked the terms of the settlement. Despite the Mayor's estimate, some observers put the cost of the settlement as high as $70 million."I do not believe any settlement which violates the guideposts to this extent is in the national interest," the President said. The President's statement was a stunning blow to Lindsay, whose prestige had been damaged as a result of the lengthy strike. Some of the Mayor's critics were even saying there were more deaths in the city than normal, as a result of the strike, although this was totally untrue.[1]

The effect of Johnson's remarks was to further undermine Lindsay in New York. In answer to reporters' questions, I had been saying that the settlement was "fair and equitable." And Dr. Feinsinger, in his special analysis to the Mayor, had stated that "all the money items involved in the proposed settlement of the present dispute are clearly within the confines of the guidelines," but he had also said that in such cases where there were long-standing "inequities or injustices" that "appropriate increases in excess of the 3.2% norm" were permissible for what he called intra-plant or inter-plant inequities. The net effect of the Feinsinger analysis and the Johnson statement was to leave a cloud of uncertainty over the merits of the whole settlement. It was far from a victory for Lindsay, although the Mayor retained his popularity with most citizens during the strike.[2] And despite the fact that the New York press was somewhat hostile, he continued to enjoy a good press in the rest of the nation, as well as abroad.

One example: Two days after the strike was over, the *London Economist* lauded the Mayor editorially: "New York's new Mayor," the publication said, "has emerged strengthened by his baptism of fire." The editorial said that if Lindsay had been more experienced, the strike might not have lasted as long nor cost the city $1.5 billion in economic losses. "Nevertheless," it went on, "the credit for peace will inevitably go to the new Mayor. . . . In fact, if the settlement is what it seems—a victory for above-board bargaining in New York's labour relations— the strike may even have been worthwhile." The editorial went on to castigate Governor Rockefeller for "political inept- ness" and because of his "appearing on the scene at the 11th hour."

We had little time, however, to evaluate the aftereffects of the strike settlement. During those first thirteen days Lindsay had virtually ignored the rest of city government and a list of critical requests to meet with the Mayor had been piling up for nearly two weeks. Lindsay had been so completely in- volved with the transit crisis, in fact, that he had not even talked to some of Bob Wagner's commissioners whom he had asked to remain on temporarily and he did not have time to respond to some of the city's other critical problems. For example, the Mayor wanted the police—and the public—to know he was concerned every day with the crimes in the city. Soon after the strike was over he began a routine of calling police head- quarters every night. The first time he called headquarters— about 11 P.M. one night—to find out if anyone had been killed or if there had been a major accident or fire, it took quite some time before anyone answered. Finally, a girl came on the line. This is the way the Mayor related the conversation they had:

"This is the Mayor," Lindsay said. "May I speak to whoever is in charge?"

"All right, honey, everything's going to be O.K."

"Who is in charge?"

"The sergeant is around somewhere."

"Where?"

"I don't know—I can't find him."

"You find the sergeant. This is the Mayor on the phone."

"Well, he's busy. He's playing checkers."

"You tell him John Vliet Lindsay, the Mayor, is on the phone and wants to talk to him."

The sergeant came to the phone. "Maybe it was the Vliet that shook her up," Lindsay later explained. "Anyway the sergeant wasn't sure that I might *not* be the Mayor, so I got the information I wanted!"

Another major problem which the Mayor had neglected for the first thirteen days was the great numbers of organized, sometimes militant citizen groups—composed mainly of Negroes and Puerto Ricans—who were anxiously awaiting the end of the strike so they could force the Mayor to make good on some of his promises. One of these well-organized groups, the East Harlem Tenants Council, wasted no time making their presence felt at City Hall. The day after the settlement was announced, they marched on City Hall at about 4:20 P.M. More than thirty-five tenants, some carrying infants, came to the gate entrance just outside of my office and demanded to see the Mayor. The plainclothes police detective on duty asked them to wait, then came into my office to ask what he should do. Fortunately, I knew Ted Velez, the head of this group, from my newspaper reporting days and I, therefore, felt that I could avoid any embarrassment to the Mayor. I told the detective I would come to the gate and talk with the tenants.

I met a man at the gate who identified himself as the Reverend Seymour Brown, housing supervisor of the Council. "We want to see Mayor Lindsay," he said, emphatically, "and we want to see him right now. We have no heat, our windows are broken in many of our buildings, ceilings are crumbling and toilets don't work. We want some action and we want it now."

I told Brown that the Mayor was busy inside his office and could not see the group at that very moment. Knowing from my newspaper reporting experience something about their grievances, however, I told them that I would arrange an appointment for them to see the Mayor "as soon as possible." I hesitated to name a date because I did not want other groups, who were sure to hear about this confrontation, to get the idea that all they had to do was demonstrate and the Mayor would see them in a matter of hours or days.

"Look here," Brown continued angrily, "I am not much interested in how busy the Mayor is. In his campaign, he told us he would help us. We believed him. Now we're here. Is there any better time than now for him to come out and talk to us?"

I went inside to talk with Harvey Rothenberg, the Mayor's appointments secretary. Harvey told me the Mayor could see them anytime the next day. I returned to the gate and relayed this message to Brown and the other tenants. Brown looked at me, paused for a moment, and then replied in a softer but frustrated voice:

"We didn't come all the way downtown just to come back tomorrow again."

"This is the best I can do," I replied, shrugging my shoulders. "Please try and realize that the Mayor has just been through a grueling strike and he needs a day to get the city in order. You know he is interested in housing and your problems and that he will see you. I think it's a reasonable delay—just one day."

The clergyman still did not agree with me, and as we exchanged more words, the conversation become heated. By this time, the Room 9 press corps had heard about the discussion and reporters were busily taking notes and photographers snapping pictures of the sit-ins. Finally, realizing the publicity implications of the hallway discussion, I said to Brown in a restrained tone:

"There are several commissioners over at the Buildings Department waiting to see you. I can arrange for you to talk with them. They are in a position to do something to help you."

"We want to see the Mayor—now!" Brown replied, stubbornly, realizing that he now had the press as an audience.

One of the tenants who was sitting on the floor then shouted: "You have to look at these buildings. There are no lights in the hallways. I have to walk around with a flashlight. The ceilings are coming down. And some of us don't even have toilets." The demonstrators, who came from twelve East Harlem tenements, then sat down outside the gate in the corridor, with their backs to the walls. One of them announced he was going out for coffee.

I went back into my office and asked Brown to join me. He agreed. I pulled out the black address book that I had kept in the top drawer of my desk at the *World-Telegram* for nine years, turned to "V" and looked up the telephone number of Ted Velez, the executive director of the East Harlem Tenants Council.

Fortunately, Velez answered the phone. "Listen, Ted," I said, "I'm asking you to go easy on us until we have a chance to get started. The Mayor knows he is carrying the sins of six generations and he wants to help—but he can't do it overnight." After some further discussion, Velez agreed to call off his sit-ins. I put Brown on the telephone to confirm the agreement. He left, along with the other tenants, at 6 P.M.

Just before the tenants had left, Buildings Commissioner Moerdler, whom I had contacted during the sit-ins, arrived at City Hall and talked with them. He told them that three of the buildings were undergoing emergency repairs already, and that a mobile inspection unit from his office was in the area. I had called Moerdler into my office and asked him to do something for this group because they were in desperate need. I knew that some $325,000 in city antipoverty funds had been allocated by the Wagner Administration to the East Harlem Tenants Council, but the group still had not received the money.

In my conversation with Moerdler, I was firm—possibly demanding. I had felt strongly about housing conditions for a decade before coming to City Hall and I felt here was a chance to do something for people who obviously needed help. Several reporters overheard our discussion, however, and within an hour I received a call from the city desk of the *Herald Tribune:* What were the commissioner and I arguing about? Was it true that I had "summoned" him over to City Hall in order to find out why his department had failed to take action in improving housing conditions for the East Harlem Tenants Council? I denied any differences between Moerdler and myself and I asked the editor on the other end of the phone to please refrain from writing such a story. He agreed, reluctantly. I hung up, amazed that the press would be so picayune when it came to a question of people's basic survival in the ghetto. I understood that the press' job was to cover the political goings-on at City Hall, but I had not fully realized up to this point that most newsmen were more interested in politics than in solving social problems.

On the Monday following the end of the transit strike, the *World-Telegram and Sun* carried a front page "exclusive" story —an interview with an unnamed mediator, reportedly one of the three who participated in the negotiations. The mediator was quoted as saying that the strike had been prolonged because Lindsay had too many inexperienced advisers—and the story named Robert Price, in particular—who confused the negotiations. "Everyone—Lindsay, Quill, the Transit Authority— couldn't figure out what was going on. It was just one mistake after another," the source was quoted as saying.

Lindsay called me into his office and asked me to get in touch with all three mediators and to release statements from each of them. He told me I could issue a one-word comment in his name about the story: "Irresponsible." From Sylvester Garrett came this statement: "The story can only be regarded as a deliberate and malicious attempt to injure innocent people." I reached Dr. Feinsinger at his home in Aspen, Colorado, and he dictated a statement to me which read, in part: "I am shocked beyond belief. . . . The story is without the slightest justification and with a complete disregard to known facts." And finally, Theodore Kheel stated: "I was in no respect the source of the story appearing in the *World-Telegram* today attributed to a mediator. Nor do I believe that it is a fair or accurate appraisal of what happened."

As I reread the story and the comments from each of the three mediators which I released to the press, I felt like the whole exercise was a mockery. In my own mind, the story was very nearly accurate. It was slightly distorted, in some respects, but it reflected the confusion and misunderstanding which had, indeed, plagued the negotiations and, perhaps, even caused the strike to last several extra days. I knew that each mediator had to deny that he was the source of the story, of course, because that is what is expected of them. The technique of leaking stories and then vehemently denying them was a sophisticated, often effective, method of making news.

Several other issues dominated the days immediately following the transit strike: The budget, a possible cut in city services, reorganization of government, charges that Lindsay was "interfering" with the Police Department, talk of a city income tax, a plan to merge all transportation agencies which aroused Robert Moses' ire, a request for $600 million in state aid from Albany and Governor Rockefeller, and public complaints about some of the Mayor's appointments. In addition, the press continued to pick on small details and to emphasize minor incidents. Lindsay, however, ignored the petty stories and began to charge ahead with his many plans. I had the feeling that he wanted to change the whole city all at once. I was all in favor of it, but I found the tempo of events hard to keep up with.

We had talked in December about bringing the Mayor closer to the people via radio and television, so it did not surprise me when the Mayor told me on Monday, January 17, that he wanted to go on television Wednesday night "live" with a message on the state of the city's finances. Ever since Murray Drabkin had joined us in December, I knew that we were going to have to ask for the first personal city income tax in the history of New York. As soon as the transit strike was over, Lindsay called in Gene Becker, the budget director, and Drabkin, along with one or two other aides, including speech writer James Carberry, and told them to get a speech ready for the 17th. He decided he would break the news to the public as soon as possible.

I arranged with WNYC's Sy Siegel for the program to be carried on two local TV channels at 9:30 P.M. Newsmen filled the Blue Room that night as the Mayor, in what I had labeled his first "fireside chat" to the public, said there would have to be a "job freeze" in city government, and an across-the-board 10 percent cut in every city department. He blamed the previous Administration for the fiscal dilemma in which the city now found itself. There had been, he said, "credit card budgeting," and a "borrow now, pay later" policy which had placed "enormous strains on this city's fiscal framework." He warned his viewers: "It should be clear to any New Yorker hearing this recital that our city will be faced with a fiscal crisis of the first magnitude unless expenses are reduced or new revenues are found." When he finished the broadcast, he seemed quite pleased. He returned to his office and I followed. "How did I do?" he asked. "Very well," I replied. Lindsay turned to Jim Carberry and patted him on the back. "A very good job, Jim," he said, " a very good job."

The newspapers reported Lindsay's call for "austerity" the next day—along with several photo spreads of the book-lined shelves which had served as a backdrop for his TV talk. The *Times* seemed so amused by the fact that we had moved books from the municipal library and had special bookshelves built for the occasion that the newspaper ran a four-column headline on the front page about an "ersatz library," referred to the "hundreds of handsomely bound volumes" being "carted over," and described the "row upon row of heavy tomes impressively in place." The *Times* news article also went out of the way to point out that the press was asked to keep quiet during the nineteen-minute program. In an off-handed, joking manner the night before, I had told a *Times* man who had a cough that "nobody with colds" would be allowed to attend the broadcast. Incredibly, he had taken me seriously—or chose to for his own reasons—and my "order" banning newsmen with colds was also reported straightforwardly on page one of the *Times*.[3]

I could hardly believe that the press could be so preoccupied with this kind of trivia that it would go to such lengths. One afternoon newspaper printed a separate article on the fact that the reporters had been asked not to smoke during the telecast or open the doors to the makeshift Blue Room studio because of the problem of noise from outside. The headline on the story: THE LINDSAY 'FIRESIDE CHAT': *Woody Burns Them Up.*

I tried to put this latest incident out of mind, only to be faced with another minor problem that ballooned to major proportions. Joseph Fitzpatrick, City Hall reporter for the Associated Press, complained to me that Price had refused to pose for a picture that an AP photographer, coincidentally named John C. Lindsay, had requested. I agreed to intervene, and walked into Price's office. He was talking on two phones at once, but paused long enough for me to urge him to "sit still" for the picture. "You're a public official," I said, "and this is part of your job."

"No," Price said bluntly. "I'm not interested. Tell him to go buy a picture from Katsy Thomas." As I protested, he waved me off and went back to his two simultaneous conversations.

Katrina Thomas was an attractive Bryn Mawr graduate and a professional photographer. She was a friend of the Lindsays and had taken photos of him during the campaign. In those early days, she was the unofficial City Hall photographer.

I returned to my office and shook my head in disgust. I was angry at Price, and I told the AP man about my encounter with him.

"Who's Katsy Thomas?" Fitzpatrick asked immediately. I told him and added that tentative plans had been made for her to join the Lindsay Administration. In response to his questions, I made some telephone calls and found out that she would receive approximately $9,100 a year on the payroll of the city's antipoverty agency. Fitzpatrick was curious about why a "society" photographer-friend of the Lindsays should be receiving antipoverty funds.

By this time, Price had learned that Fitzpatrick had told his AP office that the Deputy Mayor would not pose for a photo. Price then had a change of mind, in response to another press inquiry, and said: "It's not true. I will so pose." But the damage had been done.

The next morning the *Times* carried a three-column story on the bottom of page one with a picture of Katsy Thomas under the headline: LINDSAY CAMERA GIRL IS POVERTY AIDE. The *Daily News* went even further: a streaming six-column headline across the entire top of page three read: CITY HALL MOVES SOCIALITE PHOTOGAL INTO THE PICTURE.

I shook my head in dismay as I read the morning papers on January 21. The story was undoubtedly overplayed, I thought, but it was a "natural" in the news business. It had all the ingredients of a small-sized "scandal"—especially at a time when the new Mayor had just pledged in his inaugural address that it was his hope that the "highest levels of this Administration will establish a moral and ethical tone which will pervade every department and agency with an unshakable respect for decency and honesty." The next day, reporters checking Katsy Thomas' status were told she could not be hired by the Office of Economic Opportunity in Washington. This caused Lindsay's antipoverty staff to backtrack and I had to announce that she would be an "unpaid consultant." The announcement touched off a new rash of stories about how Lindsay had changed his mind because of the publicity. Officially, he denied any knowledge of the affair. "I didn't hear anything about it until I read it in the newspapers. I know perfectly well these matters are of more concern to the press than anyone else," he said at a press conference.

On that same morning, there was a story in the *Times* which indicated that Bob Price had been busy behind the scenes getting involved with the Police Department. I had received a call from a reporter the day before who had asked me: Was it true that Price had asked the Police Department not to fill six first-grade detective vacancies? The reporter had said Price could not be reached for comment, so I had gone into Price's office and told him of the inquiry. Price confirmed the action and told me to tell the reporter it had been "in connection with many requests to many departments in line with the Mayor's executive order to hold down hiring." When I was asked why Price had singled out jobs of first-grade detectives, I relayed the question to Price and, in turn, Price's answer to the *Times:* "No comment."

It was obvious to me that the *Times* had caught Price in an unusual power move at City Hall and the story the next day reflected this. On page one, next to the Katsy Thomas story, this headline appeared:

CITY HALL SHIFTS
POLICY ON POLICE

Orders 6 Posts Held Open,
Breaking Old Tradition

The *Herald Tribune* also carried the story under the headline:

A City Hall
Try at Role
In Police

The *Tribune* quoted a spokesman for the Police Department as saying: "Promotions in the Police Department are made on merit, and they are made by one man alone, Commissioner Vincent Broderick." It went on to report that Broderick's term was scheduled to expire February 21 and that there had been speculation that he might not be reappointed because he disagreed with Lindsay on the issue of the Civilian Review Board. It also quoted the Mayor who had answered questions about Broderick at a press conference the day before, as saying that Broderick was a "good commissioner. The whole department handled itself with distinction during the transit strike."

The *Daily News,* predictably, carried a headline:

POLICE RESENT
A 'BUTTING IN'
BY CITY HALL

And the *News* story quoted a high police source saying: "This could be the ruination of the Police Department if the commissioner isn't allowed to run his own department."

It was clear to me that Price had, indeed, wanted to reserve the first-grade detective vacancies for his own choice of a hand-picked group of men to serve the Mayor and himself at City Hall. There already were at least a half dozen plainclothes detectives assigned to the Mayor's office, but Price apparently wanted men of his own choice. A long-time friend of Sanford Garelik's, chief inspector of the department, Price also wanted to see Garelik made Police commissioner, according to some rumors I had heard. Some of the stories reported Price had used detectives to run errands for him—including delivering coffee and sandwiches—and that he had also used radio cars for travelling around the city.

I did not discuss the matter any further with Price. I made up my mind that day, however, that if I should get any further inquiries about City Hall's role in the Police Department that I would refer the newsman directly to Price.

In the meantime, there were many other stories breaking around me. Robert Moses had released a statement the day before opposing Lindsay-supported legislation in Albany to unify all the transit facilities within the city into one Transportation Administration. That story, too, received page one space in the morning newspapers and it meant that we would have to have a confrontation with Robert Moses—sooner or later. The Mayor had told me that he did not want to "take on Moses" too early in our Administration, but that unless Moses came around, he intended to use all of the powers of the mayoralty to stand up to him. No mayor ever had in the past.

It appeared that Lindsay intended to stand up to anybody and everybody, if necessary, in order to make changes he wanted. With the transit strike now behind us, I realized that the Mayor intended to make his battle for fiscal reform the next big issue. In off-the-cuff remarks at a Boy Scout fund-raising dinner for some 750 Wall Street men at a midtown hotel, I was with him when he said—much to my astonishment: "If the public does not wish to support my reform efforts, the city can go back to jungle conditions and deteriorate as before. I have a four-year job and I am prepared to put the house in order." Then he asked his listeners to spread the word so New Yorkers would "say yes to our efforts and that all will be members of a Proud City."

At the end of our first three weeks in office, I felt as if we had been at City Hall for three years. Tensions were still running high within the Mayor's office. Many of the Mayor's assistants were still unsure of the exact nature of their jobs and there was a fierce rivalry among many of the younger aides who competed to see who could spend the most time with the Mayor, either in his office or else lounging around in the small hallway leading into it. In addition, I noticed that there was virtually no communication with the East Wing of the building where City Council President Frank O'Connor and the City Council were located. In an effort to ease the "cold war" between the West and East Wings, I had a direct telephone line installed between my desk and that of Paul Bragdon, executive assistant to O'Connor. I also started a system of exchanging press releases. However, neither of us used the phone much and it didn't seem to do much good even when we did talk; our respective bosses either didn't want to or weren't capable of establishing a rapport at the top. We both resigned ourselves to accept that fact.

I thought that much of the blame for this failure lay with Lindsay. On several occasions—at small staff meetings in the Mayor's office—I suggested that the Mayor invite O'Connor and David Ross, majority leader of the Council, over to our offices more often. An O'Connor aide, Mrs. Beatrice Shainswit,[4] whom I knew socially, encouraged me to open the lines of communication between Lindsay and O'Connor. But my idea was turned down by other Lindsay aides who claimed that "you can't trust them—they're Democrats," or "O'Connor and Ross don't understand what we're trying to do." I continued to pursue the matter until one day in our third week I heard the Mayor himself say something about O'Connor "not having much to say so why should I bother with him?" I realized that Lindsay had made up his mind. He thought he didn't need the Democrats to succeed at City Hall and wanted to ignore them—at least most of the time. He had heard how O'Connor's followers, as well as the press, whose quarters were in the East Wing near O'Connor's office, had picked nicknames for him—among them "Mr. Clean," "Captain Marvel" and "Prince Valiant"—and he was not happy about being the subject of ridicule. He had also developed a habit during these first weeks of calling me every time a news story was unfavorable and asking me: "Why are they writing these stories? Why is the press so petty? Don't they realize what I'm up against? Why don't they get interested in my reorganization plan—something substantive—instead of focusing on all that trivia?"

I tried many times to explain to Lindsay the basic formula for journalistic success at City Hall: Readers want gossipy details that prove city officials often make mistakes; and the reporter who can throw the most mud on the man on the "white horse" is the biggest newspaper hero. And Lindsay was viewed as the shining white knight on a charger. But this explanation never seemed to satisfy him. When I would often side with the press in some of our discussions about the necessity for him to tell the public what he was doing, he would turn to me, annoyed, and say: "I don't have to tell the press everything I'm doing! Many of these reporters are not interested in the important issues of government, anyway. The press wants to run City Hall and I'm not going to let them. Public officials are entitled to make news in the public interest without that news being distorted by the press. That's why I want to make more use of direct television broadcasts to the public." Lindsay's attitude toward the press, unfortunately, was contagious. Other mayoral aides began to refuse to talk to reporters candidly. Bob Price was the chief problem, but there were others continuously planting rumors with the press and making my job even more difficult than it was.

Barry Gottehrer, who had left his newspaper job at the *Herald Tribune* to work for Price during the campaign, was by far the most aggressive of the young men around Lindsay. One day after the transit strike was over and I had taken the reporters from Room 9 out to lunch, he came over to me and gratuitously said: "You're doing better. But you have a long way to go." I ignored the comment. I realized that as one of Price's most trusted lieutenants during the campaign, Gottehrer was trying hard to place himself as close to the Mayor and to influence him as much as possible. He would walk with him from one place to another, ride in his car with him, sit in his office and serve as a kind of shadow adviser who was always in the background. I frequently found it difficult to conduct a conversation with Lindsay about a press release or anything else without finding Gottehrer standing within a few feet. He would either anticipate my actions by offering his own advice to the Mayor before I did, or he would second-guess me after I had made a suggestion.

Few of Lindsay's commissioners failed to recognize how selfish and power-hungry many of his assistants at City Hall had become. Frequently, when a commissioner wanted to speak with the Mayor, he would have to talk first with Gottehrer, Kriegel or Davidoff. Only Bob Sweet, Lindsay's executive assistant, was secure and wise enough not to play this kind of role. The reason these young men could grab such power was that the Mayor wanted to have a pleasant relationship with all of his top appointees, but he also wanted to feel protected by this group around him whom he completely trusted. Gottehrer soon took advantage of Lindsay's need to depend on others around him and began to tell him what to do—without any apparent reason. For example, one day we were riding uptown to a meeting and Lindsay was complaining about something which Deputy Mayor Tim Costello's office had not done. Gottehrer leaned forward and, in a flat matter-of-fact voice, told Lindsay: "Costello must go, John. You'll have to get rid of him." I was astonished Lindsay didn't respond as he continued to thumb through a pile of papers on his lap.

Of all the people around the Mayor who sought power, however, Price was by far the most deliberate and successful. Instead of acting like an official who was working in the public interest, he appeared to be much more determined to build up a power base of his own, and to continue his clandestine campaign role as "unofficial" press secretary for Lindsay. This was something about which I had been forewarned by several friends of mine in the press, so it did not come as too much of a surprise to me when Price continued to "leak" stories to the press after we began running the city.

And, while Price was a superb political tactician, it soon became evident that he could not handle public power well himself. The charges of "interference," raised by Price's order to hold open the six detective vacancies, mushroomed into a major controversy. City Council President O'Connor assailed what he called "the attempt by the Mayor's office to interfere in the professional operations of the Police Department." Lindsay tried to back away from Price's actions (which I was sure had been taken without consulting Lindsay) by stating that Police Commissioner Broderick was free to fill the vacancies, but the controversy continued against the background of the budget crisis which the Mayor had talked about in his fireside chat. Price even tried to deny knowledge of his own request. In an interview with the *Times,* he said he knew of no specific request that six detective posts go unfilled: "I don't know what the number six means in this context, to be honest with you," he was quoted as saying.

The Mayor responded to O'Connor's attack by saying that Price was "a good public servant doing a good job and has my complete backing."

It was clear to me—and to the press—that Price was trying to tie the Mayor's hands on the appointment of Broderick, too. Price's campaign to unseat Broderick had begun in December and by mid-January he was leaking a number of stories about the major differences between Lindsay's plan for a Civilian Review Board and Broderick's refusal to support such a plan. The *Post's* Maurice Carroll wrote on January 23: "Deputy Mayor Price is seeking to prevent the reappointment of Police Commissioner Broderick—although Lindsay has not yet made up his mind on this post. Lindsay was bothered by the series of planted newspaper stories to the effect that 'Broderick must go.' It is an open secret that Price has been the source of the stories."

By January 25, the Price vs. Police story developed to the point where it was page one news in every paper and a major event on TV news. Price had no alternative but to back down and settle with the police. So he conferred with John J. Cassese, the president of the Patrolmen's Benevolent Association at City Hall. Afterwards, the two men held a press conference during which Price defended himself vigorously and claimed someone else had used his name to send policemen out for coffee and sandwiches. Cassese said, "I believe we have an understanding now." The outcome was clear. The Mayor later admitted to reporters: "I think the Police commissioner ought to be completely autonomous. But, as Mayor, it is my job to supervise all departments." The *Times,* subscribing to Price's explanation that "Someone, apparently misusing the name of Deputy Mayor Price," had committed the offense, excused Price and called the incident "Trivia in a Coffee Pot."

About the same time Price's troubles with the police seemed to be clearing up, Lindsay stepped in to defend his deputy. In an impromptu press conference at City Hall the Mayor—believing the old adage that the best defense is a good offense—charged that "special interests" were responsible for the complaints against Price. After the press conference, when reporters cornered the Mayor in the hallway to ask him about his Deputy Mayor, he was visibly annoyed. "Now lookie here," he snapped. "We have a very independent Fusion non-partisan government. Nobody owns City Hall. No individuals have back door entry. When you do that, you shake up a lot of establishments and a lot of special interests—the power brokers."

"Well, Mr. Mayor," said one reporter. "Who *are* the power brokers? You mentioned them during the strike."

"Who are the power brokers?" the Mayor replied with a smile. "They know who they are!"

No sooner had the Mayor cleared the air on the police dispute, when Price caused another flap in the press by drawing the fire of a Negro clergyman, the Reverend George Lawrence, a Brooklyn Baptist minister. After a meeting at the Roosevelt Hotel with the Mayor—ostensibly to discuss the role of Negroes in the Lindsay Administration—Lawrence surprised the City Hall reporters by saying: "We told the Mayor if we had a problem we would come to him directly. He is the man we elected, not a Deputy Mayor or anyone else in this city. We elected Mr. Lindsay, not Bob Price, as Mayor. We're going to deal with the Mayor." Then, Lawrence accused Price of treating Negro office seekers "arrogantly." He continued: "I know from my personal experience that he is the most heartless man I ever met in my life. During the campaign when he was dealing with people like the Negro people, he pulled them around like cattle. I know many people have gotten a brushoff from Mr. Price. He doesn't treat them with dignity."

Price had "No comment," but the Mayor, responding to a request for a comment, said: "I have great respect for Reverend Lawrence and the others who came to see me, but I don't agree with him on that score."

As time-consuming as the inquiries about Price were, they were only a small part of the total volume of calls and requests for information from my office in the last part of January. Lindsay was moving in so many directions at once that his actions were causing great dismay among a number of segments of the city's population. The many-sided attempts at change promoted the *Daily News* to plead publicly, in an editorial on January 22: TAKE IT EASY, MR. MAYOR. The editorial referred to the Katsy Thomas and Bob Price affairs as well as the talk of a city income tax which, the editorial stated, "is sending waves of jitters coursing through the business community, and moving many a management to think of either getting the hell or staying the hell out of this city. Take it easy, will you, Mr. Mayor, please, for New York's sake and your own?"

Meanwhile, the pace of news inquiries quickened. Reporters, trying to keep up with all of Lindsay's frenetic activities, reported on scores of other developments. Among them:

• The reappointment of Seymour N. (Sy) Siegel, director of WNYC for the previous nineteen years, who had earlier handed in his application for retirement to Mayor Lindsay because, he said, he was not given an assurance the station would not be sold by the city for economy reasons. Siegel had asked Price whether there was any substance to the reports that the city was contemplating selling the municipal broadcasting system's two radio stations and Price was said to have told Siegel the matter was "under study." Left hanging, he had made plans to retire because the reported move was not refuted. I suggested to the Mayor he meet with Siegel and reassure him his job was not in jeopardy. The two men met and on January 25, I released a statement to the press saying that both WNYC and Siegel would be retained.

• A rash of calls about Mrs. Belle Davidoff, mother of Sidney H. Davidoff, assistant Buildings commissioner. She had been hired by Buildings Commissioner Moerdler at $3,750 per year as a clerk. Confronted with the disclosure, however, Moerdler denied any knowledge of the application, and said he would not approve it. The *Herald Tribune* reported the story under the headline: ANOTHER CASE OF 'UNHIRING'—with a reference to the Katsy Thomas story. The Davidoff story was a source of momentary embarrassment to the Mayor. I viewed it as another example of our new Administration trying to take advantage of power and patronage. (Author's Note: Davidoff was later assigned to the post of assistant to the Mayor in 1967 in charge of Lindsay's patronage, succeeding Constantine Sidamon-Eristoff, who was named as highways commissioner and later, as transportation administrator.)

• A story about Robert J. Mangum, a former deputy commissioner of Hospitals and a Negro, who had left the Administration to become New York regional director for the Office of

Economic Opportunity. Mangum, a competent professional administrator, had been interested in a post with us, but during the transit strike Price had vetoed him. I had known Bob Mangum when I was a reporter and I had liked him. I had recommended to Price that Mangum be retained, but Price, recalling that Mangum had once been accused of fixing a friend's ticket when he was deputy Police commissioner in the Wagner Administration, had told me: "We don't want him—not with that on his record." Because of Price's failure to retain him in city government, Mangum became bitter toward Lindsay and our entire Administration.

• A story about how the Mayor had filled a $15,500-a-year post which he had branded during his campaign as "evidence of the way in which a Democratic administration layers unwarranted expenditures on the taxpayers." The job was deputy highways commissioner for Staten Island. Lindsay had pledged to eliminate five deputy posts (one for each borough), stating: "It is obvious there is no need for these jobs." When I asked Lindsay about the appointment, he told me he knew nothing about it. I told him that he would have to tell that to the press. He did.

• A story alleging that Moerdler had threatened to quit because of the Mayor's job freeze, and that only after the Mayor and Price gave personal assurances that his budgetary and manpower requests would be screened and not lumped into the Mayor's "no exceptions" category of the job freeze, was Moerdler mollified. The story, written by *Herald Tribune* reporter Fred Ferretti, was accurate. He reported that Moerdler had called Barry Gottehrer and me a few minutes before the Mayor was about to give his fireside chat asking for municipal austerity. I did not have any knowledge of a conversation between Moerdler and Gottehrer, but Moerdler had called me, complaining about the job freeze. He told me he would resign unless he got the funds he wanted.

• The launching of Lindsay's plan to open 35 Little City Halls throughout the city, at a cost of $1.25 million a year, immediately drew the fire of several borough presidents. They complained about possible duplication of effort, waste, possible political motives, proliferation of government agencies, confusion, and non-essential expenditures in a time of fiscal crisis. Also, they were worried that the plan would pre-empt their own power in the neighborhoods. Lindsay's reply: He wanted to "humanize" government, put it into the field and the local level. "If the funds are not forthcoming," he told a news conference, "I'll take to the stump. I'll walk the streets. I'll take it to the people." Lindsay added: "It's a very modest expenditure to bring some sense of participation to the people. Our basic objective is to generate a sense of community involvement in city affairs—without regard to political affiliations—and to place city government more closely at the disposal of the people." The Mayor explained that the offices would be staffed on a completely non-partisan basis, but the suspicion that he would employ them as Lindsay storefronts for political purposes prevented the plan from getting off to a fast start.

• The final chapter in the Mike Quill story. After leaving Mt. Sinai Hospital, Quill had his final say. In a January 25 press conference at the Americana Hotel's Albert Hall—where he had been arrested on January 4 for violating an antistrike injunction —Quill accused President Johnson of having played "cheap politics with the lives and fortunes of the people of the city." He also attacked Governor Rockefeller for waiting until the last minute before he offered $100 million to help the Transit Authority and not finding the money before the strike. Surprisingly, he had some kind words for Lindsay:

"Mayor Lindsay did everything he could once he realized the seriousness of the situation. I called him a pipsqueak and an amateur in the heat of battle and under war conditions, and I will have to hold those kind of words for now." As for Senator Kennedy, Quill had nothing but praise: "He was the only top Federal official who did anything, who came in and actually tried to end the strike. He was on top of the negotiations and the situation all the time." Quill also demanded a Congressional investigation of the events that led up to the strike.

Three days later, Mike Quill was dead. He was the victim of a heart attack in bed in his five-room apartment on the thirty-seventh floor of his apartment house at 15 West 72nd Street. I learned of his death about 6 P.M. on Friday, January 28, and I immediately telephoned Lindsay, who was in New Haven for the weekend attending a meeting of the Yale Board of Overseers. I had written a few paragraphs which would be appropriate for a mayoral comment. Lindsay told me he did not want to say too much. The comment we finally agreed to release to the press: "Michael Quill's death marks the end of an era. He was a man who was very much a part of New York. My sympathy goes to his wife and family."

• A visit on January 21 from Julian Bond, a Negro who had been denied his seat in the Georgia Legislature because he opposed the war in Vietnam. Bond, a handsome, articulate young man, had been elected in June, 1965, but refused a seat on January 10, 1966, after he had endorsed a statement by a civil rights group accusing the United States of aggression in Vietnam. A meeting with the Mayor had been arranged. I sat in. The Mayor carefully listened to Bond's plea for support. Bond did most of the talking. When the twenty-minute session was over, I told Lindsay the press wanted a statement from him. "Delighted," he responded. Then he strode out to the Blue Room and declared: "It strikes me there is a very clear and interesting First [free speech] Amendment case here. If I were still in the private practice of law, it is a case I would be pleased to take on and argue." I was intrigued by Lindsay's ability to meet the challenge of supporting Bond without actually stating any agreement with Bond's position that the United States was the "aggressor" in the Vietnam war.[5]

• A dispute between the Mayor and Robert Kennedy, about a vacant lot in the Bronx. With a great deal of fanfare, Lindsay had taken his wife, Mary, Parks Commissioner Hoving, Sanitation Commissioner Periconi and a number of other officials up to a rubble-strewn lot on East 138th Street for a Saturday clean-up and a little touch football. Only a few days before the clean-up, Kennedy had suggested to Hoving that that particular lot be made into a modern park. As a result, the *Herald Tribune* ran a story headlined: LINDSAY PLAYED ON KENNEDY'S TURF. Tom Johnston, an aide to Kennedy, said the Senator's plan had been in the works for a year and that Kennedy had been "amazed" that nothing was said of his plan when the Mayor went up to clean up the lot. It was clearly a case of one-upmanship by Lindsay and, I thought, undoubtedly a response to Kennedy's performance at City Hall during the transit strike. The clean-up incident also took place the day after both Kennedy and Lindsay had appeared at a conference to discuss Harlem's future. The Mayor had arrived before the Senator, talked for a few minutes and had just invited questions from the floor when Kennedy came in and was promptly given the floor. The Mayor, in turn, sat through a few minutes of Kennedy's speech and left before Kennedy had finished. As Lindsay passed, Kennedy looked up at him and smiled and said: "Bye, John." Clearly, the two men had been publicly jousting with each other all month.

• Press releases on the appointments of Timothy J. Cooney, as interim director of Civil Defense; Arthur E. Palmer as chairman of the Transportation Council; Harold Riegelman as chairman of a Task Force on the personnel system; Alfonso Narvaez to head the new office of inspector general in the Buildings Department; Oliver Pilat as assistant to the Mayor; Robert M. Blum as assistant to the Mayor in charge of the Little City Halls program; and David Garth, the award-winning television producer, as special consultant to the Mayor for communications.

Rocked by a transit strike at the outset of the month, jolted by the news of a possible city income tax, and virtually breathless from watching and listening to the new Mayor proclaim new programs and reforms, the residents of New York City were worn out, it seemed to me, toward the end of January. Added to their problems was the first snow emergency of the winter and a cold snap, during which the temperature plummeted to near zero, causing the Governor to open National Guard armories for families without heat in their homes. The Mayor then announced that the city's antipoverty agency would pay the hotel bills at the Astor Hotel which would accommodate between 100 and 150 stricken people. There were numerous delays on the subways due to the freezing weather and, at month's end, the city found itself in a weather crisis.

Despite the many problems which had cropped up during these early days, thousands of people who worked or voted for John Lindsay wanted to join him in city government. On the last day of January, Mayoral Assistant Connie Eristoff told reporters that the Lindsay Administration had received some 3,000 applications for jobs since Election Day. "I guess there are something more than 100 members of the Lindsay campaign group working in the city government now," he said. "We've had fair success placing our people, but the job freeze has made it more difficult," he said. I read this story with particular interest because, with all the pressures of the first month, I had also been subjected to several dozen telephone calls from old friends and casual acquaintances, many of whom wanted something from the Mayor. I knew that this was part of politics, but I had not realized that everyone would descend upon us at once. My file of correspondence with job seekers in the public relations field had grown to over 100 by the time I could begin to answer the requests. Among them, telephone calls from several ex-Wagner Administration officials who offered their services, as well as notes and messages from many of the public relations men currently in government who were worried about their jobs. The pressure built up from all sides. My work was never over and continued with an unrelenting pace throughout each day and night. I had six telephone lines installed in my house—to the Mayor at City Hall, the Mayor at Gracie Mansion, Bob Price's house, my own office, a separate number for calls from the press and a private line for personal friends.

For all of us in the Administration, those early days were chaotic and extraordinarily demanding. During the first month, we seemed to be running in circles. There were many meetings, but not much action. The kind of headlines that Lindsay received were headlines having to do with his personal appearances —such as at a fire one night or at a building collapse or at an empty garbage-strewn lot which he pledged to clean up.

From the initial shock of the transit strike, at the outset, we went through a period of numbness to our broad responsibilities, and then we awakened toward the end of the month to the fact that there was so much ahead of us, and so little time to do it. The whole city wanted everything instantly. Civic, religious, business and labor groups, politicians and citizens' groups, were all after Lindsay to do everything—and immediately.

In response to this, the Mayor worked a backbreaking schedule, from about 8 in the morning to 12 or 1 A.M., averaging 16 or 18 hours a day. He was receiving about 13,000 letters and 5,000 telephone calls a week from people all wanting to reach him.

Obviously, he could respond to only a small percentage of these himself, while aides handled the others.[6] Requests to see the Mayor came from all parts of the world. Letters and telephone calls from foreign journalists were frequent. They sought his views on Vietnam, nuclear testing, NATO and almost every other major national and international topic. They came from Germany, South America, Switzerland, Israel, Ireland, Canada, Japan and other countries. Radio and TV crews and correspondents flew in from Canada and from all parts of the United States. And there were state visits scheduled—Prince Philip of Great Britain, Mayor Willy Brandt of West Berlin, Madame Gandhi of India, President Shazar of Israel, President Shick of Nicaragua, Prime Minister Holt of Australia and Governor Vilella of Puerto Rico, not to mention the many Senators and Congressmen and other dignitaries who wrote or telephoned the Mayor or Mrs. Lindsay almost daily.

It was no wonder that Lindsay, as a result, looked tired and was fidgety and short-tempered much of the time. Days went by, sometimes weeks, without any major decisions having been made, because he was caught up in such a frantic schedule of public appointments and appearances. On the evening of January 31, I spoke to Mary Lindsay about this at some length. Mrs. Lindsay, who had two secretaries of her own—Stephanie Fuchs at City Hall and Joan Gregory at Gracie Mansion—said Lindsay's calendar should be cleared away for six months while he settled down to the business of running the city. She also said there were a lot of unnecessary appointments, such as all the religious and social events he was invited to attend because it was fashionable to have him there. Harvey Rothenberg, the appointments secretary whose job it was to fit all of the Mayor's appointments, speaking engagements, dinners and ribbon-cutting ceremonies into his schedule, had told me Lindsay was receiving between 300 to 500 written invitations a week in addition to 200 to 300 telephone requests for appointments with him. Rothenberg was just as troubled by the pressures on Lindsay as I was. "My job," he had said, "is to keep John alive and you don't do that by overscheduling." The trouble was, of course, that there was only one John Lindsay and if he didn't appear on some of those occasions, no substitutes were accepted.

John Lindsay, in fact, was the whole Administration. His presence and his performing manner, his spirit and vigor were reflected throughout city government. There was no other person in those first thirty-one days, with the exception of Bob Price, who came across as a strong personality or who lent the Administration any stamp of character or humor. Although most New Yorkers couldn't detect it, the Mayor had an excellent sense of humor. Once in a while he would display signs of it in public —when he talked to a civic or political club, for example, he would open his talk by recalling the 1965 election campaign. "It's no secret," he would say, "that I got my job through the *New York Times*," referring, of course, to the fact that the *Times* supported him editorially all during the 1965 campaign. Despite everything he had going for him, however, despite his personal popularity among most of the voters, he still seemed unsure of what he should be, how he should act. He knew, of course, that he had the ability to come across in general terms. But, I sensed he still felt a lack of identity. Being Mayor of New York did not seem to come easily or naturally to John Lindsay.

5 *"I am determined that we must succeed, no matter how bloody and how costly the battle...."*

AT THE END of the Administration's first 100 days, one newsman summed up the period in terms that many of us, engulfed in the tumult of City Hall, could well appreciate. John Morganthaler of the Associated Press wrote, "John V. Lindsay has been Mayor for three months and they've been giving him a hard time."

And Edward J. Silberfarb, of the New York *Herald Tribune* City Hall staff, in an article on April 10, pointed out this uncomfortable truth: "Mayor Lindsay's first 100 days in office end today, and so ends the magical period when a new chief executive is expected to accomplish nothing less than the superhuman." He added: "In this campaign, Mr. Lindsay spelled out the problems and thus created a big one for himself—a need for immediate action in the very crisis areas that he had depicted. He has since found that 100 days is just a twinkling in the period needed to move the programs he portrayed in scores of campaign speeches, position papers and platform promises."

It was obvious that the massive changes we had planned would take time under ideal circumstances. But we were slowed further by the unpredictable, nerve-wracking events of those first three months.

Though the Mayor was faced with more urgent matters, I knew it was imperative for him to maintain good relations with the news media. The Mayor still didn't fully realize that the press had a right, indeed, an obligation, to keep a careful watch on all of his activities. "The thing I've found the hardest to get used to," he told a reporter in his office one day, "is the goldfish-bowl life here. You can't go to the bathroom without being observed. There's no such thing as a private conversation or a private visit. You're being watched all the time." In an attempt to begin improving our relations with one of our worst critics, I scheduled a luncheon with the top executives of the *Daily News* and the Mayor, Price and myself on February 2. The questioning was direct and pointed: Weren't his plans for Little City Halls nothing more than Lindsay-for-President storefronts around the city? And they particularly challenged the transit strike settlement as too costly. Lindsay explained that he was in a position where he had to make up for twelve years of inequities within the transit union, that he could not give a flat wage package to all workers, that unskilled transit workers—mostly Negroes— had comprised more than 50 percent of the New York Local and that all of this had helped to complicate the negotiations.

The *News* executives, most of them men in their sixties, listened unsympathetically to his explanation. Lindsay was equally impatient with his hosts. It was hardly a cordial or even constructive luncheon. Lindsay seemed to feel that they had no right to question him. After lunch, when we went downstairs to the Mayor's awaiting car on 42nd Street in front of the *News* building, he stepped into the car and, smiling, said to me: "A youthful bunch, weren't they? And so receptive!" His biting remark left no doubt in my mind that this would be the last time we would attempt to talk to the *Daily News* management. The paper had been attacking the Mayor editorially ever since he had declared his candidacy in May, 1965. It wasn't long after this visit that Lindsay actually stopped reading the *News*. He asked that the delivery of the *News*, which normally accompanied the *Herald Tribune* and the *Times* on a corner table of his City Hall office every morning, be discontinued.

When we arrived back in City Hall that afternoon, I joined Lindsay in a scheduled meeting with a group of about seventy-five Puerto Rican leaders, including Bronx Borough President

Herman Badillo, in the Blue Room. When we entered the room, they stood and applauded him. There had been a great deal of support for the Mayor in the Spanish communities of the city during the campaign. He had achieved an unusually high popularity in these districts, which normally went to the Democratic Party candidates. Despite this reservoir of good will, however, it was apparent from the beginning of this meeting that it wasn't going to turn out well. Among those attending were Louis Hernandez, who had lost his job as city collector when we took office; Roberto Lebron, who had been dropped from his job as assistant commissioner of Real Estate; and John Carro, who had been an assistant to former Mayor Wagner. They spoke first. They all complained that a number of Puerto Ricans had been "forced" to resign since Lindsay took office and not enough Puerto Ricans had been appointed—especially in "policy-making" positions—to replace them.

After a number of individuals finished talking, I was as surprised as anyone else in the room when the Mayor said to the group sternly: "Now lookie here. As far as I'm concerned, no particular ethnic group owns any job. City Hall is not a trading post. If an Italian-American leaves a city job, or a white Protestant or a Spanish-speaking American, they do not have to be replaced by persons of their identical backgrounds. I intend to staff city government with the very best people and to move the city forward in the public interest. I will not make my decision on the basis of pressures from special interest groups, but what I think is right and proper for the city as a whole." The group was taken aback completely. Badillo launched a heavy attack and he was followed by others. Lindsay finally backed down a little and said that if he found qualified Puerto Ricans who would best fit into specific jobs, they would be invited to join the Administration. The meeting broke up after an hour of wrangling. Badillo then held a hallway press conference in which he blasted the Mayor: "During his campaign, Lindsay promised additional representation to Puerto Ricans in government, but we have less now than we did six years ago and that's not right," he told a group of eagerly awaiting reporters.

The next day I was asked by the *Post* to "work up a list of the Puerto Ricans" we had in our Administration. I did, and then gave it to a reporter. We came out all right with the numbers, but I felt a little disgusted playing this kind of game after the Mayor had taken such a moralistic public stand about ethnic pressures. In compiling the list I was helped by John Ortiz, a mayoral assistant who had worked for Lindsay during the campaign. Ortiz said that eight Puerto Ricans had left key jobs, but that eight had been hired, holding the level at thirty-five Puerto Ricans in various middle and high echelon posts. Unfortunately, the newspaper article pointed up one inconsistency in Lindsay's statement by emphasizing that Ortiz himself is Puerto Rican, having taken over the duties performed under Wagner by Mayoral Assistant John Carro, also a Puerto Rican.

One of the ironies that resulted from Lindsay's position on this issue was that several newspapers which had previously been critical of the Mayor supported him solidly. The *Journal-American,* for example, published an editorial: "Lindsay on Target" and said: "It took political courage for Mayor Lindsay to say what he said to a group of Puerto Ricans who went to City Hall seeking more jobs in the city government. . . . Mr. Lindsay made it clear that he is trying to determine appointments on the basis of the best person for the job—any job. He is dead right in his resolution."

Coverage of every meeting Lindsay had in or out of City Hall was still intense as we entered February, so I began relying more and more on my first assistant, Warren Gardner, whose easy-going manner and even temper was a real asset to both me and the Mayor. However, during the first few weeks, Gardner had told me privately that he felt he should have received more money when he accepted the job. He had agreed to work for $15,000 a year— the same amount he was making as public relations director of Mobilization for Youth, the Lower East Side antipoverty project.

Responding to his request, I spoke to Lindsay and then sent a confidential memorandum to him requesting an immediate $3,000 increase for Gardner. I sent my memorandum to the Mayor on February 2 and gave a copy to Gardner. The next day, Gardner came to me and told me he was leaving for a job as assistant press secretary to Governor Rockefeller under Leslie Slote. I had always been on good terms with Slote so I was somewhat surprised to find that he had hired Gardner away from Lindsay and me at a $5,000 pay increase after we had only been in office for a little more than a month. I suggested to Gardner that we go in to see the Mayor and tell him. Gardner, a Negro, and someone Lindsay liked, would be the first person at City Hall to resign. I wasn't sure how the Mayor would respond to the news.

"Feel that there is no ill-will," the Mayor said in his office to Gardner. "Always do what is best for you professionally. Do what is best for yourself and your family. And when you make a decision that is right for you, stick with it. Walk tall, and when you leave, do it with style. Good luck to you, Warren." He shook hands with Gardner and, in a matter of minutes, it was over. Gardner seemed relieved—and I was, although his departure now meant I had to begin searching for a new assistant.

On this same day, coincidentally, Mickey Carroll had written a piece in the *Post* describing how our Administration was just beginning to relax. His story was based mainly on an informal interview I had arranged for Lindsay and some dozen regular "Room 9" newspaper reporters in the Mayor's small office after a weekend in which he had been to Washington to clean up the house in which he had lived in as a Congressman. Carroll, one of the most capable reporters in the City Hall press corps, wrote: "This was John Lindsay at his best—his personal warmth coming through, his tendency toward verbal imprecision that is aggravated by the television cameras disappearing now in the informal give and take. It was, too, a side of John Lindsay that is going to be seen more and more. The new Administration, jolted by a series of well-publicized flaps, is going to shift its approach." And then he quoted me saying: "We're just starting to behave the way we always intended to." The quote was accurate.

Two days later, in the Mayor's absence, Bob Price chaired the regular Friday morning Cabinet meeting, which, by now, had become a focal point of interest for the press. Newsmen were not permitted to attend, but after each session they button-holed many of the participants and several always willingly talked. On this particular morning, Moerdler gave a full report on the terrible building conditions in the East New York section of Brooklyn. Price topped Moerdler's performance with a one-liner when Moerdler had finished. "Two more cold snaps," Price said, "and Moerdler will be running for Governor." Everyone laughed.

As soon as this session was over, several newsmen who learned of Moerdler's report asked me to arrange a follow-up talk with Price. I went into his office and urged him to tell them about Moerdler's report and then to announce that our Administration intended to take "immediate action" to correct some of the conditions. Price did just that, and the afternoon *Journal-American* carried a headline: A CRASH PROGRAM ON SLUMS. The next morning, the *Times* followed suit with a long story under the headline:

CITY WILL ATTACK
SLUM IN BROOKLYN

Price Pledges Broad Effort
for 39 Square Blocks
in East New York

Other stories in the press at this time all seemed to be favorable, for a change. The *Times* carried a story, headlined: LINDSAY LIVES UP TO MR. CLEAN TITLE. It was about his plans to repaint City Hall and many of the municipal buildings in the City Hall area; the *Tribune* carried a story, photos and a big chart depicting the names and ages of all the young Lindsay appointees. Much to my surprise, I found that, at thirty-five, I was among the older men around the Mayor, older than Price and seven other mayoral assistants, older than Parks Commissioner Hoving and a number of other commissioners.

But the fast-breaking events of those early weeks seemed to be aging all of us. The controversy that had swirled around Vincent Broderick resumed on Monday, February 7, with the release from City Hall of a report by an eight-member task force on the Police Department. It recommended the creation of a police review board with a civilian majority, as proposed by the Mayor during his campaign. The *News* headlined the story: ARE SKIDS GREASED FOR BRODERICK? The *Times* played the story straight, headlining it: SWEEPING CHANGES IN POLICE POWERS URGED ON LINDSAY. The twenty-eight-page report went into great detail, suggesting new and modern methods of streamlining the department. It was compiled by the task force, with Jay Kriegel having a big hand in writing it as staff director of the task force. The *World-Telegram*, claiming a "high police official" as its source, ran a story stating flatly that "Broderick will not be reappointed when his term expires Feb. 21." Asked for comment, I talked with the Mayor and then told reporters that Lindsay had not yet made up his mind on whether to reappoint Commissioner Broderick. Meanwhile, Broderick, who had been given a copy of the report, was expected to issue a reply, possibly the next day. The Mayor had actually been in Utica, New York, on that day when the report was issued and when he returned to Kennedy Airport, he was surrounded by reporters looking for some comment. One reporter asked him if he thought the Civilian Review Board would ultimately hurt Negroes because police would be reluctant to take action against them. Impatiently, Lindsay replied: "That's utter nonsense."

Had he heard that Broderick would resign?

"I haven't heard anything along those lines."

Had he asked for Broderick's resignation?

The Mayor snapped: "Of course not. When I am ready to make any announcements, I will make them. I don't want the press to be premature in forcing anyone's hand."

Was he going to meet with Broderick?

Lindsay, without answering, turned and walked away from the reporters, heading toward his awaiting limousine. Everybody was angry—the Mayor and the reporters.

Later that afternoon—about 4 P.M., February 7—I was sitting in the Mayor's office with Jay Kriegel when a hand-carried letter from Broderick to Lindsay arrived. Broderick had held a press conference earlier in the afternoon at which he had released the letter. Lindsay opened it himself and, as he began to read the first page, anger flashed across his face. "This is the rudest letter I have ever received. I couldn't imagine writing a letter like this to the Mayor. This is incredible." As he turned the page, he added: "I ought to let this guy have it right now." When he finished the seven-page letter, he was fuming. But Kriegel and I prevailed upon him to restrain himself, despite the provocation. In the letter, Broderick had told Lindsay that the Civilian Review Board was a "cruel hoax" and a "bromide" and he had asked: "Is it not time, Mr. Mayor, for you to say that you renounce political expediency?"

Although Lindsay wanted to fire Broderick then, we urged him to respond softly—for the moment. He took our advice, and we drew up a statement saying only that the Mayor had "complete confidence" in the Police Department and that he would "study the responses submitted by Mr. Broderick in answer to the questions raised in the task force." He added: "I have and will continue at all times to act in the public interest."

Later, we learned that at his press conference Broderick had gone even further than his letter in his off-the-cuff remarks. "I am challenging the Mayor to think brave new thoughts," he told reporters. "I am asking the Mayor that, under the City Charter, the Police commissioner run the department—not the Deputy Mayor. . . ." Asked by a reporter whether Deputy Mayor Robert Price had been trying to run the department, Broderick was silent. After a pause, he said, "I won't comment on that."

The *News* headlined the story the next morning: BRODERICK DEFIES LINDSAY ON BOARD, and, in the afternoon, the *World-Telegram* carried an exclusive interview with Broderick in which the Police commissioner was quoted as saying: "There is absolutely no personality conflict involved. I think Mayor Lindsay is an intelligent, sensitive man. It's the group of young men working for him that I object to." And Broderick was also quoted: "The big difference between the new Administration and me is not this thing of the review board—not really. The big issue is over the question: Who's going to run the police in New York? The Mayor or the Police commissioner?"

The Mayor gained a brief respite from the Broderick controversy with a trip to Washington and a meeting with President Johnson. When he returned on February 9, he seemed invigorated and filled with hope. He had had a good talk with the President and a good meeting with the Washington press corps. He always seemed much happier when he was going to or returning from Washington. Once he told me while sitting at his desk in City Hall, "What do I need this job for? I loved it in Washington. I was wrestling with big issues and with big people. These people are unsophisticated and petty. I had to run for Mayor and win!" Another time, however, when his secretary, Lynn Goree, came into his office with a bill from an airline for $3,500, Lindsay looked at it and said, "I'll take care of it. One reason I ran for Mayor is because I was going broke as a Congressman."

After his trip to Washington, we left for Albany the next day on a bi-partisan trip to appeal for more state funds for the city. Frank O'Connor was on the plane with some of his aides. Lindsay turned to me and whispered: "O'Connor must have gotten some adverse mail on the positions he's been taking against me—he's softening up a bit, have you noticed?" Later at Albany Airport on the way home, I happened to be talking to O'Connor. He said: "You fellows are not in touch with us at all. The legislative program just comes down to us in the City Council without any prior warning. When Johnson wants to get something through, he calls in the opposition and makes a deal with them. That's the way to do it." I nodded my head, smiled and said nothing. O'Connor was probably right, I thought to myself, but this was not the game Lindsay wanted to play.

While the controversy over Broderick grew, I was busy answering inquiries from the press on several other fronts during these early days of February. Wall Street leaders were beginning to grumble publicly about Lindsay's proposed 50 percent increase in securities transfer taxes. Keith Funston, president of the Stock Exchange, had released a "we may move out of town" statement, and other brokers began to object to the Mayor's proposal. Several tried to reach him on the telephone, but were referred to either Murray Drabkin, his tax consultant, Harvey Rothenberg, his appointments secretary, or even my office. My response was always the same: "The Mayor's proposal is necessary to prevent the city from going bankrupt." The Mayor did not attempt to win over the bankers on those issues. He took a strong, uncompromising public stand: "If I am frustrated," he said at an Overseas Press Club luncheon early in February, "it is the people who will be the loser. I know that my program is fair because everyone is equally mad at it." Another reason there was so much objection to it was that it included a graduated tax on net income of all suburbanites who earned their living in New York. This was the first proposed tax of its kind in the nation. Other cities had flat percentage levies on income earned in the city, but Lindsay's covered all income—including dividends, interest and other private income.

The press was also requesting statements from the Mayor on the Lower Manhattan Expressway. Price had told reporters:

"The project is out—this city is for people, not for cars." It had been a spontaneous statement about a twenty-five-year-old controversy. Neither the Mayor nor I knew anything about this statement before Price issued it. Lindsay had previously taken the position that the Expressway—which was needed to alleviate the staggering traffic jams in lower Manhattan—might run around the bottom of the Island. His plan became known as "The Lindsay Loop." I confirmed, in behalf of the Mayor, that the plan now on the drawing boards—which would have destroyed many homes to build the roadway—did not have the Mayor's support. This didn't go as far as Price's statement, of course. Meanwhile, Price warmed up the battle with Robert Moses by telling newsmen—again without checking with Lindsay or me—that Moses "apparently" was an obstacle to the Lindsay Administration and that he should "remove" himself. Moses was chairman of the Triborough Bridge and Tunnel Authority and also the city's Coordinator of Arterial Highways. "I think that Robert Moses has, from time to time, not been flexible enough in working with the elected public officials," Price said. I was aware that the Mayor had instructed some of his legal aides to prepare a bill for introduction in the State Legislature that would unify the entire transit system and give him the power to name the heads of all the agencies, including those which Moses then supervised. But I felt that Price's premature attack on Moses would only enable the crusty and doughty seventy-seven-year-old Moses and our opponents to stiffen their resistance. I knew, on the other hand, that Price's political strategies often succeeded so I watched—along with millions of other New Yorkers—as the drama unfolded. Within days after Price's statement, Rockefeller publicly supported the Lindsay plan, so I figured Price must have talked with the Governor. A few days later, we announced the plan. The *Times* reported that the Mayor intended to remove Moses as head of the Tri-borough Bridge and Tunnel Authority as well as Coordinator of Arterial Highways and replace him with Arthur E. Palmer, the investment banker who had been named to head the Mayor's Transportation Council. The *Times,* on February 20, reported that "Robert Moses is a successful old hand at chopping down elected and public officials who have challenged his policies in the past or threatened to reduce his powers. He is a master of political infighting and has a command of vituperative rhetoric that few of his adversaries can equal. But he seems outmatched this time. Youth, the need to bolster the city's shaky finances and public support are on Mr. Lindsay's side."

Meanwhile, the press continued to pursue us over the lingering "power brokers" issue. Reporters like Fred Ferretti of the *Herald Tribune* continued asking us to identify them by name. Ferretti, a tough, cynical newsman who never let a good story get away from him, was among those who persisted in looking for some of the less important but bothersome and embarrassing stories which had plagued us in January. Ferretti followed up Lindsay's reluctance to identify the "power brokers" in early February by reporting in the *Herald Tribune* some of Price's answers on a Sunday TV show. His article pointed out that Price would not name names, either, except to say there were some in "government" and even in politics. Price added: "They've been running this town for their own personal interest and doing a lot for themselves and getting a lot done for their own people."

Another running news story at this time was the question of the amount of real estate taxes to be paid by the New York Port Authority's World Trade Center, the proposed $525 million project with twin 110-story office skyscrapers—the world's tallest buildings. The Mayor ordered the City Planning Commission to prepare a thorough review of the direct and indirect costs to the city. Donald Shaughnessy, a mayoral assistant, released a statement saying that the Lindsay Administration was not satisfied that the city had made the most advantageous bargain under the previous Administration with the bi-state public agency. The Port Authority was about to begin demolishing buildings when Lindsay named Price to serve as his unofficial emissary in the negotiations with Austin J. Tobin, the powerful and suave executive director of the Authority.

Lindsay continued to make news every day, and on February 14, we were ready to launch our Night Owl Watch Service, a promise he had made in the campaign. The first night, Charles Moerdler was on duty, with Lindsay supervising. The Buildings commissioner raced up to mid-Manhattan about 9:40 P.M. to check on a cornerstone of a building that had fallen on a man below, killing him. Lindsay held a press conference about 11 P.M. to explain that the "Night Mayors" would keep track of what happened in the city at night and they would sleep on a cot in the basement of City Hall. They would be available in case of any city emergency with a private phone to reach the commissioners, including Fire and Police, as well as the Mayor at Gracie Mansion. The Night Mayor, Lindsay explained, would not answer calls from the public, but would receive information from a switchboard telephone operator who would also be on duty all night. Despite the build-up by Lindsay, the experiment got generally poor reviews in the next day's newspapers.

In theory it sounded good, but I was one among those who felt there was really no need for some official to sleep in City Hall every night. A night operator, equipped with every city official's telephone number from the Mayor down, needed only to call an official at home to alert him to any major problems such as explosions or shootings.[1]

Meanwhile, newsmen continued to press for information about the Broderick situation especially after getting wind of a private forty-minute meeting between the commissioner and the Mayor. In response, Lindsay would say only that he intended to go ahead with his plan to set up a Civilian Review Board with four civilians and three police officials, but "the target date is not yet set." The split between the two men seemed to be growing and it was becoming apparent that Broderick would not be the Police commissioner after February 21, the day his term expired. With only a week to go, Lindsay summed up the situation with Broderick and the review board at a press conference: "I'm for it; he's against it."

The next day—February 15—Lindsay called me into his office and said: "Howard Leary is here. He's next door in Bob Price's office. Here's a resume of his background. Call a press conference immediately." I had known that Lindsay was talking to a number of people about the Police commissioner's job, but I had not known until the day before that Leary had been selected. I was in the Mayor's office when he had telephoned Mayor James H. K. Tate of Philadelphia to thank him for Leary. A stocky, five foot seven inch man, weighing 165 pounds with sparse, iron-gray hair, Leary was quiet-spoken. His eyes were knowing and cool and he replied in a modest way when I asked him about his background. At the press conference which followed, he talked in short, plain sentences and appeared to be every inch the "professional" that Lindsay said he was. After the press conference, Leary relaxed a bit more. Columnist Jimmy Breslin, interviewing the new commissioner, told Leary: "They have this big, sweeping talent search and when it is over they still have to come back to the basics. If you want a rug seller, get an Arab. If you want a cop, get an Irishman." Leary broke out into a big laugh. It was the most emotion I had seen him show since I had met him a few hours before at City Hall.

Actually, the search for a new Police commissioner, it was later reported by Marvin Sleeper in the *Journal-American*, began back in November shortly after Lindsay had been elected. On one of the weekends when Lindsay was in Washington cleaning up unfinished Congressional business, he had telephoned Leary at police headquarters in Philadelphia and asked him to come to his Washington home. He gave Leary a copy of his campaign white paper on the police review board and asked him to think about the whole subject. He did not make any offer to Leary because, as a matter of fact, he was still seriously considering retaining Broderick. Right up until the first week in February, a continual dialogue had taken place between Lindsay and Broderick, despite the bitter public exchange and despite Price's "leaks" to the press about Lindsay not wanting to reappoint Broderick. The Mayor had not made up his mind to let Broderick go until the incident over Broderick's letter. "I like Vince Broderick," Lindsay had told me early in February. "I think he's a sound man. It's unfortunate that he cannot communicate with me." As the public controversy mounted, however, Lindsay slowly turned away from the idea of Broderick. Finally, on the weekend before his appointment, Leary came to visit Lindsay at the Roosevelt, where he and his family were still living because the redecoration of Gracie Mansion had not yet been completed. It was then that the Mayor made Leary an offer and gave him until Monday morning to decide. On Monday, Leary said "yes" —and, on Tuesday, February 15, after spending the night at the

St. Regis Hotel in New York, Leary arrived at the Roosevelt and then journeyed down to City Hall for the press conference announcing his appointment.

Even after Leary's appointment, Broderick, unfortunately, continued to make headlines. He charged that Constantine (Connie) Sidamon-Eristoff, the Mayor's assistant in charge of patronage, had "summoned" him to City Hall to discuss jobs in the Police Department, but he (Broderick) refused to make an appointment. "If he [Eristoff] and Robert Price attempt to establish a liaison with the Police Department, Leary will have his problems," Broderick continued. "But I'm sure that Commissioner Leary will resist this sort of intrusion. I hope he's right when he says he'll pick his own men." A newsman asked if he knew that Assistant Chief Inspector Sanford D. Garelik had met with Price seven times in the last two weeks. "No. I was not aware of that. I knew about one visit, but not the others," Broderick replied. Garelik, who reportedly was Price's choice for Police commissioner, was by now expected to succeed John Shanley as chief inspector under Leary. A Democrat, Garelik was a close friend of Price's and Liberal Party leaders Alex Rose and David Dubinsky. He was virtually unknown until he was seen by the press frequently visiting Price at City Hall after we took office. Lindsay denied Broderick's charges about Eristoff saying his statements were "nonsense." The Mayor added: "We don't have any such thing as a patronage dispenser," he said at a City Hall press conference. John Lindsay was one of the two men at City Hall I knew who could flatly and indignantly deny something that was, in fact, true and make the denial believable. The other person, of course, was Bob Price.

On the forty-seventh day of our new Administration (Feb. 16) columnist Pete Hamill of the *Post* came over to City Hall. I had not seen much of him up to then because he had not been assigned to Room 9 by his paper. I had met Hamill, a creative, sardonic writer, about eight years before on his first day at the *Post* when we were both reporters assigned to cover a story in lower Manhattan. Now, he was one of the best-known columnists in the city, a much sought-after reporter with a flare for details and first-person quotes.

On this particular day, Hamill wandered through the hallways, spent a few hours in Room 9, and generally remained in the background. I talked with him for a while, but it was hard to tell what he was looking for. The next afternoon his column read:

The first 47 days of the Captain Marvel Administration are now behind us. We had been promised grand changes, flowers dropping from the heavens, fountains on every street corner. The sluggish years of Robert (Captain Easy) Wagner were over; under John Lindsay a brave new world of vigor, freshness and style would be upon us. But things started going wrong right from the start. First, the reporters in Room 9 started calling the new mayor Captain Marvel. There was the transit strike and its attendant troubles. There was the flap over the society photographer who was supposed to take pictures of Captain Marvel on poverty program funds. And then Bob Price was accused of sending cops out for ham-and-egg sandwiches. They topped everything by treating Vincent Broderick as if he had just been caught spitting at a picture of Fiorello La Guardia. Yesterday at City Hall it seemed as if everything had finally settled down. Woody Klein, an old colleague who is now Mayor Lindsay's press secretary, strode cheerfully into Room 9, gave out copies of a 54-page report on sewer maintenance, and then chatted pleasantly amidst the yawns. . . .

I suspect that most of the first month's argument was due to the nature of reform administrations. Reformers become reformers because they refuse to accept the basic assumptions which make life possible in the absolute desolation of New York. The reformer preaches the gospel of the modern in the last city in America which truly represents the 20th Century. There are none of us who do not curse the invention of the automobile at least once a day. And with all the talk of adding style and dash to our municipal architecture, I am positive that the only public act the Captain Marvel Administration could now commit to universal applause would be the dynamiting of the Pan Am building. And so, because this is a city of so many accumulated grievances, City Hall is generally filled with outraged citizens. It was so under Wagner, Impellitteri, O'Dwyer, and La Guardia and it was so yesterday afternoon.

Meanwhile, with all the commentary about the nature of reformers and the pressures of the job at City Hall, I began to realize that Lindsay was growing increasingly impatient with himself, with those around him, and with the way the public treated the Mayor.[2] Part of the reason for this, I felt, was that he was being overscheduled by his office staff. For example, one day in mid-February Sugar Ray Robinson, the popular former middleweight boxing champion who had campaigned at Lindsay's side in Harlem during the previous summer, had an appointment to see the Mayor late in the afternoon. Lindsay was already two hours behind schedule by the time Robinson's turn came. A secretary asked him to wait even longer. Robinson became insulted and stormed out of City Hall. This was not an unusual occurrence. Others were also angry at the Mayor for failing to keep appointments on time. But Ray Robinson was a "name" and the press knew about his visit that day. The result: a story in the morning *Herald Tribune* headlined: SUGAR RAY QUITS THE LINDSAY TEAM. It pointed out that Robinson, who had also accompanied the Mayor on his daily morning walks to City Hall from midtown during the transit strike, had turned down an offer from the Mayor to become a member of the city's new Sports Committee, consisting of fifteen famous athletes. "I don't want any job," he was quoted as saying. "I'm not a politician. The man [Lindsay] seems to have changed since he got elected. I hope I don't regret that I campaigned for him." The incident was not world-shaking in itself, but it pointed up the sorry dilemma in which the Mayor found himself. He did not even have a few minutes to see some of the people who had helped him the most during the campaign; although he did quietly continue to meet with members of what the *Times* called his "Kitchen Cabinet," which was headed by Herbert Brownell, the former Attorney General under President Eisenhower, and included other distinguished New Yorkers.[3]

At this time, Lindsay was moving ahead with additional municipal financial belt-tightening, which was guaranteed to make more news. I attended his regular Tuesday morning staff meetings at 8 A.M. with his two Deputy Mayors, Gene Becker, Lee Rankin, Bob Sweet, and a few other aides. At one meeting in early February, Lindsay asked Tim Costello to prepare a survey of how many city cars were in use and which ones could be eliminated. This had been a campaign pledge of Lindsay's and he wanted to make good on it. The city owned a fleet of about 1,750 cars, which cost about $9 million a year to operate. A story by Dominick Peluso[4] in the *News* started the ball rolling, with the headline: MAYOR TO TAKE CITY CARS. And, much to my surprise, Peluso wrote in the last paragraph of his story: "Already, Woody Klein, the Mayor's press agent, has been a sort of victim of the coming crackdown. Formerly, he had two cars assigned to his office, but voluntarily, as an example to possibly less enthusiastic commissioners, he had surrendered one of them." I was amused by this because it was Price who had decided that my office was to be cut back from two cars to one for around-the-clock and weekend purposes. I was very fortunate in that the two men assigned to driving me, Joseph Mandato and Mike Giaimo, were both long-time City Hall staffers and, more important, were extraordinarily helpful, loyal and pleasant men. Their presence, as well as those of my two Civil Service secretaries, Dorothy Sullivan and Gloria Cipriano, made life inside the office quite enjoyable, even if the pressures from outside tended to continuously disrupt my life. I had been skeptical of Civil Service personnel, in general, when I first came into office—and I was to remain that way—but my own personal staff could not have been more competent.

On Monday, February 21, Howard Leary and Vincent Broderick came to City Hall for a ceremony in which Broderick would hand over the five-starred gold Police commissioner's badge to his successor. Before the ceremony began in the Blue Room, the officials involved met and waited in the Mayor's inner office, as had been our custom. Leary and Broderick, who had never met before, sat almost motionless beneath a portrait of Fiorello La Guardia[5] as the Mayor tried to take up the time with small talk. "I went to the movies Saturday night with the kids," the Mayor told them, "and we had popcorn and ate ourselves sick. We saw *Our Man Flint*—a takeoff on James Bond. It was terrific." Neither Leary nor Broderick acknowledged the comment. I spoke up to break the tension.

"How do you want to handle the ceremony, John?"

He leaned over and looked straight at Broderick, "Do you want to say anything out there, Vince?"

"I think not, John," the Police commissioner said softly.

"Well, then, let's get going. I'll start it off and Howard can say a few words after me."

Shortly after 2 P.M., Broderick and the Mayor stepped into the

Blue Room and Leary followed. They made their way to the head of the room and found themselves wedged behind the Mayor's desk under the larger-than-life picture of President James Monroe, which, by now, was becoming a familiar backdrop to local TV viewers. Both commissioners wore oxford gray suits, blue shirts and vests. They shook hands and posed with the Mayor for pictures. As the room quieted down, Lindsay took hold of the microphone and said: "I'd like to express my appreciation to Commissioner Leary for coming to New York. Commissioner Leary has 26 years of excellence as a professional. . . . He has my full backing." Then, despite Broderick's desire not to say anything when the Mayor had asked him inside a few minutes before, the Mayor turned to Broderick again. Somewhat surprised, he moved to the microphone: "I offer you, Commissioner Leary, my best wishes for a successful tenure. I wish for you, that you receive the service I received . . . and I hope that the people of New York continue to have the same high confidence in the Police Department that they have now." I looked at Broderick's eyes. He seemed on the verge of tears. He took out his pipe, stuck it firmly between his teeth, and stepped back to permit Leary to take the microphone. The new Police commissioner spoke quietly, calmly, and briefly, without stressing any particular point. He kept his hands behind him and I noticed that he twiddled his thumbs as he spoke. When he finished, the Mayor made two points: Leary would have a completely free hand and he had not yet decided when he would implement the Civilian Review Board. After a few questions, the room became silent.

"Are we finished?" the Mayor asked. Nobody spoke.

"Thank you ladies and gentlemen," Lindsay said and started to walk away.

I took hold of his arm quickly and whispered in the Mayor's ear: "Don't you think you ought to say something about Vince?"

The Mayor turned back to the microphone. "Before you go," he told the reporters, "I want to express the thanks of the city and me as Mayor of the City to Mr. Broderick for his years of dedicated service."

Then it was really over. And it had been all too obvious that my last-second attempt for Lindsay to say something gracious about Broderick was just that—an afterthought. The next day, it was reported in detail, including my whispering in Lindsay's ear at the end.

As soon as the ceremony was over, Leary returned to Lindsay's inner office and I spoke with him for a while. "I was really surprised at Broderick," Leary said. "A man should never embarrass or criticize his chief publicly. If you have a difference of opinion you should take it up quietly with the Mayor in his office, not with the press." I nodded in agreement. It was clear to me that Leary was, indeed, a professional with good judgment and a sense of loyalty.

In order to dramatize the appointment of his new Police commissioner, Lindsay asked me to schedule a live television appearance for 5 P.M. that night. WABC-TV agreed to carry it so we arranged to broadcast from the WNYC studios in the Municipal Building nearby. Lindsay wanted, in effect, to introduce Leary to the public and establish some clear policies regarding his relationship to the Police Department.

The Mayor was snappish and irritable when we arrived at the studio. "Quiet out there," he yelled at reporters just before air time. Then he objected when an attendant asked him to wear his neck microphone over his necktie. "You'd think a modern network would use modern equipment," he complained. He insisted on hiding the small microphone under his tie. When he finally began speaking, he seemed a little stilted and stiff. His speech, written and edited by Jim Carberry, Barry Gottehrer, Dave Garth and perhaps one or two others, reflected the desire of some of his aides to have him sounding righteous warnings over again, as he had during the transit strike.

"I intend to offer new solutions," he said, "and every one of these solutions is going to disturb the tired, self-perpetuating bureaucratic ways of the past. Jobs will change. Deals will be canceled. Fat and easy lives will be disrupted." Then he referred to the controversies over police autonomy and the Civilian Review Board. "Today it is the police issue that is bringing a storm of abuse around my ears. Tomorrow it will be tax reform. The day after it will be transportation consolidation or the poverty program or hospital or smoke pollution. I cannot promise you a peaceful, quiet Administration. I cannot promise you that you will not continue to hear the howls of the power brokers. I cannot promise you the ominous silence of unanimity. But I can promise you change and reform and progress."

In this speech, the Mayor also made it clear who would run the Police Department. "Desperate voices which have spoken in the past weeks about the relationship between the Police Department and the Mayor have come perilously close to missing the basic principle of a democratically elected government. They have suggested—no, they have stated—that the Police Department is a law unto itself. They have stated that the duly elected civilian government of New York is not responsible for the Police Department as it is for the other departments of the city. . . . The ultimate responsibility lies with the Mayor, and I intend to exercise that responsibility."

Before the broadcast, the Mayor had told me to tell the reporters he would not answer questions afterward, so I found myself in an unexpected cross-fire. Who are the power brokers? Several newsmen began to press me for an answer. I thought we had left that behind us during the transit strike, but here it was again. All I could do was to give them the same comment Lindsay had issued before: "They know who they are," I replied. And, of course, I was quoted the next day—February 22—in the stories about Leary's swearing-in.

On February 24, after briefing Frank O'Connor and members of the City Council, Lindsay asked me to call a press conference to clarify some of the rumors about his tax program. Minutes later, he was telling the Room 9 press corps that "there isn't anything that is not an option at this point." One of the Mayor's reasons for wanting to clarify the tax question was a story in the morning *Times* by Robert Alden, who was covering the tax program and had developed some inside sources in the Administration. His story stated that the Mayor would sponsor both a personal and business income tax as the keystones of his program to overcome the city's current fiscal deficit of more than $400 million. The Mayor did not confirm that he would ask for any specific tax. As a result, the newspapers carried various stories during the next few days, saying he wanted everything from increased water fees, a lottery, a boost in real estate taxes, a general business tax, offtrack betting, a commuter tax, and many others. I knew that Price had been opposed to an income tax because he did not think it was politically palatable.

Opposition to reports of tax raises mounted quickly. Lindsay responded by saying that if his tax program was blocked by the Legislature, "I'd have no choice, I'd have to take it to the people." Pressed for how he would do this, Lindsay said that he would "take it to the streets, if necessary." This remark was quickly picked up by many state legislators. Fourteen from Nassau—all Republicans—marched into City Hall at the end of February and told the Mayor flatly they would not support him on the tax issue. "I can't believe he is serious about this," remarked Senator Edward J. Speno. "If he came out to Nassau County and campaigned against us, it would be a plus for us." Other legislators also "invited" the Mayor to come ahead. Lindsay's poorly timed remark had been made as a threat in what he probably thought was the public interest. But it was an untenable position to be in: campaigning against local legislators just because they did *not* want to raise taxes! It was an empty threat and it created a flap in the press. The *Journal-American,* for example, carried an eight-column banner headline in huge type on page one:

TAX OPPONENTS DEFY
A LINDSAY 'PURGE'

Legislators
In a Protest
At City Hall

On February 27, the Mayor and a group of aides, including myself, went to Albany to meet with the Governor and legislative leaders about our tax program, including Assembly Speaker Anthony J. Travia and Senate Majority Leader Earl W. Brydges. Most of the legislators we talked with were wary. While we were visiting in Albany, Bob Price was making news on radio supporting the tax program. "The fact is that the commuter and the suburbanite must begin paying for a share of the city's burdens," he said. "For too long the commuter and the suburbanite . . . have benefited from our streets, our subways and everything else." Then, much to my amazement, Price took the same line as Lindsay. "If the Mayor presents a package and goes to the people with it, and I know he will, and it can't get through the Legislature because of political reasons—this is an election year, if I remember correctly—then it's irresponsibility on the part of the Legislature."

Despite the gloomy picture in Albany, I got the impression there was a growing optimism back in City Hall, especially after Frank O'Connor issued a statement saying that the income tax was "probably the only answer to the financial problems of New York City at this time." Another reason was Lindsay's insistence on taking the full "blame" for the tax. He made it clear during our trip to Albany that a local legislator could tell his constituents he was going along with the "Lindsay tax" because of the city's desperate fiscal plight and the Mayor's persuasive insistence that only an income tax could save the day. The argument had some appeal and would enable the Mayor to get a tax package passed with some three and a half years to go before he had to run for reelection.

Meanwhile, more shifts in the Police Department were making headlines again. Howard Leary announced a major reshuffle of his staff and, as expected, promoted the forty-seven-year-old Sanford D. Garelik,[6] who had been in charge of supervising the special agencies of the department such as the Safe and Loft Squad, the Narcotics Bureau, Auto Theft Squad and Confidence Squad to the number two post in the Police Department—chief inspector. He also named Lloyd Sealy, a Negro, to be assistant chief inspector.[7] In being named to his new job, Sealy was jumped over two intervening ranks, assistant inspector and inspector. He received the highest uniformed rank ever achieved by a Negro in the Police Department. I had known that Sandy Garelik was going to be Leary's right-hand man, but I had not known about Lloyd Sealy. I was enthusiastic about both appointments. It seemed, as the press itself reported, that the "Irish Mafia" in the Police Department was finally going to be broken up. As Leary himself stated with the announcement of the Garelik and Sealy appointments, this was the start of a "top to bottom" reorganization of the department.

By the end of February, I felt exhausted from the pace. If I thought that things would calm down after the transit strike, I had been mistaken. The number of telephone and in-person requests for comments from Lindsay seemed endless. Every time I managed to get home for a few hours rest, even late at night, the telephone would continue to ring. And, of course, Lindsay announced more appointments, in addition to Leary, including William H. Booth, as chairman of the Human Rights Commission; Samuel J. Kearing, Sanitation commissioner; Jay L. Kriegel, assistant to the Mayor; Mitchell I. Ginsberg, Welfare commissioner; Mrs. Eugenia M. Flatow, a housing official; Peter Paul Meagher, first deputy commissioner of Rent and Rehabilitation; and finally, on February 28, James L. Marcus, as an assistant to the Mayor. Jim Marcus had come into my office two days earlier on a Saturday morning, introduced himself and said the Mayor was going to appoint him. Lindsay had told me Marcus would be in to see me. He was mild-mannered and likeable. I asked him to type out a resume at another desk in my office. Based on this biography, I wrote a press release, inserted some quotes from the Mayor, showed the release to both Lindsay and Marcus and issued it to the newspapers. The handling of an appointment from City Hall was by this time routine procedure. I shook Marcus' hand and wished him luck. He thanked me and offered to deliver the release to the papers himself. I agreed and I was favorably impressed, particularly by the fact that he had volunteered to work for Lindsay at no salary.

I had put out seventy press releases in February—more than two a day—and I was, therefore, relieved when Robert Laird, twenty-nine, a good friend of mine from my days on the *World-Telegram* whom I had succeeded in persuading to join me as assistant press secretary, came to work. I had first suggested Laird to Lindsay on February 17. He had previously met Bob when Laird had worked for a short time during the newspaper strike in Lindsay's campaign, but he did not know Laird well. He was seven years my junior, quiet, well-mannered and good-humored. He was a good writer and he was highly regarded by newsmen who knew him. I felt he would be an asset in my office because I knew his work, I got along well with him and I knew I could count on him. Lindsay's initial reply to my suggestion, therefore, came as a surprise. "He's a nice guy," the Mayor said, "but what will his appointment do for our image? He's not from Room 9 and he doesn't work for the *Tribune,* the *Times,* or the *Journal-*

American. He's a *World-Telegram* man like you. We don't score any points with the other papers." Lindsay was also under some pressure from other aides—Barry Gottehrer in particular—to bring in someone from Room 9 in order to appease the local press a little. Martin Steadman, a good investigative reporter from the *Journal-American,* was one suggested.[8] However, I was told that if he did join me, he wanted it to be on an equal basis —for which I did not blame him. Still, I needed an assistant— not another press secretary. So I pursued my request for Laird and, after much discussion, Lindsay agreed. We may not have "scored points" because he was from the *World-Telegram,* but I honestly felt that his everyday reliability and pleasing personality would be a great asset to both Lindsay and myself. Not only would he be able to help us in our relations with the Room 9 press, but I felt that his easygoing manner would tend to relax the tense atmosphere within the Mayor's office itself. The Mayor had reached the point where every time I stuck my head into his office he would look up and almost automatically ask: "What's wrong now?"

Stories in the newspapers about every member of the Administration continued unabated. Parks Commissioner Tom Hoving, by now, was getting almost as many headlines as Moerdler and Price. On March 1, a story in the *Times* reported his proposal to ban automobiles from Central Park's east and west drives on weekends. I asked Lindsay if Hoving had told him he was planning the announcement. "No, but it sounds like a good idea," Lindsay replied. "Hoving's all right. He's the rabbit of this Administration. Let the other commissioners do half as well in trying to catch up with him and I'll be happy."

That same day, somewhat to my embarrassment, the *Times* also carried a story about how the John Birch Society's national publicity director, former Congressman John H. Rousselot,[9] had come to the City Hall gates with a request to see the Mayor so he could disclose the names of the 500 policemen he had said were members of the John Birch Society. The Mayor was not in City Hall, however. The week before, Lindsay—in response to a rash of stories about alleged Birch Society membership in the Police Department—had called the organization "terrible, infamous and hostile to everything I think is decent." The Mayor's criticism came after Howard Leary had said he would permit policemen to belong to the Society if their membership did not "impair their efficiency." I went out to the front gate and told Rousselot that the Mayor's schedule did not permit any time for a visit. A reporter, anxious for a story, however, introduced Rousselot to Bob Price, who happened to be coming into the building. Price shook hands, but quickly told the photographers who were standing nearby: "No pictures, please!" I had to ask Rousselot not to come through the gates at one point. Harvey Rothenberg suggested Rousselot go across the street and have a cup of coffee while he was waiting for the Mayor. Lindsay arrived and told us to station a plainclothesman outside of City Hall to keep a watch out for Rousselot. For a while, I also stood outside. Rothenberg then ordered lunch in for Lindsay. Finally, Rousselot left. Unfortunately, this whole story appeared in the newspaper. The truth of the matter was that it seemed necessary for us to resort to elusive tactics in order to protect Lindsay against anyone who wanted to buttonhole him for any reason whatsoever—possibly with a photographer standing by ready to snap a picture.

In the next few weeks, the pressure really began to build up on the Mayor to get his tax program passed, even as charges of City Hall "interference" still plagued Howard Leary ("I haven't spoken to Mr. Price relative to any appointments, either before or after any appointment has been made.") We also sandwiched in a trip to Washington on March 1 to meet with some Federal officials and to attend a reception for politicians and the press in the Capital in John and Mary Lindsay's honor given by Senator Jacob K. Javits and his wife, Marian. Someone at the cocktail party asked Lindsay how he liked being Mayor. "The job is like picking your way through a mine field," he replied, with a smile. "The trick is to keep the city moving forward, while putting out the brush fires along the way."

As the party was about to break up, Vice President Hubert H. Humphrey arrived, smiling and ebullient. "Mayor Lindsay," he told reporters gathered around him, "has one of the most important jobs in the country, and I'm glad to see he's enjoying it." Then Representative Adam Clayton Powell joined the impromptu news conference. Powell put his arm around Lindsay and bellowed: "Mayor Lindsay has done more for New York City than any man since Fiorello La Guardia. But from here on in, he's going to have to work like hell." Powell broke out into a big laugh and was joined by the others around us.

When we returned to La Guardia Airport the next afternoon, I told Lindsay as we departed from the plane that there would be reporters awaiting him in the lobby. He said he was tired and did not want to answer questions. I reminded him that he was obligated to at least stop and tell them that. As we reached the terminal, I could see a group of a dozen newspaper reporters and television cameramen waiting for the Mayor. They surrounded us as we walked into the terminal.

"Mr. Mayor," one reporter cried out, "do you deny that City Hall is running the Police Department?"

Lindsay's face flushed with anger. "That's ridiculous," he snapped. "I don't have to answer any more of your questions." And he started to walk away.

Television and radio reporters, their microphones projecting from their outstretched arms, ran after us all the way to the upper ramp where Sid Davidoff was waiting for Lindsay in his own car. The Mayor jumped in the passenger seat in front. The window had been rolled down. One radio reporter stuck a microphone into the open window and shouted: "Lindsay, you'd better answer our questions—or we'll get you." The Mayor looked intensely at the newsman. His voice reflected his incredulity at the harassment he was receiving. "I don't have to answer your questions," he said softly—almost pleadingly. "I don't have to talk to you—I am the Mayor and you have an obligation to treat me with respect."

Lindsay then rolled the window up as Davidoff pressed his foot down on the accelerator and they sped away. I stepped into my car—which had been waiting behind Davidoff's—and Joe Mandato drove me to New York as I sat quietly in the back seat pondering the incident which I had just witnessed. It seemed to me that the Mayor was justified in his outburst, but I knew only too well how the press would report the incident. The next morning, the *News* ran a story, headlined: MAYOR BACK, ANGRY, SILENT.

I recall this incident exactly the way it happened because in the coming months and years, the phrase—"I am the Mayor"— was to be used against Lindsay, with the clear implication that he had said it in arrogance. Actually, it had been in a moment when he was perplexed and disturbed by the fact that a newsman could insult—even threaten him—because he did not wish to answer any questions.[10] The Mayor, it was clear to me, was still having a great deal of trouble learning how to deal with the press.

At the end of February, after interviewing Lindsay, writer Nat Hentoff later wrote in *The New Yorker*[11]: "I had been impressed by his resiliency. But never before in his political life had he experienced such persistent turmoil . . . there had been a transit strike, opposition from many quarters to the plans he had advanced for reorganizing city agencies, sharp criticism of some of his appointees, and a growing awareness nearly everywhere that the city's financial problems were so severe as to make new taxes inevitable. There had also been difficulties with the press. The dry humor and spontaneity that had characterized Lindsay's friendship with most reporters in the past were absent from the interviews with the new Mayor . . . on the evening television news he usually looked taut."

Hentoff then quoted the Mayor's response: "It's certainly different from my experience as a Congressman. Here the press is commenting on you all the time. I've got coldblooded about it. Well, not entirely. Once in a while, my blood begins to boil a bit. But listen, I figure, I'll do my best and that's it. There's no sense getting coronaries about criticism. There's no point lying awake nights about a newspaper story."

At exactly 6:05 P.M. on March 3, 1966, Lindsay made history by announcing on live television from Studio 41 in the CBS building on West 57th St. the long-awaited details of the tax program. In a brief fifteen-minute talk, he confirmed all the unpleasant news that the people of the city and the suburbs had expected. A city personal income tax, an increased income tax on business, a stock transfer tax, an increase in water fees, and a real estate tax were the principal revenue raisers in the plan. The tax program was, in effect, a breach of a promise Lindsay had made during his campaign, but this is the way he handled it in his speech: "I said last fall that a personal income tax would be a last resort. I believe it is a last resort. We have canvassed the other possibilities and there is no other choice." Lindsay said the sources of income he named would bring in $520 million of the $600 million he needed to balance the upcoming budget. The remaining $80 million, he said, would be made up by economies—mainly elimination of 13,000 city jobs.

The *Times* editorially greeted the program by saying: "No one can be happy about them [the taxes], least of all the Mayor. But they are essential, inescapable, if this city is to re-establish its good credit standing and serve the people in adequate response to need. Mayor Lindsay . . . has met the challenge bravely and without evasion. He deserves—and must have—the cooperation of both political parties here and at Albany in balancing the city's books." The editorial concluded: "The Mayor will win no popularity contests by his tax program. But he had no honorable escape if he was to be worthy of the trust placed in him by the voters of New York. He has taken the cold plunge, and early. We respect him for it."

Of course, that was only the *New York Times*. When I finished reading the editorial that morning I realized that hard work lay ahead. We had the City Council to contend with and, also, public opinion. The next day, at an Overseas Press Club luncheon, the Mayor decided to head into the eye of the storm. In a brief talk, he said of his tax program: "It must be fair because everybody is equally mad." And, he added: "I'm probably the only one in history who has got both organized labor and the New York Stock Exchange against him." Reminded by a newsman that opposition was rising rapidly, Lindsay responded: "I don't accept defeat for a minute. The program is fair. We'll fight for it, including that portion that has the commuter make a reasonable contribution to the city." At the same luncheon, the Mayor tried to put to rest, once and for all, the dispute over who runs the Police Department. In answer to a reporter's question, he said: "A Police Department is not an unguided missile." He endorsed the appointment of Sandy Garelik and added: "He reports to Leary—and Leary reports to me. The Mayor, as the highest elected official in the city, must see to it that the Police Department is operating at top efficiency." The *News*, as could be expected, headlined this remark the next morning with: MY JOB TO KEEP COPS ON BALL: MAYOR.

After a successful—and unexpected—song-and-dance appearance on March 5 at the political writers' Inner Circle lampoon show, an annual affair for newsmen and politicians, Lindsay had some of the newsmen smiling who previously had not thought he had much of a sense of humor. The *News'* political columnist, Edward O'Neill, who played the role of the Mayor in the newsmen's skit, was particularly impressed with this new and lighter side of Lindsay which he had not seen before. Lindsay actually topped the press at their own show, "New faces of 1966," at the New York Hilton. The *Times* thought enough of his appearance with professional singer-dancer Florence Henderson to assign a reporter to do a lengthy story on how his "vaudeville debut" had been "kept under wraps" for a month before the show and how it drew a roar of applause and a standing ovation. In addition, Harold Harris' column in the *Journal-American* was headlined: LINDSAY DANCE HARD ACT TO TOP.

The battle over the tax program resumed shortly after this event. Several state legislators warned that the program had little chance of passing unless the City Council sent a "home rule" message meaning that the state wanted the local legislators to take the brunt of the criticism. At the same time, Lindsay's transportation reorganization plans were being roasted at a public hearing in Albany. Robert Moses, one of the witnesses, labeled the unification "vicious and unjustifiable." Moses then revealed a secret visit the Mayor had made to his apartment at 1 Gracie Terrace after succeeding trips to Moses' apartment by Arthur Palmer and Judge Samuel I. Rosenman had failed to persuade Moses to resign his posts. Lindsay, on the spot, conceded to newsmen that he had, indeed, gone to Moses' house and that they had "a very engaging and pleasant chat." He added: "Mr. Moses did not agree with the reorganization." The Legislature soon afterward voted to return the transit reorganization plan to the City Council for a local vote. It marked the second time in a row the Legislature had voted to shift responsibility to the City Council for approving a touchy piece of Lindsay legislation.

However, the Council, headed by Frank O'Connor, was in no mood to do business with Lindsay. They felt bypassed and by this time O'Connor had been firing almost daily salvos at the Mayor. On March 11, however, word came to us that O'Connor wanted to end the "feud." A reporter came into my office and gave me the news. His statement read: "I have no fight with Mayor Lindsay. I wish that we can bring it [the feuding] all to an end and get on with the matter of running the city."

Did I want to make a statement, the reporter asked?

Yes, I did. I said: "The Mayor feels there should be no feud. The Mayor has a very great respect for Mr. O'Connor and he hopes they can work together in true non-partisan fashion."

On March 12, Jim Marcus was sworn in as unpaid assistant to the Mayor. Marcus, the Mayor said, would be assigned to devote most of his time to water supply problems. The water shortage had been a major issue in the campaign and the city was still in some trouble in early March. The reservoirs were only at 57.2 percent of capacity (although this was an improvement over the year before when the supply stood at 37.2 percent on March 11, 1966). At Marcus' swearing-in, Lindsay also announced that his new assistant would coordinate the Mayor's campaign to clean up Times Square and the "mess on MacDougal Street"—referring to the narcotics and coffee-house problems in Greenwich Village. Marcus' wife, Lilly, the attractive daughter of former Connecticut Governor John Davis Lodge, stood smiling by his side during the ceremony. Afterwards, she posed with her husband for photographers, holding an empty glass into which Marcus poured some water from a pitcher. They appeared to be very happy with the whole ceremony.

Shortly after this event, the *Post's* Joe Kahn scored a major journalistic "beat" when he revealed that Buildings Commissioner Moerdler's father-in-law and Deputy Buildings Commissioner Bill Diamond's mother-in-law were both members of private corporations which owned slum properties with violations on them.[12] Moerdler said he had made this fact known to the Board of Ethics before he considered accepting appointment to the commissionership and that the Board had found no conflict. He also said he had told his father-in-law to sell the properties. Still, it was a very revealing news story, the kind I would have enjoyed writing for the *World-Telegram* if I had still been a reporter. As the *Post's* Joe Kahn, who was an old friend, said to me in my office shortly after he broke the story: "You know you would have written it the same way yourself!"

On March 20—the seventy-ninth day of our Administration—the *Journal-American* ran a lengthy analysis of our progress, or lack of it. Written by William McCullam, it hit on the key to our problems: "Mayor Lindsay—besieged and perhaps a little bewildered—today begins his 12th week in City Hall as the lonesomest man in town," the article began. "An army of opponents, political and otherwise, appear—as of now—to be closing in on the 44-year-old Republican-Fusion Mayor, some clearly on the warpath to get his scalp. The question observers are asking: Can John V. Lindsay survive the onslaught? Standing virtually alone with a badly chipped sword, can he turn the tide of battle? Can he re-polish the image that won him his office? Can he go beyond the political dead end of City Hall and up the national stepladder?"

No sooner had this story appeared, when Human Rights Commissioner Bill Booth started a new controversy by attacking two prominent labor union leaders who had been considered virtually untouchable for years by the Wagner Administration—Harry Van Arsdale, president of the city's Central Trades and Labor Council, and Peter Brennan, president of the Buildings Trades Council. Booth issued an ultimatum: Each had one week to show in detail how their unions had integrated since 1963. The attack touched off a series of denials from the union leaders. Finally, a meeting with the Mayor was arranged and Van Arsdale and Brennan came to City Hall. I was hardly objective about the whole matter because I had attacked Brennan when I was a reporter and I had not been impressed with the meager effort his union had made to integrate. Nevertheless, I attended the meeting with the Mayor. It was not one of Lindsay's better performances and I felt that neither Van Arsdale nor Brennan was particularly won over by our frontal approach to the problem.

The next day, Brennan, responding to Booth's charges, attacked the city for delaying the start of large-scale construction work. Taking the initiative instead of being defensive, Brennan issued a statement saying that more than 45,000 members of his 255,000-member council were unemployed and might demonstrate to protest the situation. He called for a speedup in the work schedule on several arterial highway projects such as the Lower Manhattan Expressway, the Bruckner Expressway, the Richmond Expressway and the widening of Grand Central Parkway and Queens Boulevard. The Mayor, of course, had already expressed strong opposition to several of these projects—particularly the Lower Manhattan Expressway and the Richmond Expressway through Staten Island's so-called greenbelt. But it was a clear rebuttal on Brennan's part. Writing about him and his union had been one thing—it had been easy to charge him with bias in the construction unions—but dealing with him as an insider at City Hall was another.

In late March, the Mayor opened still another campaign—this one against air pollution. "It is imperative," he told the City Council hearing on an air pollution bill, "that we speed up our controls if this problem is to be kept from getting out of hand. I am informed that we now have the most serious air pollution problem of any city in the United States . . . and it is a problem that affects the health and well-being of every resident."

We moved, almost daily, from public crisis to private crisis and back. March 23 was a day of mourning for the death of Mrs. Emanuel Celler. I accompanied Lindsay to her funeral at Temple Beth Elohim on Park Slope in Brooklyn. The turnout for Stella Celler was impressive—Borough President Abe Stark, Mayor Lindsay, Senator Robert F. Kennedy and President and Mrs. Johnson. I stood next to the Mayor in the middle about ten rows from the front. Directly in front of us—alone—stood Robert Kennedy. Directly in front of him stood President and Mrs. Johnson. I had never seen Johnson before. He towered over everyone in the Temple. He was a huge, impressive figure. Kennedy seemed almost like a young boy standing behind him. Kennedy exchanged a slight smile with Lindsay, but, as far as I could see, neither Kennedy nor Johnson spoke to each other. The President's friendship with Celler went all the way back to 1937. Celler, seventy-seven, was then in his forty-fourth year in Congress.

The evening of March 24 was a difficult—and memorable—one for me. Rarely had I seen Lindsay in such a petulant mood. Scheduled to speak at the annual awards dinner of the prominent Citizens Budget Commission, he had not had time to change into a tuxedo, but had rushed directly from his office to deliver his talk. I sat in the audience and listened as he warmed up. Within moments, I knew he had departed from his text. "If my tax programs are not passed," he said, "I will take to the streets to remind the voters in the fall that Albany—all of Albany—is responsible." That could only mean Rockefeller—who up to that point had failed to offer strong support—as well as the legislators, I thought to myself. Raising his voice, he continued: "Police Commissioner Leary has requested funds for 300 patrol cars that he feels are necessary for the safety of the citizens of the city. And if my tax program is defeated in Albany and the police force is cut and the streets are not safe, the people will know who is responsible. And if they do not know, I will take to the streets in the fall before election to remind them." The Mayor's extemporaneous words in the Sert Room of the Waldorf-Astoria showed his increasing anger. He continued:

"I am determined that we must succeed, no matter how bloody and how costly the battle, so that your successors and mine will fall heir to the greatest single urban community in the world." Lindsay added that unless municipal government elevated the "great cities to great accomplishments," the national government could not succeed because the nation was a collection of great cities. "The battle for greatness is being fought on the side streets and gutters and alleys of the great cities," he added. Then, turning to a friendly audience, he said: "Your commission recommended a city income tax and I am proposing a city income tax. . . . Yes, everyone is for change, providing it doesn't interfere with their own particular area. But the most prideful and self-righteous citizens are the first to shout the loudest when the changes affect them."

I expected what followed. Legislative opposition to his tax program stiffened. "This threat is going to get him nowhere—the campaign is over. He ought to start acting like a Mayor," said Assembly Speaker Anthony J. Travia. Senate Minority Leader Joseph Zaretzki of Manhattan was even more critical. "If he [Lindsay] wants to come into my district, I'll be glad to show him around. I'll introduce him to every voter in the area. . . . I'm sure he'd be the greatest campaign manager I've ever had."

Stung by increasing criticism, Lindsay told me he thought he needed a rest. So he went off to Vermont for a long ski weekend. It was apparent that the pressures and the long hours were having a marked effect on him. He would start out each day strong, but as the hours passed he began to look harried and to act impatient.

He tried to extend himself every day to the limit. I was glad that he could squeeze in a ski weekend in Vermont.

When he returned from Vermont on Monday, March 28, I accompanied him to Albany where we met with Senate Majority Leader Earl Brydges and Assembly Speaker Travia. Lindsay also met privately with Rockefeller. The Governor, always cordial and smiling, was a polite and proper host. He made us feel comfortable, even though we also had the feeling that we were not going to get what we wanted from him. This was one of Rockefeller's great political talents. When we left Albany that day, it was without any commitment from either the Governor or the legislative leaders for a tax program. They all wanted the City Council to approve the package first, for obvious political reasons.

As March drew to a slow close, I particularly enjoyed the swearing-in ceremony of George F. McGrath as commissioner of Correction. It took place on Wednesday, March 30. A former head of Massachusetts' state prisons, McGrath was a pleasant Bostonite, forty-nine years old, an assistant professor at Boston University and a former assistant dean and professor of criminal law at Boston College. He came into my office before the ceremony and we talked about the job ahead of him. He was gracious about his predecessor, seventy-five-year-old Mrs. Anna Kross, a former magistrate, who had served as commissioner of Correction since January 1, 1954. Mrs. Kross, known as a reformer among prison administrators, had been a tireless worker, but I was told she had put in her retirement papers and wanted to leave public service. The Mayor thanked her for her "long, constructive and rewarding service" and then he swore in McGrath, calling him "the most qualified man for the job in the United States." It was one of the smoothest transitions that we had made since we had taken office.

On April 1, we had a press conference that I considered a milestone. The previous year, Mayor Wagner had set up a tripartite committee of union leaders, city officials and impartial labor experts to seek a new means to avert strikes by city employees. The transit strike in January gave impetus to this search. Mayor Lindsay renewed the committee's mandate and named Tim Costello and J. Lee Rankin to join the panel. The plan we were about to announce was the result of the group's efforts, and was cemented by a written agreement of the labor, city and public members of the committee.

The new formula called for the creation of an Office of Collective Bargaining to resolve differences between the city and its employees. The OCB would determine proper bargaining units, certify unions and bargaining representatives, and administer procedures for mediation, fact-finding and grievance arbitration. In contract negotiations, the OCB could step in and name one or more mediators from its register. If necessary, the OCB could set up an impasse panel, which would be empowered to conduct fact-finding and make recommendations for a settlement. It was not the only answer to labor problems in New York, but it was one answer, and I, along with other Lindsay aides, felt it could help in the future. At the news conference, labor leaders representing 113,000 municipal employees signed the agreement with the city.

Also on April 1, Jim Marcus made headlines by stating that he would recommend universal water metering in a report he would soon turn over to the Mayor. The reservoirs at this point were at 70.4 percent of capacity. Normal storage for this time of the year was 82.4 percent. The story was headlined: WATER OFFICIAL TO ASK METERING. The next day, the Mayor's tax program was introduced into the City Council. Immediately afterwards, Majority Leader David Ross, a short, cigar-smoking, tough-talking Bronx politician, charged that the Mayor had lost "10 valuable weeks" by not going to the Council in the first place. "The city administration should have known better. Certainly, they were forewarned," he said. And so the long-expected fight between Lindsay and the Council had finally begun. We didn't make much progress. The following day, the Commerce and Industry Association charged that the Mayor's tax program would lead "toward economic chaos" and "drive many firms away from the city." Fortunately, this attack fell on silent ears because most of us were out of town for the weekend. Lindsay went to Vermont with his family again; so did Bob Sweet. And I took a long-awaited break myself by driving up to another part of Vermont with my family.

No sooner had we all returned to town, when we received more bad news. A press release had been put out by a council of twenty-six leading business executives rejecting the tax program, calling it "self-defeating" and potentially injurious to the city's economy. The statement was issued by the prestigious Economic Development Council. Lindsay responded in a lengthy fifty-minute news conference on April 5, his longest since we took office. Looking relaxed and suntanned after his second consecutive ski weekend in Vermont, where he had been reading the newspapers and had kept in touch by telephone, he was prepared, he said, to respond to the attacks from the two business groups. Informally, sitting around a table with the Room 9 newsmen in the high-ceilinged, oval Committee of the Whole Room of the Board of Estimate on the second floor of City Hall, Lindsay said: "These attacks have been coming from banking and insurance fields. It's about time these elements begin to give greater support to the city and its needs. Up to now they have made no contribution in business taxes—not so far. None. Zero."

I had given some thought to this particular press conference. It was so close to the first 100-day mark that I had briefed Lindsay on what I thought were his major accomplishments during his first ninety-five days in office. (See Appendix, page 308.) Several of the reporters had asked for an informal session on his first 100 days. As a result, the following day the *Times'* Terence Smith offered this summation in his lead: "Mayor Lindsay was asked yesterday to assess the first three months of his own Administration and, not surprisingly, he decided he'd done a good job."

Smith quoted Lindsay as saying: "It's been a productive period with change for the city. Some parts of my Administration have been a little turbulent, but that's all to the good—that's what the city needs." Lindsay then cited seventeen examples, including his proposed tax reorganization, the job freeze in government, the virtual liquidation of the Office of Civil Defense and the creation of the Office of Collective Bargaining. Lindsay also mentioned his plans for a Civilian Review Board, for Little City Halls, plans to open a New York City office in Washington, to launch a self-funding business development corporation that would issue bonds, the elimination of "pothole inspectors"—a practice which he said was a "massive boondoggle"; an expanded vest pocket park program and the proposed reorganization of city government. In explaining the need for reorganization, Lindsay told the newsmen: "The bureaucracy has become so big and insensitive. The way these ninety-nine or so agencies are set up, they're often dealing with fractions of problems, and yet even the fractions sometimes transcend what the agencies' jurisdictions should be. The system is so damn divisive that the city departments have to deal with each other almost by treaty. We've got to get moving," he continued, pounding the table for emphasis. "I think we ought to act like de Gaulle—go in and do it and answer questions afterward. We have to have doers, gentlemen, and that's all there is to it."

Continuing to list his accomplishments, Lindsay told the reporters there had been "significant" appointments of non-whites, that Police Commissioner Leary was moving ahead "effectively," and that, "I did everything in my power to work with Broderick. I could not control the decision on his part and others to make a public war—strike the word war—a public contest out of the issue of the Civilian Review Board." Lindsay also reminded the newsmen that he was "looking forward" to the two major studies being conducted for the city by Mitchell Sviridoff, in antipoverty, and Edward J. Logue, in housing. And he said he had begun to initiate "long-range budget planning" in the city as well as removing the "clubhouse atmosphere" from judicial appointments.[13]

Buoyed by a good press response to this lengthy interview, Lindsay asked his speech writer, Jim Carberry, to come up with some good quips for a talk he was scheduled to give the next day, April 6, at a luncheon meeting of the International Radio and Television Society at the Waldorf-Astoria. "One of my predecessors, Fiorello La Guardia, used to read funnies to children," Lindsay told the group, "but this Mayor reads tragedies to adults." More "one-liners" followed. He had the crowd laughing heartily. The broadcasting society presented the Mayor with its "first annual Owl of the Year award" for instituting the City Hall Night Owl Mayor program.

At the same moment the Mayor was winning over a good part of this crowd by making fun of himself and his Administration, Paul R. Screvane, a former City Council President and Deputy Mayor under Mayor Wagner, was visiting Room 9. Fred Ferretti's story in the *Herald Tribune* on April 7 began: "On the 96th day, Paul Screvane came down to City Hall and said he sensed 'a feeling of arrogance and contempt stemming from the top' in the Lindsay Administration. Screvane, who had turned down an offer (presumably as a third Deputy Mayor) in the Lindsay Administration stated: 'Lindsay offered it to me . . . I didn't think it would work. I turned him down. . . . I thought there would be a personality clash. The Mayor had a lot of mellowing to do.'" The *Daily News* story was headlined: SCREVANE SMASHES LINDSAY'S IMAGE. Screvane's visit to City Hall was followed the next day by another from Albert S. Pacetta, a former Markets commissioner under Wagner, who also dropped into Room 9 and voiced strong criticism—this time of Screvane: "It's time someone discredited these tired old pros to get them out of the political picture so the Democrats can reunite under competent leadership," Pacetta said in an impromptu press conference. The outbursts by Screvane and Pacetta, although seemingly unusual, served no useful purpose except to give the local reporters something to write about.

On Friday, April 8, it was my turn to take the Night Owl Mayor shift. I decided to have a look at our Administration's clean-up program in Times Square and in Greenwich Village. I lived in the Village and I was not satisfied with the conditions there. I notified Jim Marcus, Lindsay's "trouble shooter" in the Village, and he offered to accompany me. We also had a guest —an Associated Press reporter whom I had not met before. We drove up to Times Square and parked on a side street.

"Let's have a look at some of those dirty book stores," the reporter said. We stopped for a few minutes in one store filled with pornographic books. When we came out we met a police captain who recognized Marcus and offered to show us around. We walked with him for a half hour around the area and then got into our car and headed toward the Village. There, on Bleecker Street, we could hardly make our way through the heavy crowds. Even though it was not a warm night—the temperature was in the 40s—there were hundreds of beatnik types wandering along the streets and standing on corners, and there was bumper-to-bumper traffic. It was about 9:30 P.M. I asked Marcus what he thought had been accomplished in Times Square.

"There are fewer drunks and panhandlers than there have been in the past," he said, matter-of-factly.

The Associated Press man asked me if I ever went out in the

Village. "No," I replied, "My wife and I don't enjoy going out here at night because of these crowds. And I certainly wouldn't go through here on a Saturday night." Marcus, however, said he thought the Village was "much improved" since the clean-up had started. After talking about the two areas for a little while, the Associated Press man left for his office and I returned to City Hall. There, about 11:30 P.M., the plainclothes detective at the gate came downstairs to the room beneath the Mayor's office where I was preparing to get some sleep and informed me that some fifty angry young men and women were outside of City Hall demanding to see someone. They were protesting a police raid on a party they had been having in an artist's loft in the Village to raise money to fight against the war in Vietnam.

I came upstairs and agreed to meet with three of the protesters in my office. One of the women was a reporter from the *Village Voice* who kept asking me why Lindsay wasn't interested in protecting the civil rights of the people at the party. She demanded an "immediate" investigation of the police who had broken up the party. I asked the delegation to send me a memorandum about their problem and I assured them the Mayor would see it. One of the women kept on insisting that I should call the local precinct and tell them to permit the party to continue. I couldn't resist the opportunity to tell them: "You know I can't do that. We never interfere with the operations of the Police Department."

Finally, about 1 A.M. I managed to fall asleep in the basement of City Hall, although it was cold by that time and I was not very comfortable. At about 6 A.M. I was awakened by a telephone call from the policeman upstairs. I had asked him to get me up then because I wanted time to go home, shave and shower, have breakfast with my wife and daughter and be back at my desk in the press office at 8 A.M. when the Mayor was due to arrive. I rushed home and made it back to City Hall by 8, ready to begin my 99th and 100th days on Saturday and Sunday with John Lindsay.

On the 100th day—Sunday, April 10—in an exclusive interview with Marvin Sleeper of the *Journal-American*, Lindsay referred to some of the pressures he was under and some of the biggest internal problems he felt were obstacles to our success. I was with

Sleeper when he talked to the Mayor in the back seat of the Mayor's car en route to City Hall one afternoon in early April. It was one of the frankest and most open interviews I had heard Lindsay give. "The people in the middle echelons of city government don't want the responsibility of making decisions," he told Sleeper. "So decisions get bogged down in red tape and bureaucracy. Even decisions that just need a little common sense on the part of the people in charge don't get made because they're afraid. I say make decisions—even if once in a while they're wrong." And Lindsay also complained about everyone wanting to see the Mayor. "They won't settle for the Buildings commissioner, or the Police commissioner or the chairman of the City Commission on Human Rights. They want to see me. They wait until I arrive at City Hall and get my ear. Or they can wait until I leave and catch me. You've got to be on top of everything."

Another frustrating aspect of his first 100 days, Lindsay said, was the never-ending delay in capital construction projects. "The backlog of schools, hospitals and offices to be built is appalling. So I'm trying to get a bill through the Legislature that would permit one general contractor to do the entire job instead of letting it out piecemeal for public bidding. These are the kinds of frustrations that send me through the roof."

Talking about the Presidency to Sleeper, Lindsay declared: "The President's job is much bigger because of the button. Outside of that, running City Hall is just as tough."

6 "It's about time we started asking what are the priorities in this country—Vietnam or Brownsville?"

ON APRIL 12, I was sitting in the back seat with the Mayor as his official limousine, a big black Lincoln, sped up the East River Drive en route to Yankee Stadium where Lindsay was scheduled to throw out the first ball. He did not really enjoy watching baseball, but he had been persuaded by Barry Gottehrer—who was also riding with us—that his appearance at a luncheon held by the Yankee management, as well as the baseball game itself, was a "must" for a New York Mayor.

The three of us were talking and somehow we got on the subject of pensions in city government. Lindsay commented, matter-of-factly: "I just joined the pension fund the other day. They have some kind of arrangement where your widow gets half of your salary for life if you get killed on the job. You never know when someone is going to take a shot at you. In this job, you can never tell." I was surprised to hear him say it. We had all realized from the moment he was elected that he must live each day with the thought in the back of his mind that he—like John F. Kennedy, a popular hero—could be cut down at any moment. But this was the first time I had ever heard him say anything about how he felt. It gave me a strange feeling. It was soon forgotten, of course, when we arrived at the Yankee Stadium's New England Room and had drinks and lunch. Then, we watched the Detroit Tigers beat the Yanks, 2–1. Much to his surprise, and mine, Lindsay was roundly booed when he got up to throw out the ball to begin the game. It was, in fact, a tradition for most fans to boo the Mayor—but I was still slightly disturbed by the reception.

The Mayor also attended the Mets opener against the Atlanta Braves three days later, which the Braves won by a score of 3–2. Despite these two outings, Lindsay's moments of leisure were limited. And whenever he did take an hour out for recreation, most of the time it was not a spectator sport. By mid-April, he had already started to work out in a gymnasium a few times a week at the Downtown Athletic Club in lower Manhattan. He asked me not to publicize this aspect of his daily schedule because he wanted to appear to be on-the-job at all hours and also because this particular club reportedly restricted its membership. I had no information to support rumors that neither Jews nor Negroes were allowed into this club, but after joining the Mayor on several workouts myself, I mentioned this to Bill Mattison, the commissioner of Public Works, who had invited me to work out at the Downtown Athletic Club—and he said there were "a few" Jews. Nonetheless, Lindsay and I and several other City Hall aides continued to exercise there because, I think, we all desperately needed it. I know that once I discovered how it eased tension, I could not go more than a few days without a workout. Lindsay enjoyed throwing around a medicine ball with Sid Davidoff, swimming a half dozen laps of the pool and then sitting in a sauna for as long as he could stand it. He exercised with an almost fierce determination, the same way he worked. The first time I joined Lindsay at the Downtown Athletic Club, I tried to keep up with him. That was a mistake. By the time we had completed the hour, I became sick from the strain and had to go home. "What's the matter?" he asked, "Can't you take it? You're getting soft and fat." Compared to him, I was.

The pace on the job continued to be as hectic as ever. In the press area, I discovered that Barry Gottehrer had gone ahead without consulting me and had urged the Mayor to completely reorganize the public relations functions in city government. He had a plan to take all the public relations men out of local agencies, place them in a central "pool," and then use them as a team for various campaigns, depending on what the daily or weekly need was. When I heard about the idea, I told the Mayor I was strongly opposed to such centralization. Nevertheless, much to my surprise the plan just seemed to be moving ahead and on April 15, Marvin Sleeper wrote a piece in the *Journal-American* entitled: ECONOMY SHAKEUP UNDER WAY: FUNERAL BEAT FOR CITY DRUM BEATERS? He said that a "top-to-bottom shakeup" in the city's $5.5 million public relations operation was under way. "Wholesale cuts in personnel, to streamline the publicity setup in 30 city departments, is contemplated," he wrote. His story said that I organized the Task Force and that Gottehrer was the head of it. Working with us, he said, was Arnold DeMille of the city's Personnel Department. The project was an outgrowth of the survey which I had taken myself back in December. There was only one problem: Who was going to do the firing? I resolved that it wouldn't be me. It had been difficult enough listening to the stories of several older city public relations men whose wives were sick or who had a few years to go before they retired when they had come to see me at the Roosevelt in December. I decided that I would not sit in judgment over these men, whether or not this was politics. So when neither Price nor Lindsay pressed me to follow up my survey with recommended firings, I had let the matter drop. When I saw Sleeper's story, however, I had some strong fears that Lindsay might go ahead with the concept of tightening up. The reporters in Room 9 were opposed to this move, of course, because many of their ex-colleagues were among the public relations men in government.

On this same day—April 15—the Mayor presented the biggest expense budget in the 300-year history of the city to the City Council. It amounted to $4.6 billion, a 19 percent increase over the budget which Bob Wagner had adopted in July, 1965. Observing a tradition which apparently had been in existence for some years, the photographers asked for some shots of the Mayor carrying the 2,906-page document which weighed 20.2 pounds. The Mayor, wearing a gray pinstripe suit, a blue shirt, and a red and blue figured tie, cradled the document on his left hip and, as

we approached the gates just outside of my office on the way upstairs to the Board of Estimate chambers, he paused just long
enough to permit the photographers to get their pictures. He
smiled broadly, almost self-consciously, as we walked upstairs. He
had often told me that he did not enjoy posing for pictures and,
up to that time, he had tried to avoid them on many occasions.
He had, in fact, refused to put on a hat, any kind of hat, two or
three times when photographers had asked him to during various
public events at which he officiated.

Holding the two huge volumes under his left arm, the Mayor
then climbed the steps to the second floor of City Hall and
called to order a special meeting of the Board of Estimate. In a
short address, he told the meeting: "The budget is large, but the
needs of the people of New York are great. The budget is frugal,
because the demand for economy in our government is compelling. The budget is ambitious, for it embodies an aspiration
shared by all New Yorkers: to protect and enhance their city's
standing as the most exciting metropolis in the world." He added:
"The budget I present to you today offers an unusual challenge:
It can mark 1966 as the year in which New York City faced up to
the financial facts of life." He advised the grim-faced Board of
Estimate members[1] to "take the budget home and read it over
the weekend, page by page, line by line."

The next day, the *Times* complimented the Mayor on his
budget in an editorial entitled: "The First Lindsay Budget." The
editorial said Lindsay's first executive budget "restores integrity
to city finance, stops the deficit financing," and it is "honestly
balanced." It also complimented him for proposing an unpopular
tax program and concluded: "He has met every test of prudence
except to demand an increase in the transit fare—which must
come."

Over that weekend, the press reaction to the Lindsay budget
was generally favorable, but the big question still remained:
Could he get support for his tax program from Governor Rockefeller and could he get it passed by the State Legislature?

On April 17, the Mayor's normally crowded Sunday schedule
started off with a WOR-TV interview. In answer to a reporter's
questions, I was surprised to hear Lindsay bluntly challenge
Governor Rockefeller. If his tax program were not passed, the

Mayor told his TV audience, there would have to be a massive "lopping off" of city employees. "It is necessary," he said flatly, "at this point that the chief executive of the state as well as I, chief executive of the city, give a very clear statement of support for this important piece of legislation."

By the time Lindsay addressed the City Council on Wednesday, April 20, the opening two days of hearings, the controversy over his tax program was swirling. Dressed in a navy blue suit, white shirt and blue tie, Lindsay spoke for twenty-eight minutes and then answered questions for twenty-three minutes more. He urged the Council to support his "entire" $520 million package. He was particularly strong in his argument for a commuter tax. "Commuter incomes," he said, "are in large part due to New York City's unparalleled complex of rail, highway, air and water transportation—the very transportation system which is the vocational lifeline of the commuter. In our judgment, the non-residents who use the spokes of that system should recognize the dangerous irony in exploiting the hub."

Asserting that his budget had been "cut to the bone," Lindsay told the Council "that no more destructive effect can be imagined" than exempting commuters from the proposed city income tax. "If the City Council or the Legislature exempts commuters from the tax," he declared, "I submit that the reprieve will accelerate the flight of middle- and upper-income families from New York City." As the Mayor spoke, I was concerned about interruptions from the gallery where angry shouts and screams rose from one group which opposed rent controls and real estate taxes. They pushed against police who were trying to prevent them from entering the Council floor. The property owners were also shouting, storming and shoving into the lobby of City Hall demanding to see the Mayor and police had to block the corridors that led to the Mayor's office. Outside, on the perimeter of City Hall park, another taxpayer group assembled what it called a "chamber of horrors"—a coffin, whipping post and a hangman's noose—to dramatize Lindsay's tax program. That group, the United Taxpayers Party, a perennial critic of former Mayor Wagner, carried picket signs, one of which read: "All forgiven, Bob, please come back." City Hall was in a state of virtual siege.

Wrote *Herald Tribune* reporter Edward Silberfarb: "City Hall observers could not remember its equal in recent years."

Lindsay kept calm and delivered his speech strongly and carefully. He urged "prompt passage" of two "home rule" messages and three other resolutions which would call upon the State Legislature to enact his proposals. These included the first local personal income tax in New York City history, which would be levied at 50 percent of the state rate; a package of business income taxes on general corporations, banks, insurance companies and utilities; a stock transfer tax at half the state rate; and a rise in the real estate taxing limit.

His presentation went smoothly, but when members of the Council began to question him, the Mayor grew impatient. The press began to sit up and take notes. They could always count on getting a good quote out of the Mayor when he was pressed. By now, they had learned that he often snapped back a fast answer and did not control his temper.

One Councilman directly challenged his $4.6 billion budget and said it could be cut more. Lindsay, raising his voice, countered: "We will have to attack the budget with a meat cleaver. And we'll need your help. You gentlemen will have to tell me how many policemen to cut, how many firemen, how many hospital workers, how many teachers." In answer to a similar question from another Councilman, Lindsay responded: "I wish you could sit in my seat for a while and hear the complaints of city departments responsible for our hospitals, our old people and the education of our children as they tell me that I have been too stingy with them. This budget has been cut to the bone." After the two days of hearings, it was clear that the vocal opposition had captured the headlines and that many members of the Council were not particularly enthusiastic about endorsing a city income tax. Nevertheless, when the hearings finally recessed at 10:35 Thursday night after 107 witnesses had been heard, it was also clear that they had little alternative if the city was to balance its budget.

On April 24, despite a meeting the day before between the Mayor and publishers from the local newspapers, The Newspaper Guild of New York went on strike against the *Herald*

Tribune, the *World-Telegram and Sun,* and the *Journal-American.* The strike had been threatened for many months and was triggered by the publishers' plan to merge the three corporations and combine the two afternoon newspapers into one and continue to publish the *Herald Tribune* in the morning. I had told the press in Room 9 that the Mayor called the meeting on April 23 "in the interest of helping to resolve the present newspaper impasse." But most of my ex-colleagues knew by this time that there was little chance the publishers would call off the merger. I talked on the telephone with representatives of Governor Rockefeller and Senators Javits and Kennedy to work out a joint plea from the group for around-the-clock bargaining and inclusion of a fact-finding panel. But the plea failed and the Guild struck. I felt particularly bad about the closing of the *World-Telegram,* where I had spent nearly ten years of my professional career.

The same day the newspaper strike began, Frank O'Connor confirmed the general impression that the City Council would reluctantly support Lindsay's tax program. O'Connor predicted that the Council would vote for the home rule message "but only because its hands are tied." At the same time, he added: "The Council has to be responsive to the city's needs as well as responsible." His announcement received page one treatment in the *Times* the next day, Monday, April 25, and was, I think, instrumental in helping to get the local legislation passed. O'Connor, I had found up to that point, was always ready to criticize Lindsay, but he was a reasonable man. This piece of political maneuvering on his part had actually made him look good. It was obvious that the Mayor had laid down his case before the Council and that it was a compelling one. O'Connor had little to lose by supporting the tax program, since everyone knew it was the Mayor's idea to ask for taxes—not the Democrats or O'Connor.

That same Monday, the first day of the newspaper strike, was the same day on which I had scheduled the Mayor's first press conference for weekly newspapers exclusively. It was the first time, as far as I knew, that a New York Mayor had invited editors and reporters from New York's seventy-five weeklies to City Hall for a separate press conference. A great deal of preparation had gone into this conference, almost all of it coordinated by Alfonso (Al) Troche, a twenty-nine-year-old Puerto Rican-born Army captain whom I had hired as a second assistant press secretary after Bob Laird had joined me. Troche, who proved to be diligent and capable, had written me a letter earlier in the year from his base in New Jersey stating that, after five years in the Army, he was impressed with John Lindsay and wanted to join city government if there was an opening. His background was impressive. A graduate of New York University, experienced in journalism and social welfare, he had worked for the city's Welfare Department and had served as a public information officer in the Army. Married and the father of two daughters, he appeared to be the picture of the ideal press aide when I first called him to City Hall for an interview with the Mayor and myself. After some problems arranging for his discharge from the Army (we had to call upon Senator Javits to intervene), he came into my office and immediately began to take on the responsibility of responding to weekly newspapers and the Spanish press as part of his duties. It was obvious that these media had been severely neglected during the early weeks of our Administration.

On the day of the weekly newspapers' press conference, I alerted the Room 9 daily press corps, and invited a good many commissioners to attend so they could answer specific questions about what we were doing in the city's neighborhoods. We had asked each of the newspapers coming to send in their questions beforehand so that we could research many of the answers from the various departments in advance. As *Town and Village,* a newspaper with a paid circulation of about 8,000 residents of Stuyvesant Town and Peter Cooper Village in the lower East Side of Manhattan, later described the press conference: "In large part, the event was a reflection of the Lindsay storefront philosophy which acknowledges that the City is made up of innumerable little neighborhoods, many of which are serviced by aggressive weekly newspapers." The questions from the weekly editors and reporters dealt with local matters and we had the answers on small cards. As the questions were asked (the newsman identified himself and his paper), I shuffled through the cards and handed the Mayor the answer. In the event the reporter had additional questions, the Mayor called on the commissioners to give further details. It was a complicated, somewhat rehearsed format, but it worked. The news conference, if not exciting to the regular TV and daily newspapermen who attended, provided a great deal of specific information to the weekly papers. For that reason, I thought it had been helpful to the Mayor. Apparently the weeklies agreed. A few wrote editorials lauding the Mayor.[2]

By the end of April, Lindsay had succeeded in attracting more talent to government. Several appointments had been newsworthy. The new officials included: Richard H. Buford, thirty-six, Philadelphia's commissioner of licenses and inspections, as an assistant to the Mayor in charge of the city's summer antipoverty programs; and Dr. Nachman Bench, thirty-one, a university professor and an Israeli citizen, as a deputy city administrator.[3] Added to his previous appointments, these helped Lindsay in his quest for a non-partisan professional team. He began to express confidence privately that his "team"—as he called his top officials in Friday Cabinet meetings—was beginning to take definite shape.

Still, I noticed Lindsay was growing so tense that he always seemed to be slightly distracted when someone was with him. When he focused on another person in conversation, he focused hard. But he didn't always focus. He could be looking right at someone and his mind would be somewhere else. He smiled and he tried to act friendly, but when he became preoccupied, I noticed that he looked at least ten years older than he did when we first took office. The muscles along the sides of his jaw flickered when he was angry or fatigued. I began to wonder if his nerves wouldn't become so taut that he might actually snap, but I realized that his workouts in the gym and his abundance of nervous energy somehow kept him in balance. His job, after all, was more than any normal man could stand. It was while riding from place to place in the spring that Lindsay showed extreme tension. He would never relax. Instead, he would make one telephone call after another on the car phone, or sign papers, or stare out of the window with his bleak blue eyes. Occasionally, he would become too impatient to even remain in the car when the traffic slowed us down; he would get out and walk and tell the driver to meet him at our destination.

Once when we were trapped in a particularly bad side-street in heavy traffic for about fifteen minutes, he got out of the car and yelled down the street for a policeman on horseback to "give all of these cars tickets and clear out this place." Recognizing the Mayor, the astonished police officer immediately dismounted and began furiously writing tickets.

April, then, was a time of uneasiness and discontent. Spring had arrived and we had been in office for four months. And Lindsay himself began to say regularly at the beginning of each speech, "Yesterday, I celebrated my seventy-fifth birthday . . ." or, "When I took office I was forty-three years old. Now I am seventy-five. . . ." The theme was clear: He was beginning to feel the impossible pace.

For me, April was an even busier month than March. My office put out forty press releases and the tax program was beginning to take up almost all of my available time—day and night. I looked forward every week to 9 P.M. Saturday, the last copy deadline of the *Times* for the Sunday morning edition. Of course, there were the radio and TV stations calling with questions—especially on Sundays—but most radio and TV reporters did not call me as often as the daily press.

Several of my friends in Room 9 reported to me, however, that there was still a deep-seated resentment against the Mayor in some quarters of the press. "Finesse," one reporter said in regard to our Administration about this time, "is the last word in their vocabulary. As Cousin Joe would say (Cousin Joe is a New Orleans blues singer), finesse and them haven't talked in years." I half hoped it wasn't true, but all around me I continued to see signs that the Mayor and many of my colleagues in government were still exercising power as if it was something to be worn on one's sleeve and exhibited in public. Perhaps I was guilty of some of this showmanship myself—I had a chauffeur-driven car—but I tried to be as inconspicuous as possible. Power, I found, was a difficult commodity to be burdened with unless you knew exactly what to do with it. One of the discoveries I made as press secretary was that although I had not changed, many people who knew me casually actually treated me differently because I was so close to the Mayor. They attributed some hidden powers to me that I could not thoroughly understand.

And many of my former friends in the press seemed to feel that my increased salary had somehow changed my values. By the beginning of May, it was clear to me that our Administration needed to make a lot of progress in communicating our story to the public.

For some months, for example, we had been discussing the possibility of asking all city employees to work normal hours during the summer—9 A.M. to 5 P.M.—instead of the summer hours of only until 4 P.M. to which they had become accustomed. Lindsay felt that a great deal of work could be accomplished in that extra hour and that it would help him in his "economy" drive. Although no formal announcement had been made yet of our intentions, word had leaked out and union opposition was beginning to mount. I felt there was nothing wrong with asking city employees to work a full day in the summer. I had the same attitude toward most civil servants that the Mayor did: tolerance but not much respect for people who basically did not want to work hard—winter or summer. City employees, we learned, had been working short days ever since James J. Walker had been Mayor and they were not about to give up that extra hour. On May 1, several city unions began to distribute leaflets around City Hall expressing dissatisfaction. The leaflets warned that the 4 P.M. quitting time was a condition of employment. "We will not let anybody take it away from you," said the pamphlet. Abel (Al) Silver of the *Post,* whose paper had "broken" the story a few days earlier, came to me for a comment about the union leaflets. As Silver stood in front of my desk, notebook and pencil in hand, I looked up at him and slowly dictated the following: "It is the Administration's policy to ask all city employees to work a full day in summer as they do in winter in the interest of economy and increased productivity."

On May 2, in a special televised talk originating from television station WPIX in the *Daily News* building on East 42nd Street, Lindsay and Howard Leary announced the creation of the Civilian Complaint Review Board. The Mayor named a panel of eleven men, including three Negroes, and a Puerto Rican, to recommend civilian candidates to be appointed by him to the revamped review board. The Mayor's plan, for which he had campaigned, called for the board to have three police officers and four civilians with a civilian executive director, its own investigating unit of police officers and conciliation procedures.

I accompanied the Mayor to the studios and watched while the announcement was being aired. Commissioner Leary appeared tight and nervous, but he performed with discipline. The Mayor explained that he had taken to the air-waves because "public understanding of the need for and the purpose of the board is essential to its success." But he was also nervous before the program was aired. Nevertheless, he came across well once he started talking. The press were not permitted inside the main studio, but were given a studio in which they could view the program "live." As might have been predicted, the *Post* called the plan "an excellent beginning," the *Times* also endorsed his plan, calling it a "constructive step," and *The News* labeled it "the property of bleeding hearts and cop-haters in about equal proportions." The other three newspapers had been out on strike since April 25.[4] Strong opposition was immediately registered by the Patrolmen's Benevolent Association, led by its President, Patrolman John Cassese, who said: "We consider the Mayor's proposal improper, illegal and undesirable." Within a few days, additional criticism was leveled at the board. Surprisingly, the National Association for the Advancement of Colored People said it had "serious inadequacies," and additional attacks came from the Congress of Racial Equality.

The Patrolmen's Benevolent Association then announced it would seek a citywide referendum on the issue in the fall. "We intend to mount the biggest campaign against the board ever seen in New York City," one spokesman said. The Patrolmen's Benevolent Association said as part of the campaign it would attempt to test the constitutionality of the Lindsay concept. There was no doubt in anyone's mind by now that there would be serious and worrisome opposition to the board. Despite Cassese's warnings, however, I never actually felt at this time that the issue would reach the point where it would be taken before the public in a referendum on Election Day.

One reason I did not worry too much about the attacks on the board is that I had not directly participated in the formulation of the specific plan. That had been left mostly up to Jay Kriegel. And the TV show had been arranged and carried out by Kriegel, Dave Garth and Barry Gottehrer. I was, in a way, an outsider to the plan, even though I was familiar with all of the details. I was, of course, in favor of it; it seemed logical to me and I, therefore, did not find it difficult to believe that it would succeed. After it had been announced by Lindsay on May 2, I had accompanied him to a dinner of the Urban League at the Hotel Americana where the Mayor was greeted with some enthusiasm. Many of the other dais guests congratulated him on announcing the board. He was scheduled to be the first speaker and, as I leaned over next to him conferring for a moment before he went on, he asked me: "What should I say?" I told him former Mayor Wagner was present and to mention him and to talk about civil rights, possibly even the review board. His talk was short and adequate. About twenty minutes later, he called me over from the side of the dais. Interrupting a conversation he was having with someone next to him, he whispered to me: "Get me out of here. This is a bore." I said, loudly, "Mr. Mayor, it's time for us to be moving along. You're half an hour late for your next appointment." He apologized to his neighbors on both sides and got up to leave. We walked off the dais together straight into the kitchen on the side, passing about a dozen waiters, all carrying cake in one hand and strawberry sauce in the other. Much to their astonishment, Lindsay smiled and bellowed: "Why don't you fellows dump that stuff on a few of them out there? I can think of several offhand."

The night of May 4, my wife and I went to a dinner given by the United Jewish Appeal in honor of Harvey Rothenberg. Lindsay was scheduled to drop in—and he did. Rothenberg had put the United Jewish Appeal dinner on Lindsay's schedule, and of course, the Mayor said a few words praising Harvey and the United Jewish Appeal. Rothenberg, forty-one, owner of Philip Rothenberg & Co., a shirt manufacturing concern started by his father with offices in the Empire State Building, worked for Lindsay as a $1-a-year man. A cool, competent administrator, he had won the Mayor's friendship and trust by helping and advising him since the early 1950s when both men were among the more vocal liberals in the New York Young Republican Club. Rothenberg had helped out in all of Lindsay's campaigns, including the mayoral campaign when he ran the headquarters. He somehow managed to run his own business and handle the scheduling and administrative chores at City Hall as well. "If I went through life just making shirts," he had told a reporter once, "I wouldn't feel I'd accomplished what I could have. I think I can do some good by spending all the time I can at City Hall." His wife, Elaine, also helped out at City Hall as a girl Friday—drawing $3,000 a year for twenty-five hours a week. I thought Lindsay spoke well at the dinner and I told him so the next morning. "No, I didn't," he replied, coldly.

Lindsay at this time was frequently snappish in public as well. At his weekly press conference on Friday, May 6, he was once again asked by a newspaper reporter about Governor Rockefeller's failure to support his tax program. Lindsay shot back: "If the Governor has any better alternative, I haven't seen it." He said the Governor had an "obligation" to support the plan unless he had any better ideas. The *Post* immediately picked up his comments as a new challenge to the Governor and the already strained relationship was growing even more difficult to mend. I had been in touch with Leslie Slote, Rockefeller's press secretary, on several occasions—mostly about joint press conferences and statements. Even though I had known Slote when he was Wagner's press aide and I was a reporter, that did little to cement any working relationship between us. Slote had hired Warren Gardner away from me without any warning earlier in the year and it was clear to me that, in his own way, he was just as tough, cool and shrewd as his boss, the Governor. This did not diminish my respect for Slote's abilities—he was a first-class press secretary with a good sense of humor who knew how to handle newsmen—but he was obviously no fan of John Lindsay's. Our relationship was a peculiar one, too, because we would often meet in Washington Square Park in the city on weekends accompanying our daughters to the children's playground. Rarely, if ever, did we talk shop on those occasions.

Life had become so hectic for Lindsay during May that he had to literally hide from the public and the press to have dinner with his wife. On May 10, for example, we were attending a reception at the Plaza Hotel for newspapermen who had won Pulitzer Prizes, when I received a call from Bob Laird that someone "important" had to talk to the Mayor. Lindsay stepped out into the lobby and, seeing a pay phone on the wall, he stopped, leaned against the wall, put a dime in and made his call. Suddenly, a teen-age girl came by and, realizing it was the Mayor, shrieked: "It's him. It's John Lindsay. I've never been so close to a Mayor before. I can't believe it." Lindsay tried to continue his conversation, but by now a TV camera crew from one of the networks was setting up a few feet away from him to film him talking on the telephone. I asked them to leave the Mayor alone, but they refused. When they were about ready to shoot, however, Lindsay hung up, turned on his heels and, running after him, I saw him leave the Plaza by a side door. The camera crew ran after us, but Lindsay merely ran around and into the front entrance. We had shaken both the TV crew and the young teen-age fan. Slightly out of breath, he calmly went back inside to the dining room where his wife, Mary, had reserved a table for them for dinner. It was 9:45 P.M.

There were, of course, some lighter moments in May, like the Cabinet meeting we held in The Arsenal, the Central Park headquarters of the Parks Department. The Mayor had instituted a policy of taking the regular Friday morning Cabinet meetings out in the field almost every week, moving from one department to the next so each commissioner could "host" the meeting and tell the others something about his department. One morning in early May, we had all arrived in the old Arsenal, when John (Bud) Palmer, the ex-Princeton University and New York Knickerbocker basketball star and then commissioner of public events (the official city greeter), announced to the group that he was going to Moscow on a personal trip to study how to attract tourists to New York.

Bob Price turned to Palmer and kidded him about "picking up a few inches in the newspapers" in the publicity race usually led by Parks Commissioner Tom Hoving and Buildings Commissioner Charles Moerdler. Fire Commissioner Bob Lowery noted that Palmer hadn't yet made *Life* magazine and that Hoving had.

"Hoving used up all of his credit cards sewing that one up," Price said. Price then asked Palmer who was paying for the trip to Moscow. Palmer said he was paying for it himself and then asked Price why he was so concerned with the trip.

"Bob, do you have some friends over there?" Palmer asked. The room broke up in laughter.

By this time in May, the newspaper strike was beginning to drag—Lindsay had appointed David L. Cole, a veteran mediator, to try and settle the dispute. And there were other running battles, not the least of which was a new one with the Board of Education over a remark the Mayor had made at a weekend country outing of school principals that compared to Los Angeles and Detroit, "our educational system is not demonstrably better." School Superintendent Dr. Bernard Donovan and a number of other school officials objected publicly and Lindsay was forced to issue a statement reappraising the city's public schools system as "the finest in the country, but one which still can be improved." I objected to Lindsay backing down, but other advisers said the time was not yet ripe for him to be taking on the entire public school establishment with so many other fights still unresolved.

One of the more difficult problems we had was the struggle for clean air in New York. Lindsay appointed Austin Heller, fifty-one, an expert from Cincinnati, early in May and on May 9, the Mayor released a report from a ten-member Task Force, led by *Saturday Review* editor Norman Cousins, which shocked even those of us working in City Hall. New York, the report stated bluntly, "has all the ingredients for an air pollution disaster of major proportions." Our city, the report continued, had the most polluted air of any major city in the United States. It added that city government itself was "the worst violator of its own laws against pollution" because of its incinerators and buses. Lindsay, trying not to look bewildered by the bad news, held a press conference to release the report and promised firm action to improve the air. I listened to him and wondered how we were ever going to save New York from a pollution disaster. If we put all of our energies into the fight for better air alone, it would be a big job—and we had so many other problems to worry about, too.

One small legislative victory we did win was City Council approval of the tax plan, voted on May 9 late in the evening. But in voting to support the Mayor the Council also asked for an additional $100 million savings in Lindsay's expense budget. The package was also approved with the understanding that the subway fare would remain at 15 cents. As soon as we got the word, Lindsay asked me to prepare a statement. I did, and then released it to the press. It said the Mayor was "delighted" by the Council's action and that "the city now speaks with a unified voice as a result of this approval by the Council and its president. Albany must now listen and act promptly in order to prevent the loss to the city of substantial millions." The *Times* called the Council approval "a constructive and essential first step," but chided the Council for not giving the Mayor his entire tax program. "The Council succumbs," the editorial stated, "to the temptation to stage-out, over several years, the immediate fiscal reform that Mr. Lindsay courageously proposed."

Meanwhile, trouble was brewing on the labor front. In addition to the newspapers, the taxi drivers and the city's nurses were threatening to walk off their jobs. Fearing an emergency in city hospitals if the nurses were to strike, the Mayor grew more and more concerned over this threat. On May 12 the cabbies went out, leaving New York virtually without taxi service.

While these emergencies were breaking out all around, I accompanied Lindsay to a press conference at the Hotel Astor for a joint announcement of a $600 million housing and industrial development for lower Manhattan. On the way to the Astor, Lindsay was interviewed by Frank McMasters of the *Long Island Press,* an old-timer who had been around City Hall for many years. Lindsay told McMasters, off the record, that he thought very little of the quality of the press in Room 9. McMasters agreed. "Don't worry so much about newspapermen or what they write," McMasters told the Mayor. "Never let them bother you." Lindsay replied: "They don't bother me one bit!"

By the time we arrived at the press conference, Rockefeller had already distributed press releases. There was no doubt that he intended to turn it into his show. But when it came time for

Lindsay to speak, he had picked up just enough of the spirit of the conference to state that the new housing along the waterfront would be a "great asset" to New York. As we left the hotel afterwards, I told him I thought he had taken some of the thunder out of Rocky's press conference with his talk. "I was winging it," Lindsay replied with a smile. "Whenever you wing it, you just make up your mind to take off and keep going no matter what happens."

As we stepped into the Mayor's car outside, a British journalist, Charles Wintour, editor of the *London Evening Star,* was sitting in the back seat waiting for a car-ride interview back to City Hall. He asked the Mayor: "How did it go in there?" The Mayor replied, smiling: "I winged it all the way." Wintour smiled politely, but I don't think he had any idea of what Lindsay was talking about. On the way back to the Hall, the British writer asked the Mayor about his background. Lindsay's grandfather had come from the Isle of Wight. His British ancestry was a source of great interest to Wintour. "My grandfather," said Lindsay, "probably left Scotland or was driven out at some point. I once asked him about it when I was a little boy and he said he didn't know." When the subject turned to the United States' involvement in the Vietnamese war, Lindsay praised Secretary of Defense Robert S. McNamara, but added: "He's a great Secretary of Defense, but a lousy Secretary of State."

Friday, May 13, 1966, was not, as we might have expected, a very lucky day. Renewed efforts by the Mayor to break the impasse in the taxi negotiations yielded no progress; the Mayor's tax programs appeared to have run into a political stone wall when Democratic leaders in the City Council informed him that they would do nothing until his tax plan was endorsed by the Republicans and Governor Rockefeller; some 1,400 of the city's 3,500 nurses were threatening to resign in 10 days causing the Hospitals Department to warn that 21 city hospitals could close; the Mayor lost his temper by attacking the State Legislature at a press conference, accusing its members of "irresponsibility" in holding back action on his transportation bills; and there was little progress reported in the newspaper strike. It was a very hard day, indeed. It almost reminded me of the labor crisis during the transit strike. City Hall began to look as it did during those early days after the first of the year.

In the midst of this long and difficult day, Lindsay, at one point, got up from his desk and walked over to a table in his office on which lay a portfolio of lithographs of the city done by Luciano Guarneiri, of Florence, Italy, which had been presented to the Mayor two days earlier. "These are really beautiful," he said softly, slowly turning the pages. "Look at these pictures of his wife. Beautiful work." Murray Drabkin, Bob Laird, Dick Rosen and I were in his office at the time. He seemed genuinely moved by the paintings, I thought. This was another side of John Lindsay which few New Yorkers knew; this was the quiet, compassionate John Lindsay who had held the hands of several children suffering from muscular dystrophy, in a Brooklyn hospital weeks before, and who had nearly cried when they asked him to sign his autograph. I had stood by his side as he knelt down next to the children, many of whom appeared grotesque to the average observer. And, no matter how cynical the press may have been about the publicity which resulted from the Mayor visiting the sick children, I believed that Lindsay meant everything he said to the youngsters when he crouched down on the floor of the hospital room and talked with them. It was not often that he permitted people to see this part of him. I often thought that he considered this deep sensitivity almost a weakness and that he, therefore, did not permit himself the luxury of showing his true feelings much of the time he was in public.

About the middle of May, the requests for interviews began to increase once again. We were reaching the six-month mark and the newsmen and columnists were beginning to take aim again. Pete Hamill of the *Post* came in for a long interview. He caught the Mayor on a cold, gray Monday morning. "Monday morning should be abolished," he quoted Lindsay as saying. He described the Mayor as looking "a bit drawn, the hair ruffled." Hamill asked him what his toughest problem was. "In the end," Lindsay said, "the hardest job is to keep open the lines of communication, to let various people from all the power interests know that they can at some point talk to the Mayor.

It's part of a charade that goes on at all times, and I suppose that is something that never can be changed." Finally, after an hour with Lindsay, Hamill concluded: "No one is quite sure how John Lindsay will work out as the months go by, including Lindsay himself. But one thing is certain: He has gotten past that fragile point he had reached a few weeks ago, when you were almost sure he would be replaced by Ralph Houk. Perhaps now, with a little luck, he can begin to function as the Mayor."

By May 17, the labor problems began to fall into place. Lindsay announced on the evening of May 16 a settlement of the six-day-old taxi strike, after a lengthy session with Harry Van Arsdale. It was an unusual dispute because both sides settled and agreed to let the Mayor himself decide the wage increase for the cabbies. Lindsay, who had taken part in the twenty-two-hour marathon bargaining sessions, looked weary when he made his announcement. I had remained with him during most of these negotiations and I felt about as exhausted as I had during the transit strike. The Mayor had helped solve the strike by threatening the taxi owners with issuing 1,700 new hack medallions, which would have flooded the market. Both the drivers and the fleet owners recognized in Lindsay a new toughness which they had not seen before and he was able to settle the strike in a much shorter time than, for example, the transit walkout.

The next day, the log-jam in the twenty-three-day-old newspaper strike broke as the merged corporation and the New York Typographical Union No. 6 reached an agreement, which the Mayor announced at the Commodore Hotel. The settlement had been made through the efforts of David L. Cole, the labor mediator, but still no agreement had been reached with the Guild. I accompanied Lindsay into the hotel suite where the negotiations had been conducted. There, we found Matt Meyer, president of the new publishing enterprise, whom I had known as business manager of the old *World-Telegram*. He nodded in recognition as I entered. In the past, I had been one of those reporters sitting outside in the hallway, waiting, for hours, sometimes for days, before there was a piece of news. Now, I was standing with Lindsay in the hallway next to Cole behind the scene of the negotiations. It appeared it would only be a matter of a week or two before agreements could be hammered out with the other unions and the newspapers would be publishing.

Former Mayor Robert F. Wagner had said publicly sometime during the first few months of our Administration that he intended to wait six months before he evaluated Lindsay's performance. On May 17, however, Wagner broke this pledge and, in a speech at the division of urban affairs of the University of Delaware, he said that he viewed the Lindsay Administration as "amateurish, lost in an organizational thicket and failing to meet campaign promises." He said Lindsay spent more time streamlining city government than in solving city problems. "There can be improved efficiency, but there is certainly no miraculous magic in the merger and reshuffling of government departments and agencies," he said. "In my judgment," he continued, "concern with governmental structure—as important as it may be—can be a diversion from the main attack on the critical problems of government and of the cities." His observations were by far his strongest criticism of Lindsay up to that time. He also attacked Lindsay for ignoring experienced persons in government to take on newcomers for "on the job training," and for claiming too much for newly announced, untried programs. "I would say," Wagner added, "that he had better start running faster to catch up with where he was." And, at another point, Wagner said: "It is indeed dangerous, as Mayor Lindsay is finding out, to claim that all urban problems can be solved straight away by the waving of a magic wand and 'presto' fiscal problems will be solved, housing will be built, the ghettos abolished, crime reduced, employment provided, schools improved, opportunity equalized, segregation abolished and the flight of industry reversed."

The next day, May 18, Lindsay responded at a press conference to Wagner's criticism. He declared: "I believe my appointments to top jobs have been outstanding. I think the former distinguished Mayor is aware of some of these appointments. I should think he would be delighted to see this talent added to the city's Administration." Then Lindsay mentioned by name Police Commissioner Leary, Correction Commissioner McGrath and

Fire Commissioner Robert Lowery. Also, for the first time in many months he answered a question about Vietnam. Up to now, I, for one, had urged him not to become involved in national or international issues—he had run on a non-partisan platform and had promised he would not run for national office. Still, when asked at a press conference on May 18 what he thought of the Johnson Administration's conduct of the war in Vietnam, Lindsay could not resist the temptation. Without hesitating, he told the newsmen: "It's about time we started asking what are the priorities in this country—Vietnam or Brownsville? In the absence of new resources coming into cities, the government ought to reexamine this and where the cuts can be made in the massive fund pouring into Vietnam. If urban centers are ever going to solve their ills, the government is going to have to reallocate expenditures and set up its investment in the cities of the nation."

Later that evening, I became involved in the settlement of the nurses' strike, but by issuing a statement in the Mayor's name I almost inadvertently unsettled the settlement. About 8:30 P.M., the Mayor asked me to call in the Room 9 press corps and tell them that the nurses were on their way down to announce an agreement. I told the newsmen: "The nurses have settled. They are on their way down." They went to the telephones with a bulletin. About twenty minutes later the nurses' representatives arrived at City Hall. When the press converged on Mary Finnin, assistant executive director of the New York State Nurses Association as she arrived at City Hall about 9 P.M., she declared: "We have accepted nothing." Then, Eugene Becker, the acting budget director and chief of the city's negotiating team, added: "There is no truth in the statement whatsoever." I was stunned. Less than a half hour before, the Mayor had told me there was, indeed, a settlement. I did not know whom to believe or what to say to the press. I told the reporters I would join the group behind closed doors with the Mayor and attempt to clarify the situation.

Thirty minutes later, leaders of the negotiating teams were gathered around the battery of microphones in the Board of Estimate chambers, flanking the Mayor, who formally announced the settlement. "This is a fair and proper settlement," Lindsay said. "It makes up for many years of insufficient attention. Nurses in the past have too often been underpaid and over-worked. The most important thing is that their profession has not been properly recognized." The settlement, I later realized, had been carefully worked out to satisfy the 1,480 nurses in the city's 21 municipal hospitals and they wanted to share in the announcement. When they were asked to confirm the settlement at City Hall, their first reaction had been to deny any agreement until they were ready to announce it. And Becker, fearing that the settlement would fall apart, felt it was necessary for him to deny it also. As it turned out, it was all a meaningless charade —but the press did not appreciate the confusion, and I could not blame them. I explained to the nurses' spokesman in the Mayor's office what had happened and I accepted responsibility for the early release of the settlement.

With the taxi and nurses' strikes settled, and with agreement apparently close in the newspaper dispute, the Mayor began to turn his attention back to his tax program. Several close advisers were urging him to make an appeal to the public on TV, since his program appeared to be stalled in the State Legislature. There was divided opinion among the staff about the advantage of going to the public. I told the Mayor I thought he should work it out privately. I was anxious to avoid any further polarization between City Hall and the state politicians. Yet, there were others in our group who wanted to see Lindsay lay down the gauntlet in the same manner as he had been doing since we first took office.

For a change of pace, on May 21, I accompanied the Mayor on a fog-shrouded circumnavigation of Manhattan Island and a crossing of Long Island Sound for a luncheon at the U.S. Merchant Marine Academy at Kings Point, Long Island. With us were Congressmen from twenty-three states and their families, who were on a four-day tour of New York City. The Mayor was the host on this trip and, as a former Congressman, he knew most of the twenty-three aboard. At one point in the trip, the Mayor told the group: "If we don't get the support we need in Washington, we'll pull the plug out of the boat!" He added: "I know you all and this makes me nostalgic about the simpler life of a Congressman." When we returned to the mainland, the press asked the Mayor what kind of trip he had had: "It was fine," he said with a smile, "except for the fog which was quite dense, but which members of Congress are used to operating in." All in all, it was a pleasant trip—despite the weather, and I rather enjoyed being away from pressing city problems for an entire day.

On Sunday, May 22, the tax program really began to take shape when Lindsay—after receiving some word from Bob Price—announced on radio that he would be willing to compromise on the commuter part of the tax package. Lindsay said: "We realize the commuters ought to pay only half of what residents would pay." In the same program, Lindsay charged that many suburban legislators had "dug their heels in. I think," he added, "that there's more support among commuters than they themselves realize, and I would hope that they would not in the long run be judged guilty of political cowardice on this question." The next morning, Price flew to Albany to meet with Rockefeller and work out details of a tax program. Once again, Price was operating behind the scenes and all I knew about what he was doing I read in the newspapers. Lindsay remained silent.

The *Times* ran an editorial on May 24 stating: "Mayor Lindsay has shown political courage in his tax program; but, in the handling of that program, he has not demonstrated much diplomacy. At the very moment that he was making his first gesture of compromise, in conceding the 'reasonableness' of taxing commuter income in New York City at half-rate, he was implying that legislators from surburban counties were showing 'political cowardice'—a challenge that brought immediate counterattack yesterday in Albany." The Mayor had, indeed, attacked the surburban legislators and it was a source of great concern to me and other aides. Moreover, when he read that he had been quoted saying he would cut the commuter tax in half, he said he had merely tried to indicate he was open to compromise but not necessarily that exact formula. This led to great confusion among the press.

In the middle of the tax controversy, still another one broke out—this time it involved the construction union leadership again. Peter J. Brennan, president of the Building and Construction Trades Council threatened a one-day work stoppage in the construction industry on June 22 to protest what he called the Lindsay Administration's "practice of impeding and postponing work on several major projects in the city." Brennan named such projects as the World Trade Center, the Lower Manhattan Expressway, the proposed civic center and the Richmond Parkway. Brennan made his statement in a City Council hearing on the Mayor's proposed transportation merger. Brennan also complained that he had failed in repeated efforts to see the Mayor and that he had sent him a new telegram in an effort to meet with him.

The Mayor, hearing of Brennan's charges, called me in and we discussed a reply. We decided I would issue a statement in his behalf. I said the Mayor "flatly denies bottling up any projects" and that he had, in fact, moved ahead on the Richmond Parkway. I also said the Mayor denied not wanting to meet with Brennan and that anytime he wanted to see Lindsay "all he had to do is ask for an appointment." I also told the reporters—not for attribution—that I thought the reason Brennan had attacked the Mayor was because Brennan was angry at Bill Booth, Human Rights commissioner, for putting great pressure on him to hire Negroes. After the story appeared, Brennan replied that he had been "cooperating fully" with Booth and that 10 percent of the membership of his union was Negro.

Returning to the tax dilemma, the Mayor decided after listening to Price that he would fly to Albany on May 24 to soothe the feelings of some of the legislators he had offended with his "cowardice" remarks on Sunday. He made the trip after two Republicans, Senator Earl W. Brydges, the senate majority leader, and Assemblyman Perry B. Duryea, Jr., the minority leader, had both indicated that his comments had seriously damaged their efforts to reach a compromise on the city taxes in the Legislature.

On the same night Lindsay was in Albany trying to make peace with the legislative leaders—May 24—I was covering for him at a dinner of the Encampment for Citizenship honoring two great civil libertarians, Roger N. Baldwin and Norman Thomas, both in their eighties and both men who were in the forefront of the battle for individual rights for more than seven decades. I had the job of presenting to both men the highest honor which the City of New York can bestow on a citizen—the Gold Medal of the City of New York. I did so— in the Mayor's name—with a comment that with the medals goes "the Mayor's deepest affection and appreciation." Lindsay was chairman of the board of sponsors of the Encampment— an experiment in international living which brought students of all nations together every summer in New York. I had a personal reason for feeling very gratified at the opportunity of presenting the medals: I had been close to the Baldwin family for many years.

On Thursday, May 26, I sat in on a crucial Blue Room meeting with Peter Brennan and some other labor leaders which had resulted from Brennan's telegram a few days earlier. Brennan opened the meeting by stating that he considered discrimination a separate issue and that he had been meeting with Commissioner Bill Booth on the subject. He told Lindsay there were unemployed men in the union halls—men who had not had steady work for a year or more. He said thousands of his men had obtained jobs outside of the city—therefore, unemployment figures had not increased. He complained about the "red tape" on getting building permits and approvals by city agencies. Lindsay responded by saying that he had "thrown out" old red tape procedures and "shrunk it by one-third." Quietly, patiently, the Mayor told Brennan: "We have set up test cases—to push architects on larger projects, for example. I have asked Bill [Public Works Commissioner William C.] Mattison to cut out all the nonsense on all public works projects," Lindsay continued. And he then displayed some figures which showed that construction commitments in public works in the city had risen from $22.5 million in 1964 to $31 million in 1965 to $72 million for 1966. "This stuff is committed," Lindsay went on. "The money is in the capital budget. It breaks all records. Architects have actually signed."

On specifics, Lindsay told Brennan and the members of the buildings and construction industry that there had been some delay on construction on the World Trade Center, but this was because the city took the view that New York was badly shortchanged in the Port Authority deal. "By the time this is settled,"

Lindsay added, "the city stands to get out of this a passenger terminal—four to six piers in Brooklyn and Staten Island. The city will strengthen its economy by making a fair arrangement in return for these properties." On the Staten Island highway, Lindsay conceded there was a holdup on one section, but he said there was no reason the remaining two could not go ahead. In addition, the Mayor told the gathering that the Board of Education had increased its construction from $30 to $37 million during the first five months of 1966, that he did not agree with the route for the Lower Manhattan Expressway, and that he opposed one or two other projects that were on the boards. I listened to the Mayor, knowing that he had been well briefed by Mattison, and I was impressed by his candor. I did not see how Brennan could argue with his figures, although he might disagree with some of his views.

Brennan responded: "We were down on Bob Wagner for the same thing. Construction wasn't moving fast enough. So it's not just a matter of this Administration, Mr. Mayor. That much I want to make clear." Lindsay, with Bill Mattison at his side, responded by pointing out that total citywide construction commitments were up in 1966 and that he expected it to continue that way. All in all, it was a quiet, reasonably friendly meeting and neither Lindsay nor Brennan pushed too hard. Lindsay, I was certain, construed the meeting as a partial victory even though Brennan still publicly claimed he would carry out his threatened one-day work stoppage on June 22.

About this time, Lindsay's troubles with his antipoverty program resumed. It was sparked by an attack by Robert J. Mangum, northeast regional director of the Office of Economic Opportunity. He charged that despite prodding from Washington, New York City's "only response was delay" in submitting its budget for neighborhood programs. The city at this point was slated to receive some $36 million, but it had been pressing for the allocation to be increased to $60 million. In the meantime, some formal paperwork had not been completed and Mangum, a Democrat and a Negro who had not been reappointed by Lindsay (he had been serving as a deputy commissioner of Hospitals) earlier in the year, took the opportunity to play a little politics with the Lindsay Administration. Lindsay replied the next day by blaming the delay on "intensely complicated procedures that his Administration inherited." At one point, I was asked by several newsmen why there had been such delay. I responded by stating openly: "There are too many people involved, and they can never get together. We hope to revise the operation soon and streamline the procedure."

The underlying reason for the delay was too scandalous to tell the press. What was actually causing the delays was the fact that Lindsay had retained Wagner's antipoverty officials much too long while he was awaiting a definitive report on the city's poverty program from Mitchell Sviridoff, the former New Haven poverty expert. In the meantime, Mrs. Anne Roberts, a holdover from the Wagner Administration, was trying to run an outdated, bureaucratic agency which, at the same time, was also being directed by several of Lindsay's so-called whiz kids—such as Sidney Gardner, an inexperienced twenty-three-year-old youth, who had a cool, even-tempered appearance and who had impressed Lindsay during the campaign. He was now executive director of the unwieldly eighty-member New York City Council Against Poverty—composed mostly of Wagner holdovers. Barry Gottehrer, whose only experience in this field had been writing some newspaper articles on this subject when he was with the *Herald Tribune,* was working with Gardner. Thus, for the first five months of our Administration, literally nothing had been accomplished—except perhaps for some hearings in the ghetto communities—and everything stood still while we awaited the Sviridoff report, which, ostensibly, would merge the antipoverty agency with welfare and one or two others under the umbrella of the Human Resources Administration. This was scheduled to be part of Lindsay's governmental consolidation.

Gardner had been a source of trouble—aside from the poverty program. Earlier, *Daily News* reporter Bill Federici had found out that Gardner had not served in the Army and he wanted to know why. I told him I didn't know, but that he should check with Gardner. He did. And then he wrote a story which was published at the end of May stating that Gardner had joined the New York National Guard after receiving a pre-induction notice from his draft board in California. When he was ordered to take a physical, the story said, he requested a deferment on the grounds that his job was essential and he asked also that all his records be forwarded to New York City, where he was now living. Despite tight quotas, Gardner enlisted in the Guard—presumably to avoid the draft, the *News* reported.

As the month drew to a tired close, one more problem made the headlines: Joseph E. O'Grady, the chairman of the Transit Authority, warned that the 15-cent bus and subway fare would have to be hiked by July 1 unless the Legislature came through with a subsidy. Some $69 million had been earmarked for such purposes by Governor Rockefeller after the transit strike had been settled—but the Legislature had not as yet acted to pass enabling legislation. There was considerable resentment in some upstate communities to keeping the city fare at 15 cents when upstate residents in many places were already paying 25 cents for similar bus rides.

After five months, I viewed the mayoralty as a near-impossible task. As I sat near the Mayor, day after day, I could see his time and energy being slowly drained away—mostly by labor disputes. It seemed ridiculous that the Mayor himself should have to deal with every one of the almost 100 municipal unions representing the 300,000 city employees—but it had become an established custom under Wagner and there seemed to be nothing Lindsay could do to escape the pattern, particularly since he had become so deeply involved in the crippling transit strike. Pressures in all areas continued to build up. The tax program, which the Mayor had hoped would be law by now, still was not a certainty. There appeared to be little hope that it would become law by July 1—in time to begin the fiscal 1966–67 year. I was still proud to be a part of the Administration, but I couldn't help but feel that John Lindsay was taking on too much, too fast. About the only consolation was my belief that, despite our troubles, we felt the majority of the public was still behind us.[5]

Perhaps the *Wall Street Journal* summed up my feelings better than any other newspaper in mid-May when it had published a lead article which was headlined: TROUBLES PLAGUE NEW YORK'S MAYOR LINDSAY. It criticized him for taking uncompromising positions and then having to change them in order to pick up some support. "A hallmark of the Lindsay Administration has been," it stated, "the graceless backdown." It praised him for taking some steps, but added: "He has yet to demonstrate that he can come to grips, in those private, hard-driving sessions where the doors are barred to the press, with the big, difficult problems." The article then touched upon a sensitive nerve which I could not argue with. It said: "And there is, finally, that puzzling tendency of John Lindsay to go it alone. 'This has been a complaint about John for years,' says a man who once worked for him. 'He persists in trying to play a lone hand. He would do so much better if he just talked to a few people. It's a psychology that's harmful to him. He views every other politician as his natural enemy. There's a wariness about him. He just doesn't understand the art of cooperation and compromise.' "

The article continued: "It is ominous that after just four months in office Mr. Lindsay has antagonized so many people and so many groups of people. Governor Rockefeller has become increasingly cool to him. . . . The Republican organization is disappointed in him because he refuses to recognize party workers. . . . City Hall Democrats, whose cooperation Mr. Lindsay must have if he is to succeed, are angry at him because he has tried to bypass them. Business leaders are angry because of his tax program and because they were never consulted about it. The policemen are furious over the review board; some civil rights leaders are disappointed because the board won't be enough. The list of complaints, real or imagined, is endless. If John Lindsay wants to run for President—almost everyone here presumes his ambition ranges that far—he will have to do better. So many indignities have been heaped upon New Yorkers. They hope and pray that this young man isn't another."

Even *Fortune* magazine, in a long piece by Richard J. Whalen, commented: "Under this appealing and aggressive young Mayor, New York can expect a succession of stirring battles over large public questions—that much is certain and welcome. But the city is still awaiting its first substantial victory." The article continued: ". . . Lindsay's performance so far suggests that his militant campaign ideology may be getting in the way of the achievement of his very ambitious proclaimed objectives. He remains in a highly combative posture, continuing from inside City Hall the outsider's attack on various 'Establishments.' His Administration is still basically a campaign organization, and most of the bright young men suddenly elevated to power incline naturally to the tactics of frontal assault. Whether they will settle down to learning the subtle art of government depends on how they interpret their painful rebuffs."

By June 1, the unresolved tax program was a major source of concern to the Mayor. We discussed the tax problem in his office and he decided to issue a statement to the press which would attempt to break the logjam. "I have advised the Governor and the leadership of the Senate and the Assembly that I am prepared to meet with them as soon as possible," the statement ran, "and for as long as necessary to resolve the legislative impasse which now threatens the city's tax program." The next day, June 2, after a Cabinet meeting on Welfare Island, the Mayor told reporters: "We need the income tax. If we don't get it the city will be in a crisis and we will have to cut back on essential services." The reporters tried, as they had for several months, to draw him out on Rockefeller's failure to take a stand on the issue up to then. Rockefeller had said only that he would be an "honest broker" and help to resolve the impasse. It was obvious, however, that in an election year the Governor did not want to risk the voters' ire by coming out for the program. The Mayor, who by now was beginning to learn how the press works, parried questions from the reporters as they tried again and again to bring out his true relationship with the Governor. For example, here is how one exchange went:

Q. Is the Governor doing enough to help the tax program?
A. We can judge only by the ultimate results.
Q. Is the Governor's "honest broker" stance helping?
A. If it will produce a tax program, I have no objection to it.
Q. Would you prefer a more muscular approach?
A. If it will do the job.
Q. Has the "honest broker" policy failed so far?
A. Our program is still before the Legislature.
Q. Is Governor Rockefeller doing enough for you?
A. I hope the Governor will urge the Legislature to give us the taxing power we are seeking.

Q. Should the Governor do something to help the city?
A. All I'm saying is whatever effort is needed to help our program should be done. I'm not saying how it should be done.

On Monday, June 6, the Mayor flew up to Albany for private talks with the legislative leaders. But after spending the day trying to rescue his embattled tax plan, the Mayor told the Albany press corps in the press room of the state capital: "The impasse is there. I've done everything in my power to break it—to press, push, to fight. They remain immobile. I've done everything I can in Albany today." In mid-afternoon, the Mayor called me from Albany. He sounded depressed. He said there was nothing much to report and that he would have to wait until after 5 P.M. to see Rockefeller, who had been away from Albany during the day attending a funeral in Boston. He wound up his conversation: "I'm going to be available later on." I said: "Where?" He replied: "The usual place." I realized he meant the New York City offices in the Hotel Ten Eyck, and that he was attempting to avoid letting anyone know who might be listening what his plans were.

Other troubles continued to pile up. Comptroller Mario A. Procaccino asked Corporation Counsel J. Lee Rankin for a ruling on the legality of some of the Lindsay-appointed commissioners who were not living in New York City at the time of their appointments, thereby possibly violating a local law which required they be city residents. It seemed like a trivial matter, but Procaccino claimed he had been "asked by newsmen" to make an inquiry. Included among the appointees of the Mayor who lived beyond the city limits when appointed were: Police Commissioner Howard Leary; Air Pollution Commissioner Austin Heller; Corrections Commissioner George McGrath; Mental Health Commissioner Marvin E. Perkins; Markets Commissioner Samuel J. Kearing; Dr. Efren Ramirez, narcotics coordinator; William Tobin, assistant to the Real Estate commissioner; Richard H. Buford, an antipoverty official; Raymond Rivera, executive director of the City Human Rights Commission; and Harvey Rothenberg, administrative assistant to the Mayor.

Also in early June, the negotiations with New York Port Authority Director Austin J. Tobin, which had been going on since we took office, blew up publicly when Tobin angrily charged our Administration with demanding what he called a "preposterous" $3 billion payoff to the city as its "price tag" to approve the controversial twin 100-story World Trade Center for lower Manhattan. A memorandum raising the questions of conditions for approval from Bob Price, chairman of the city's eight-man negotiating committee, had apparently angered Tobin, who then let loose in the press. Price had indeed asked for payments of close to $30 million for 99 years and he had charged the Authority with short-changing New York City and favoring the New Jersey side of the river.

On June 8, for the first time, Governor Rockefeller brought out into the open the rift between himself and the Mayor.[6] He accused Lindsay of reneging on a deal that would have assured passage of a tax package for the city. He also accused Lindsay of being "misinformed and totally irresponsible" because of his warning that across-the-board cuts in city services would be needed unless the full tax plan as originally proposed by the Mayor was adopted. Although the Governor did not say so, the newspapers reported that it was Price who had made the "deal" for a $407 million program. But when the Mayor was told of the arrangement, he turned it down after talking to Alex Rose, the union leader and chief political tactician of the Liberal Party, who was firmly opposed to any form of a payroll tax on the working class. Rose also objected to a compromise in the commuter tax, which had been part of the so-called deal which Price had made with the Governor and the State Republican leaders in late May.

The weekend of June 10 was crucial. On Thursday, June 9, Rockefeller had announced he was calling the Mayor to Albany the following Monday to begin round-the-clock negotiations on the city tax program. That night, in a 6½-minute television address at 6 P.M., the Mayor said the tax crisis was not the result of a "personality fight" and added: "I am not engaged in a feud with anyone." The overriding issue, he said, "is the survival of a great city." In his telegram of invitation, the Governor said: "Despite serious efforts to compromise the differences of opinion regarding solutions to the financial problems of New York City, the situation has reached a stalemate. The city must adopt a budget before its fiscal year begins July 1. The stalemate can and must be resolved in the immediate future . . . by all parties with only one objective, the interests of the people of the city and the state as a whole." The Governor's invitation, we knew, meant that he was putting his prestige on the line—at long last—and that he was prepared to do whatever was necessary to reach an agreement. Even before the talks got started, the Governor compromised. Lindsay had requested that Frank O'Connor, City Council president, and David Ross, City Council majority leader, accompany him as part of the city delegation. Rockefeller said no at first, but then changed his mind when Lindsay said he would not come alone.

I felt at the time that Lindsay's position at this point should be conciliatory, despite Rockefeller's public charges about the deal which Price had made. We discussed the position the Mayor should take in Albany the following Monday with Murray Drabkin, Gene Becker and one or two other aides. Lindsay seemed willing to change his ground in order to resolve the problem. But he was still hoping that the final package would total the $520 million that he was told he needed to meet all the items in the existing budget.

On Saturday, June 11, I flew down to Dallas, Texas, with Lindsay and his wife, Mitchell Sviridoff, J. Lee Rankin, and one of the Mayor's police bodyguards, Pat Vecchio, to attend the annual United States Conference of Mayors. Upon arrival at Dallas' Love Field, several members of the local television press wanted to interview the Mayor at the airport and I advised the Mayor to cooperate fully. He did and the next day the *Dallas Morning News* carried a major story about his arrival as well as his comments about the problems of the cities. It quoted Lindsay: "Our greatest common problem is clear and proper planning for the future, discovery of sufficient resources to get the job done and greater involvement by the federal government." The story was accompanied by a large, two-column photograph of John and Mary Lindsay next to a smaller photograph of Los Angeles Mayor Samuel Yorty, another member of the conference. Before the meetings began on Saturday, Lindsay shook hands with many other Mayors from small towns around the country. I was amazed to see how many of them wished him good luck. One Mayor from a small Southern city came over to me and said, quietly: "That's a mighty fine fellow you work for. He's genuinely modest. I hope he goes a long way." At one point, a group of Southern Mayors gathered around Lindsay and photographers started snapping pictures. It was as if they were sightseeing and he was the famous landmark. As soon as the picture-taking was completed, Lindsay turned to me and snapped: "Don't let that happen again. I don't want my picture syndicated all over the country with those reactionary bastards."

The next morning, Lindsay participated in a nationwide panel TV show with Yorty and several other Mayors. He stated that the United States should be prepared to cut back in Vietnam and put more money into the cities, a position similar to that taken by Mayor Jerome P. Cavanagh of Detroit. The other speakers, Mayors John F. Collins, of Boston, Ivan Allen, Jr., of Atlanta, and Richard C. Lee, of New Haven, were all articulate and sharp. It was a good program for Lindsay and when we left I was pleased with how well the weekend trip had worked out.

On Sunday night, we flew back to New York from Dallas and began preparations for our meeting in Albany the next day. Our next mission: to successfully negotiate with Governor Rockefeller and city and state legislators the first personal income tax program in the history of New York City.

7 "I'm getting to the point where I don't trust anyone."

ON MONDAY MORNING, June 13, we arrived in Albany and checked into the city's legislative office in the Hotel Ten Eyck. We walked three-quarters of a mile up to the Governor's century-old, Victorian red brick Executive Mansion at the top of a hill in time for the first day's 11 A.M. meeting. On the way, reporters asked Lindsay for a comment. He smiled and said only that, "I'm an eternal optimist." He appeared to be in a good mood, but he was a little nervous, too. When we reached the Mansion, the Governor stood inside the front entrance and greeted everyone as we came in. The press was asked to remain out front on the lawn where Les Slote, the Governor's press secretary, told them he would keep them posted. As I walked up the front driveway, I noticed many of the newsmen I knew well from the city, including several columnists who were looking for some "on the scene" stories for their newspapers. This was a big news event with many political overtones.[1]

Once inside the Mansion, I saw that the Governor's staff had set up the normally opulent dining room adjoining the large foyer for the meeting. I noticed that when Frank O'Connor, the

City Council president, arrived, Rockefeller gave him a particularly warm welcome. Prominently mentioned as a contender for the Democratic nomination for Governor for the 1966 election in November, O'Connor smiled and clasped Rockefeller's hand. "Hello, Frank," Rockefeller said, smiling, "I guess sometime you would like to look around." Others who arrived included Malcolm Wilson, the lieutenant governor; Assembly Speaker Anthony J. Travia, Democrat of Brooklyn; Senate Majority Leader Earl W. Brydges, Republican of Niagara; Senate Minority Leader Joseph Zaretzki, Democrat of Brooklyn; Assembly Minority Leader Perry B. Duryea, Jr., Republican, of Suffolk County, Long Island; the Democratic majority leader of the City Council, David Ross; and Angelo J. Arculeo, Republican, the minority leader.

They sat down at a long rectangular table in the dining room about 11 A.M. with Rockefeller and Lindsay at the head of the table, the city officials on one side and the legislative leaders on the other. "All right, Frank O'Connor," Rockefeller began, "tell us your position." And the meeting had begun. When O'Connor finished, the Governor moved on to Ross and so on around the room. The Governor appeared to be trying to play the role of mediator and the Mayor, sitting by his side, was cast in the role of silent partner. From time to time, the participants, working in their shirtsleeves, split up into smaller negotiating sessions in other rooms of the Mansion. I was surprised to see the emotion slowly drawn out of the talks as the day wore on. As each man presented his position, there was less and less antagonism, although nobody showed any sign of giving ground. I did not sit in on most of the first day's talks, but I was told by Lindsay that it was only what he called "the early stages of maneuvering." After a break for lunch at the Mansion, the talks resumed all afternoon, another break for supper, and then on into the evening. I spent much of my time inside Rockefeller's living room admiring the many fine paintings on the walls where he exhibited part of his vast art collection. I did not officially talk to the press because Slote and I had agreed that he would make all the announcements from the Mansion. Once or twice I accompanied him outside to the front where the press corps, by now, had decided to sit down outside of the iron gate entrance. As the evening wore on, Murray Drabkin, the Mayor's tax consultant who had drawn up much of the controversial program the men inside were discussing, came over to me and said: "Did you notice how nervous and fatigued Lindsay is? He's cracking up—I know it," Drabkin added, half in jest. Finally, about 10:30 P.M., the meeting broke for the night, some eleven hours after it had started. Little had been accomplished. I accompanied Slote down to the front gate where he told the newsmen: "I think we can say we're making progress and the staffs are continuing their work." The staffs which Slote spoke of included Drabkin, Deputy Mayor Robert Price, Budget Director Eugene Becker and myself from the Mayor's office; and a host of other secondary officials accompanying the other members of the conference.

As I left with Lindsay to return to our hotel downtown, the press gathered around us. He answered a barrage of questions with one simple off-the-cuff statement as I stood by his side: "We're making some progress," he said with a smile. "I've learned never to be unhappy. Anytime you're making some progress there's hope." A small cheer went up from across the street, where several of the Governor's neighbors had been perched to see and listen to Lindsay. And, with these few words, Lindsay had indeed upstaged the Governor on the first day without even trying. Yet, as we walked down the hill to our hotel, Lindsay's outward mood changed quickly and he let his real feelings show. I was the only aide with him as he strode, head down, hands in pocket, troubled by the long day behind him. "You know," he said, "I'm getting to the point where I don't trust anyone." I listened, but didn't say anything. I had seen him in this type of mood before and I knew from experience that the best thing was to let him talk and just listen. "These talks," he continued, "are much tougher than the transit strike. I've never been involved in anything like this." The next morning, Tuesday, June 14, even though he was not happy about what had happened the day before, Lindsay dominated the headline in the *Times*. It read: LINDSAY REPORTS ALBANY PROGRESS ON CITY TAX PLAN. It was the "we're making some progress" quote which the Mayor had given the night before almost as a formality upon which the *Times* based its report. They had little else to go by. There were other stories on the meetings inside (including one in which Comptroller Mario

Procaccino complained that he had not been invited to the talks and proclaimed: "Everyone is playing politics"), but Lindsay was the main story.

Columnist Murray Kempton started his column in the *New York Post* this way: "Through 11 hours of heroic exercise of delicacy and imagination, Governor Rockefeller seems yesterday to have transported all partisans in the great city tax quarrel from the heights of passion to the pit of boredom."

The second day went a little smoother than the first but was much grimmer. There still wasn't any apparent progress. The negotiations resumed at 10 A.M. The issue of whether or not to raise the subway and bus fares in New York City seemed to be the biggest stumbling block. Nor was there any agreement on how much money the city needed and how much the various taxes would produce. Toward the end of the second afternoon, it became apparent that everybody in the room needed to get away from the Governor's Mansion for some fresh air.

A dispute over the presentation of the city's 15-cent transit fare had dominated the second round of negotiations. The Republican leaders of the divided Legislature insisted the fare should be raised to reduce the city's total tax package; the Democratic leadership of the Legislature and the City Council, as well as the Mayor, had been equally firm in insisting that the fare remain at 15 cents. The stalemate became so intense that at one point in the afternoon, Rockefeller, in his shirtsleeves, poked his head out of a ground floor window of the Mansion and told reporters: "These are the toughest negotiations I've ever been in." There was a lot of table thumping and a good deal of shouting, too, and just about everyone in the room lost his temper at least once with the exception of Rockefeller and O'Connor—both of whom managed to remain calm throughout the session.

At about 5 P.M. Speaker Travia got up and announced: "As far as I'm concerned, we'll have to start from scratch. If the Mayor and the Council can agree on a package, I will accept it." There was silence. Then the Governor said he was serving scallops that night for dinner and he invited everyone to stay. Few of the men accepted. Instead, everyone headed out for downtown Albany. "The one thing everybody wanted was not to see anybody else, preferably ever again," one of Frank O'Connor's aides later told a newspaperman.

I got into a car with Lindsay and a few other aides and we drove to a restaurant called Joe's Delicatessen. Moments after we arrived and sat down, we were surprised to see Frank O'Connor, Dave Ross and their aides walk through the front door. In our desire to escape from the confinement of the Governor's Mansion, and each other, we accidentally ended up in the same restaurant. We all laughed about it for a few minutes and then went to separate parts of the restaurant. The mood was different that second night when we returned to the Mansion. There was less hope. As the talks neared midnight, it became clear that nothing could be served by staying any longer. So we agreed to recess. I wondered how long it could go on without any breakthrough. Most of the participants, I felt, did not really think a tax package could be worked out. Most of the newsmen covering began to grow pessimistic, too. I went to sleep that night at the Ten Eyck Hotel depressed by the fact that a group of men as skilled in politics as these men were could not find a compromise which would save John Lindsay's tax program.

I later learned that Rockefeller was as upset as we were by the way the talks were going that night and that after we left he had ordered his fiscal staff to stay up all night to produce a tax package that could be put on the table the next morning. They did. The arguing resumed at 10 A.M. the next morning, Wednesday, June 15, and continued all day.

I was almost certain that the talks would fall apart. About 7 in the evening, Slote turned to me and told me he was going to go out on the lawn and tell the newsreel cameramen to move their equipment in front of the Mansion's entrance. He told them to be ready for "something" in the next few hours. Everyone outside thought that meant that a solution to the deadlock was developing. The truth, however, was quite the reverse. The talks inside had broken down and everyone at the conference, I was sure, had just about given up. Two situations kept the talks from collapsing at this point. I realized that although many of the participants felt further discussions would be fruitless, no one wanted to be the first one to walk out. The other was that the

Governor, although admitting there was no hope, asked everyone to stay for dinner. At first, Rockefeller got no response. Then Joe Zaretzki began walking slowly to the buffet table off the downstairs foyer. Travia followed, and soon all of the participants began to fill their plates. After the roast beef and Yorkshire pudding, the Governor made his move. He talked them back to the conference table.

After dinner, discussions started again and they continued well into the night. After seven slow and painful hours—at 2:30 A.M. (I had been napping in the Governor's living room on and off awaiting some news)—Slote was called in by the Governor. He came out and told me that he had been instructed to tell the press that the men had reached a limited accord on how much money was to be raised. And so, some seventeen hours after the third session had gotten under way, there finally appeared to be a break in the negotiations.

A little before 4 A.M. on June 16, the wilted and unshaven group of men who had been working continuously for nearly twenty hours emerged from the conference room. Lindsay was so tired he appeared to be staggering. His shirt was soaked from perspiration and his hair completely uncombed. He came over to me and as I started to talk to him he stared at me blankly. He seemed oblivious to anyone around him. Hammering out the agreement had taken everything out of him. As the *Times* described him in the next day's newspaper, the Mayor "looked like someone had just rescued him from the sharks." Under the terms of the agreement, the city would receive a total of $283 million in various taxes, or some $237 million less than the $520 million Lindsay had been seeking for months.[2] Nevertheless, the three-month deadlock over new taxes had been broken. At 4:10 A.M., Rockefeller—who somehow still looked fresh in a light blue unwrinkled shirt—announced the details to the bleary-eyed press corps, with Lindsay standing by his side and all the other men who had spent some forty-three hours inside the Mansion since Monday, huddled around them on the front steps of the Mansion. Lindsay, his voice flat, declared: "The essence of compromise is that you give more than you want to, and nobody is totally happy with the result." After the press conference, Lindsay took me aside and whispered: "Get a hold of a bottle of

Rockefeller's good Scotch for the plane ride home." I did, and we boarded the Governor's private plane an hour later in Albany Airport and arrived in New York City about 7 A.M. I went home and fell asleep.

When I awakened sometime after noon, I turned on the radio and was amazed to find out that Lindsay had gone down to City Hall directly from the airport after showering and changing into a fresh suit of clothes at Gracie Mansion. He held a press conference while I was asleep and had optimistically told the press that while the yield from the tax package was "somewhat short," he felt that "we've done the best we can and the situation is far better than I thought it might be originally."[3] He called the substitution of a business income tax for a gross receipts tax "a major step forward in the history of this city." He also said the concept of a city income tax for residents and commuters was something "that's growing in the United States for the big cities as they seek their salvation." Lindsay emphasized that a principal reason for going to Albany was to minimize the difference between what a city resident and a non-resident would have to pay so that there would be as little incentive as possible for people in the middle and higher income brackets to move to the suburbs. "And this we have won on," he said. "The differential averages out at not more than two to one, which is regarded by most economists and most other students of this subject as a fair differential." Summing up the Albany negotiations, Lindsay told a crowded City Hall news conference: "All who participated in three arduous days and nights of negotiations compromised. Everyone who was in Albany dealt in good faith and everybody did their best. We think we've won on principle[4] and we think we've also won on the question of revenues."

8 *"Don't worry about the fare raise. We've done everything we can."*

DURING THE NEXT FEW WEEKS, while we were waiting for the State Legislature to act on the tax program, the subject of a possible fare hike began to take over the front pages of the newspapers. When Lindsay had reported on the Albany tax negotiations, at his June 16 press conference, he said he would ask the city's Corporation Counsel for a ruling on whether or not it was legal to transfer to the Transit Authority $84 million set aside in his expense budget to hold the fare at 15 cents. "If the opinion of the Corporation Counsel is that I cannot in law do it," he said, "I'm not going to be a party to an illegal act." Without the subsidy, the Transit Authority would have to raise the fare, since under the terms of its charter, the Transit Authority's expenditures must meet its income. Finally, after persistent questioning about a fare raise, the Mayor said: "I can only say that the 15 cent fare is in doubt." It was a thorny political issue for Lindsay, of course, because he had campaigned on the promise that the subway fare would not be raised. He had also campaigned on the promise of no further taxes, but we had worked our way out of that one by stating early in the year that the tax program was a "last resort."

I wasn't sure how we were going to work our way out of the fare increase, which, by now, appeared to be inevitable.

During this time, one potential labor problem cleared itself up. On Friday night, June 17, Peter Brennan disclosed in a letter to the Mayor that a meeting of his Building and Construction Trades Council, the delegates had voted 232–1 to put off the threatened work stoppage. The Council came to its decision, Brennan said, as a result of the conferences with Lindsay on May 26 and with Bill Mattison on June 8, at which the Council was assured that the city would move ahead soon with millions of dollars worth of construction. In addition, Brennan's letter was conciliatory in regard to the employment of more Negroes in the building trades. "We hope," Brennan wrote, "that [construction projects] will provide more job opportunities for qualified members of the minority, as well as our present membership." The Mayor was pleased that he had been able to avoid the bad publicity of a "labor holiday."

On Wednesday, June 22, an entirely unexpected problem raised a new controversy in the city. Saudi Arabia's King Faisal was in Washington on a state visit. The next evening, June 23, Mary and John Lindsay were scheduled to give a dinner in the King's honor at the Metropolitan Museum of Art. A great deal of preparation had gone into the plans for the evening. But on the 22nd, the day before he arrived in New York, Faisal, under heavy questioning from Washington newsmen at a newspaper luncheon, was reported as saying, "Unfortunately, Jews throughout the world provide assistance to Israel and we consider those who provide assistance to our enemies as our own enemies." The first I heard about Faisal's statement was when a newsman from Room 9 asked me for a comment from the Mayor on a statement from City Councilman Theodore Weiss demanding that the Mayor cancel the dinner because so many New Yorkers were Jewish. My immediate response, after talking with Lindsay, was to tell the press that we would try to obtain a transcript of the news conference the King had held. I also told the reporters: "King Faisal is here on a State visit. The request came from the State Department and Mayor Lindsay is honoring that request, as did President Johnson." Later that afternoon, we received the exact text of the King's statements. Bob Laird took it down on the telephone

from the Associated Press and the *Times*. I brought it into
Lindsay and he said simply: "We'll still have to check this out
before doing anything. I am not anxious to cause a major
incident." Then he left to go to a concert in Central Park and
told me that he wanted to speak with Secretary of State Dean
Rusk before making any final decision.

I went home and answered telephone calls from various newspapers, radio and TV stations in New York and Washington. At
about 10:30 P.M., on June 22, I received a call from Lindsay. He
was in Sardi's West for dinner and said he would try to reach
Dean Rusk from there. Shortly after midnight, I got another call
from Lindsay. He had just spoken to Rusk. He related his conversation: "Rusk said he didn't want me to cancel," Lindsay told
me matter-of-factly. "He said he admitted it would be difficult
for us to have the dinner, but he wanted time to talk to Faisal.
He said Faisal had gone to bed. I told Rusk, jokingly, 'Maybe
he's in bed with some Jewish girl.' Rusk didn't think that was
very funny. Anyway, he said I should stay in touch with him. He
said he would reach Faisal before 10:30 A.M. tomorrow."

Throughout the night I kept getting calls from the morning
newspapers. The *Daily News* seemed to be pushing hard for a
cancellation, I suppose because it would make a good front-page
story. I tried to nap on and off, but it turned out to be a sleepless
night. The next morning, the *Times* carried a page one story
headlined: MAYOR RECONSIDERS PLANS TO GIVE DINNER FOR FAISAL
and the story indicated that pressure was building up against
holding the dinner. It quoted Frank O'Connor as saying he
would not attend and the Mayor was sharply criticized by Theodore Weiss and Manhattan Congressman Leonard Farbstein, both
Jews, for not cancelling immediately. Farbstein had sent a wire to
Lindsay in which he said he considered it "reprehensible" that
the city should welcome the head of a nation "that openly and
unashamedly boycotts American business and discriminates
against Americans of the Jewish faith." Weiss' telegram was in a
similar vein. "Has the city administration no sense of decency
and rights?" he asked. The *Daily News* story on page three on
Thursday morning, June 23, was headlined: FAISAL'S RAP AT JEWS
PUTS LINDSAY ON SPOT and it went into the same background as
the *Times*. The situation brought to mind a previous incident in

1957 when former Mayor Robert F. Wagner had barred any official welcome or reception for Faisal's older brother, King Saud, who had also been on a State Department visit, then under the Eisenhower Administration. Wagner had virtually precipitated an international incident. A candidate for reelection that year, he had accused the King of being anti-Jewish, anti-Catholic and an upholder of slavery.

By coincidence, Lindsay had been scheduled to be in Washington on Thursday morning to testify in behalf of the U.S. Conference of Mayors and the National League of Cities before a Senate subcommittee. At 10:30 A.M. I received a call in my office from Lindsay who was at the Washington Airport. "I talked with Rusk," he said. "What do you think I should do, Woody, if the President were to ask me to go on with the dinner?" Lindsay asked.

"I think it would be hard to dispute the President," I replied.

"Well, Rusk is working on something like that now," Lindsay went on.

"I would still advise you not to hold the dinner, John," I said. "I don't think you should let it go that far, I mean letting Johnson ask you publicly to hold the dinner. I would call Rusk off that course of action, if you can."

"I'll call you back later," he replied, and hung up.

About a half hour later, he called back. "It's cancelled," he said flatly. "Take this down." I reached for a pad and a pencil. "This is the statement I want you to put out for me from New York," he continued. "I don't want to issue anything from Washington. Just say: 'Under the circumstances, the Mayor has concluded that it would not be feasible to proceed with the dinner.' That's all. Nothing more. I'll issue another statement when I get back to New York. I'll hold a press conference later in the afternoon. Ask Jim Carberry to work up a longer statement for the conference."

I typed out the short statement Lindsay had just dictated to me, issued it to the local press and read it for the radio and TV reporters at City Hall. I also called John (Bud) Palmer, commissioner of Public Events, and asked him to officially notify the State Department. By this time the Mayor's office had been compiling statistics on phone calls and telegrams which indicated a heavy majority of people were against holding the reception for the King. Telegrams ran about 9–1 in favor of cancelling; telephone calls ran about 100–1 against the reception. At 2:30 P.M., I met Lindsay at the Battery heliport in lower Manhattan where he had just arrived via helicopter from La Guardia. I was joined by Harvey Rothenberg and Ernie Latty, a plainclothes detective. The Mayor brought back from Washington with him mayoral aides Sid Gardner and Jay Kriegel. As he swooped out of the helicopter and ducked his head as if to avoid the chopper blades, he stuck out his hand to me with a big smile, said: "Shalom, where do we go from here?"

We drove back to City Hall in the Mayor's limousine and I told him that Bud Palmer had wanted to meet Faisal at the airport in behalf of the city, but that I had told Palmer he (the Mayor) did not want a reception of any kind. Lindsay nodded his head in approval of my action. Then, in the few minutes it took to drive from the Battery to City Hall, I filled him in on other developments that morning: Harlem rent strike leader Jesse Gray had been arrested; O'Connor and Ross had held a joint press conference demanding that Lindsay sign a "message of necessity" retaining the 15-cent fare; Rent Commissioner Frederic S. Berman's office had been ransacked by demonstrators; and a City Councilman was demanding that New York City secede from the State of New York.

"Oh," Lindsay said with a broad smile, "a normal day like any other day." As we arrived at City Hall newsmen converged on the Mayor from all sides. He told them he would have a press conference at 4 P.M. and that seemed to satisfy them for the moment. By this time, a draft of a statement for Lindsay had been prepared and was sitting on his desk when he returned to his office. He asked me to call Federal Judge Charles M. Metzner, a longtime friend and adviser of his, whose views he respected almost more than anyone else in New York. Charlie Metzner made some suggestions which I conveyed to Lindsay and then Lindsay finally sat down at his desk and wrote out the statement in longhand himself, with some final touches from Kriegel, Laird, Rothenberg and myself. He read it to the press and the TV cameramen about 4:30 P.M., saying, in part, that Faisal's unfortunate comment ". . . has made it impossible for me, as the Mayor of New York, to extend the official welcome of the city. The remark is extremely offensive, not just to Jews, but to all citizens of New York. I, personally, was very deeply disturbed. But more importantly, I, as Mayor, have an obligation to prevent, wherever possible, abrasive divisions in our city." Despite the snub, Faisal, with grace and good humor, made it clear at a news conference at the United Nations (where he met and talked with U.N. Ambassador Arthur Goldberg) that he was not angry at the United States.

On the Sunday following the cancellation, Lindsay had to vigorously deny that politics played any part in his decision. Interviewed on the ABC-TV "Page One" program, Lindsay said: "It was a very difficult decision over a very serious statement by the King." Lindsay added that his decision was not influenced by any fear of reaction from the city's 1.8 million Jews if the dinner had been held. "I was not aware of any public pressure," the Mayor said.

The Faisal Affair, as it had become known, momentarily took the pressure off Lindsay on the transit fare problem. But just as soon as it was over, O'Connor and Ross came down to our end of the Hall to meet with Lindsay for more than an hour. The outcome: Lindsay refused to send a "message of necessity" on a bill to save the 15-cent fare because he had not yet received an opinion from J. Lee Rankin about the legality of transferring the $84.3 million budget item to the Transit Authority. I asked Lindsay what he wanted me to say when newsmen asked about his position, which was not altogether clear. "Just say it's a complicated legal matter," the Mayor replied.

On Monday morning, June 27, at an early morning City Hall meeting with Louis Craco, Don Elliott, Bob Sweet and myself, we discussed the Mayor's plan to reorganize the city's scattered fifty or more departments and agencies into ten superagencies or "administrations." One of Lindsay's campaign pledges had been to streamline government and it was now time, he said, to get started in this direction. Craco outlined his carefully worked-out plan and then suggested that Lindsay or someone representing him get in touch with Bob Wagner to try and get his support on the reorganization plan. The strategy, Craco suggested, would be to tell Wagner that this plan was an extension of the kind of planning that the Wagner Administration had laid down and that the Lindsay plan was an outgrowth of what had gone before.

"I'll ask Bob Wagner to meet me at Gracie Mansion in the near future," Lindsay declared. "I'll explain the whole set-up to him, but I don't think we should publicize the meeting unless Wagner wants it," he continued, looking straight at me. Craco suggested that Wagner might not be too receptive to just talking about reorganization and that the Mayor should offer to talk about a wide range of topics and to seek Wagner's advice on several matters. We left this up in the air, but the Mayor did say he would try and get Wagner to come to the Mansion.

The next morning, at the regular breakfast meeting of Bob Price, Tim Costello, J. Lee Rankin, Eugene Becker, Don Elliott, Bob Sweet, Connie Eristoff and myself, Lindsay said that he was worried about the tax program in Albany. At one point he said: "I have my doubts if it will pass." He then asked Becker to get ready recommended budget cuts in the event that he had to announce large-scale cutbacks in city services. Then he turned to Bob Sweet and said: "If it doesn't pass, what's the next step?" Sweet replied: "I'm not really certain, but I would guess you would have about a week in which to decide to either make severe budget cuts or try to impose a bunch of nuisance taxes." Lindsay said: "I don't think the City Council will pass a payroll tax at this point." Becker disagreed and said he thought the Council might. Either way, the uncertainty about what our course of action should be surprised me a little. It was as if we had prepared to go to the brink, but had no definite strategy after that. I was certain after those three days in Albany that it would just be a matter of time before the Legislature agreed to pass the bills into law. Yet, here we were on Tuesday morning, June 28, with a few days to go before the city budget must be adopted, and we did not know what our next step would be. On this same day, I was pleased to read in the morning *Times* that the sixty-five-day strike by the New York Newspaper Guild against the *World-Journal-Tribune* had been tentatively settled and the settlement had to be ratified by the membership.

Two days later, on Thursday, June 30, just when we had about given up hope for our tax program, I received a call from the

Mayor about mid-afternoon on the one-way black telephone from his office to mine.

"I just got the word," he said, excited. "The Senate in Albany is going to vote on the tax bills sometime before 4 P.M. today. Look, postpone the press conference we have scheduled today to announce Herb Haber [as director of labor relations for the city]. I don't want to be in the middle of a press conference when the news breaks from Albany. I'll want some time to get a statement ready." I agreed and told Room 9 that the Mayor's news conference would be called off that day.

About 6:30 P.M. I wandered into his office to see if he had received any word from Albany. "Not yet," he said. "We'll stay here at the Hall. They are going to vote on it and then the Assembly will vote. We'll go out to Whyte's for supper around 7:30." I declined to join the Mayor for dinner that night because I hadn't been home for dinner for more than a week. I told him so and he said he understood. I planned to go home and return to my office at 8:30 P.M. At 7 P.M., however, while I was still in Lindsay's office, he got a call from the Governor. His face lit up.

"Good work, Nelson," Lindsay nearly shouted. He stood up at his desk, smiling. "That's a good piece of work." He hung up and told me that the Senate had passed the tax bill 37–27. He was obviously pleased. I shook his hand.

"Well, we're halfway home," I said.

"Yeah, and we had to give away half of New York to do it," Lindsay responded wryly. The Mayor told me he had also discussed the problem of the fare raise with the Governor. They agreed it was inevitable and that the Transit Authority would be the agency to announce the increase to 20 cents. It would happen immediately after the long Fourth of July weekend.

We waited until 11 P.M. that night, but were disappointed to find out that the Assembly had adjourned without taking any action. With the City Council on standby notice to meet at 11 A.M. the next day to pass the local laws putting them into effect, it now appeared as if everything would have to be put off at least twenty-four hours.

The next day, Friday, July 1, the Assembly passed the bill and Rockefeller signed it. By the time it went to the New York City

Council it was early evening. Lindsay told me he wanted to remain at his desk while the Council voted upstairs in the Council chambers. He said it was "anticlimactic" because the outcome was certain. Nevertheless, he had waited three long months for this moment and he did not want to miss it.

I strolled into his office about 7 o'clock to see how he was doing.

"Let's get out of here and get something to eat at Whytes," he suggested.

At about 8 o'clock we walked down the five long blocks from City Hall together to the restaurant, along with Bernie Bitterman, one of the regular plainclothes detectives who had been assigned to work the shift that night. We all sat down at one table and Lindsay pulled out a sheaf of papers. "Read this," he said to me. "It's Lee Rankin's opinion on the fare raise business." As I began to read it, a waiter stepped up to the Mayor and told him he had a phone call. After Lindsay left the table, Bitterman, a pleasant-mannered, soft-spoken detective, looked at me and commented:

"You know, John is quite a guy. In all the years I worked for Bob Wagner, I never once sat down to dinner with him." As we were waiting for dinner, we ordered a round of drinks. The tab for the whole dinner came to nearly $28. Lindsay picked it up and we returned to City Hall. Once back in the office, I started closely reading Rankin's eight-page opinion. It concluded that it was not legal for the City Council to allocate $84 million to the Transit Authority to enable the Transit Authority to meet its operating deficit. In essence, the opinion stated that the State Constitution did not permit the City Council to enact local laws changing the powers and duties of the Transit Authority, since the Transit Authority had been created by the state as an independent agency.

By now, City Hall was almost deserted, except for the Mayor, Bob Sweet and myself. The beginning of the long Fourth of July weekend had seen a complete exodus from both ends of the Hall. Lindsay asked me to start preparing a press release stating that "as a result of having read Rankin's opinion, it was now clear that the City Council's bill to transfer $84 million from the expense budget to the Transit Authority was invalid." He telephoned Rockefeller and O'Grady and began to draw up an elaborate plan to break the news of the fare raise. We worked out a strategy: I would announce that Lindsay had received Rankin's opinion and state that the Mayor was studying it. Sunday, I would release it for the Monday newspapers with a short statement from the Mayor about the City Council bill being "invalid." Then, on Monday, July 4, with the city virtually empty, the Transit Authority would announce the fare raise. I stayed at City Hall long after the Mayor had returned to Gracie Mansion (he was scheduled to leave for a long weekend on Long Island the next morning). Late Friday night, the City Council enacted the income tax on residents, the earnings tax on commuters and a business income tax to replace the gross receipts—all of these had, of course, been authorized by the Legislature.

On Saturday morning, I returned to my desk in the press office and, after speaking with Lee Rankin at his summer home in Connecticut, I typed out a summary of his opinion, turned it over to Bob Laird, who was in the office with me, with instructions to have it delivered with a short press release and a copy of the opinion to all the newspapers for release Monday morning. (See Appendix, pages 309–310.) Then I left with my wife and daughter about 2 P.M. to visit friends in Massachusetts.

On Sunday night, while in Massachusetts, I learned from a radio report that the news about Rankin's opinion was already out. I called Lindsay at his Long Island house. He said he had read it in the *Times* Sunday morning (I had not seen a newspaper), but he didn't seem to mind the fact that it had leaked out early. Rankin had spoken to the *Times* a day before we had planned for the news to be released.

Lindsay seemed unperturbed. "You know, Woody, I've been sailing and swimming all day and I got some sun, for a change. I feel pretty good. Don't worry about the fare raise. We've done everything we can. Just relax. By the time we get back Tuesday the other shoe will have dropped and that'll be that." This, I decided, was one of those rare moments when John Lindsay really sounded relaxed and more like the man I used to know before he took office. I took him at his word and didn't even listen to the radio for the next twenty-four hours—something unusual for me. Whenever I left the city, even if it was just for a few hours, I always turned on the news to stay in touch.

The Monday, July 4 *Times* carried a story that the 5-cent transit raise was reported to be "imminent." Written by Robert Alden, who had been covering the tax program from the outset, it was accurate and anticipated by one day the Transit Authority's announcement. The next day, Tuesday, July 5, when we all returned to City Hall—and a mayoral press conference—the fare had been raised by the Transit Authority at 12:01 A.M., as we had planned, and the *Times,* predictably, carried the story as its lead on page one. As the story pointed out, the fare raise affected some 4.6 million passengers who ride the subways daily and the 1.5 million who use the Transit Authority's bus lines. This was the first fare raise since July 25, 1953—nearly thirteen years before.

Just before his afternoon press conference on Tuesday, July 5, Lindsay seemed nervous and anxious. It was obvious to me that he was concerned over the possible impact of the strategy we had decided upon a few days before. He opened the press conference by first expressing his "gratification" to the Legislature and to the City Council for completing the tax program over the weekend. "New York is now a healthy place to live, economically," he said. After some lengthy explanation of why the new taxes would be much better for all New Yorkers, he then eased into a statement on the fare raise. "Naturally," he started slowly, "we have all wanted to avoid an increase in the transportation fare. I regard the transit fare as something in the nature of a form of tax. It's unfortunate that the Transit Authority had to raise the fare. However, in the course of doing that, there is no doubt about the fact that everybody who is concerned and deeply concerned did everything in his power to hold the fare at its present level. No question but what Governor Rockefeller, Speaker Travia, Mr. Zaretzky, minority leader of the Senate, Mr. O'Connor, Mr. Ross, Mr. Arculeo, of the City Council—as a whole all of them—have fought valiantly to keep the fare. Under all of the circumstances, however, that was not possible."

A reporter then informed the Mayor that O'Connor had charged earlier in the day that he and Rockefeller had "conspired" to have the fare go up and that as far back as before May he had agreed to a fare raise. Was that true?

I remembered the telephone conversation the Mayor had had with Rockefeller the previous Friday arranging for the details of raising the fare.

Lindsay's face reddened. "That's absolutely untrue. There is no truth in that whatsoever," he snapped back.

"Then, Mr. Mayor, who killed Cock Robin?" asked Gabe Pressman, WNBC-TV's veteran correspondent.

"The Transit Authority acted on the basis of very clear and unequivocal opinions that were handed down by the Corporation Counsel and by the general counsel to the Transit Authority . . . ," the Mayor replied before he was interrupted.

"Was it Senator Brydges with his little hatchet?" Pressman continued.

"Well," Lindsay replied, a little more at ease, "everybody knows—it's no secret—that Senator Brydges and the commuter representatives in the New York State Legislature were very strongly disposed toward a fare increase in New York City. There's no doubt about that."

Lindsay was then asked what he proposed to do with the $84 million which had been earmarked to preserve the 15-cent fare, and he replied: "Well, that's not extra money. The City of New York needs every cent it can find in order to carry on city services and to build for a great city in the future. And remember this: the city tax reorganization program produced far less in revenue than the city asked for and what my Administration thinks that we need and should have. It's still short. And for that reason we are keeping on the job freeze—which will continue, and we shall keep a very tight fiscal control. New Yorkers may be assured that they are going to get a dollar's worth of service for a dollar's worth of revenue produced. Bear in mind that although the budget stands in balance, it is in very tenuous balance."

The next day, Lindsay offered a little different version of the fare raise. In a taped interview for the *Merv Griffin Show*, Lindsay was asked if he thought the subway fare was his fault. "No. I really don't think so," Lindsay replied. "It was a collective chain of events, the march of time, and the inevitability of today." Then he broke out in a broad smile and said, "I inherited a city with no subway fares at all because the subways weren't running."

9   *"Let's cool it!"*

DURING THE HECTIC WEEK after the fare raise, Jimmy Wechsler of the *Post* talked with Lindsay and wrote a column that accurately summed up the way the Mayor felt at this point in time. "It is probably John Lindsay's salvation," he began his column on Thursday, July 7, "that he is an optimist by instinct and a lawyer by profession. The first has sustained his belief that he has begun to salvage this city, despite the numerous frustrations of these six long months; the second permits him to contemplate without panic the possibility that City Hall may be his political graveyard." Wechsler then observed that "a visitor can only conscientiously report that Lindsay shows no sign of disarray or despair." Finally, he quoted Lindsay as saying: "I just know we have to make the effort—and I don't believe New York City is willing to admit it's through."

One practical step Lindsay was taking at this time in his fight to save the city was to recruit a top-rate budget director from Washington. As part of the "effort" he told Wechsler about, he had offered the post to Frederick O'Reilly Hayes. Hayes, forty-two, a former official of the Federal Bureau of the Budget, was then working as a top aide in the Office of Economic Opportunity. Lindsay finally persuaded Hayes, a Democrat and a professional in his field, to take on the job which Eugene M. Becker had relinquished in order to return to private industry.

Lindsay was now more confident that the city's financial problems would be kept under control and that he would have more planning in this area. Another important appointment at this time was Roy M. Goodman as head of the Finance Administration. Goodman had invited a throng of friends to speak on the day he was appointed, including Senator Jacob K. Javits. Lindsay, however, had no idea that Javits would be present. Still, once he saw the Senator in the audience, he felt compelled to ask Javits to say a few words. Javits, never a man to turn down an opportunity to speak, said that the city was still in deep financial trouble, but despite "what has happened in the first six months, the Mayor might eventually solve the problems." He added: "I am sure that Lindsay's first six months are no real indication of what he is capable of."

Holding back his annoyance, Lindsay rejoined: "Thank you, Senator. I still have two or three commissionerships open. I'll be glad to swear you into any one of them—any time!" Lindsay was still furious after the press conference. When we returned to his office he told me: "Javits doesn't have the key to City Hall. Let the press know that we were laughing at his lack of humor, his stuffiness and his nerve. He is no friend of ours. You can leak that to the boys."

I replied: "Javits and Rockefeller always seem to treat you like a son. They have such a paternal, condescending attitude toward you. It bothers me, too, but I don't really think we should pick any more public fights right now."

Lindsay responded: "Nelson doesn't treat me that way any more. Not after I let him have it in Albany."

On the same day as Roy Goodman's appointment, Thursday, July 7, the Patrolmen's Benevolent Association placed an eleven-volume bundle of 51,852 signatures atop the walnut desk of the City Clerk, Herman Katz, in an effort to make sure that a referendum to bar the Civilian Review Board would go on the ballot the following November. In addition, William F. Buckley, Jr., led a delegation of outspoken supporters who carried a five-volume bundle containing 40,383 signatures, bringing to 92,235 the total number of signatures. Only 30,000 were required by law to place the matter before the voters. We had known that the police would resist the review board, but the extent of opposition was greater than we had anticipated.

Lindsay told me he was anxious to respond right away to the two petitions at a press conference. We scheduled one for the next day, Friday, July 8. He took the offense by charging that "highly organized, militant, right-wing groups" were seeking to kill the review board. The referendum, he said, could cause an "inflammatory situation" in New York. "I hope people will listen carefully to the issues," he said slowly. "Otherwise it could cause a difficult time." And then he disclosed that he was studying possible ways to block the referendum. Speaking slowly, at times pensively, Lindsay made an impassioned plea for New Yorkers not to be inflamed against the board. Quietly, and with conviction he said the fight would cause only harm to the city. "I'll do my very best," he added, "to mobilize the community to sustain the review board."

On Monday, July 11, Lindsay was scheduled to announce the composition of the Civilian Review Board. He flew in by helicopter from Syosset where he had spent the weekend with his brother, Rod, to the Wall Street heliport. At about 8:30 A.M., I walked into the Mayor's office for a pre-press conference meeting with the new board members. Mayoral aide Jay Kriegel, and Sylvan Fox, a friend of mine and a former city editor of the *World-Telegram and Sun* who was then working as deputy Police commissioner in charge of public relations,[1] were also present. In response to a request from Police Commissioner Leary, I had suggested Fox's name shortly after Leary was appointed.

As the meeting got started, Lindsay seemed relaxed and calm. He asked the seven men to be "moderate and reasonable" and he told them that the Patrolmen's Benevolent Association's fight against the board would be "a tough one." He said he planned to talk with John Cassese at Gracie Mansion, but added quickly: "I doubt if it will do much good." He asked the board's chairman, Algernon D. Black,[2] to keep in mind the fact that the entire city would be carefully watching the new board. Black responded by assuring the Mayor that the only proper way the public could judge the board would be by its record. Howard Leary then said he would tell the forthcoming press conference that, in his opinion, the review board would not hamper the "efficiency" of his department. The mood of the meeting was formal and serious. Many of the board members had not met each other before. They were quiet and reserved.

Al Black then spoke to his new colleagues in quiet, measured tones. "All I ask," he said, "is that we try to work in harmony and that we work out our differences privately." The Mayor chimed in: "The press will pry and push, cajole and stick you —they will do almost anything to stir you up and try to make you angry. But just remain calm and be careful what you say. I know it is unnecessary to tell you this, but I will do so anyway just to satisfy myself." The Mayor was firm but restrained. He had the respect of everyone listening, I felt, and he would start out with a review board that would be working as a team and a Police commissioner who would cooperate with both the board and the Mayor. We had come a long way, I thought at that moment, since the early months when controversy swirled over Vincent Broderick's disagreement with the Mayor's plans for a review board.

The next morning, July 12, the *Times* carried the review board story as its page one lead. The board, headed by Black, included two Negroes and a Puerto Rican. Black, the sixty-five-year-old senior leader of the Ethical Culture Society, was featured along with the others.[3] It also carried the Mayor's plea for the police and New Yorkers to "give the board a chance." He said the newly named members "would have a deep and abiding respect for the professionalism of the Police Department," and that they would be "balanced and fair" and that they would "provide stability to the community." Within hours, of course, the Patrolmen's Benevolent Association called a press conference to respond. John Cassese's reply: "They [the board] couldn't be impartial if they wanted to." He lashed out against Lindsay and the board, and he pledged to continue his campaign to put it to a referendum in November.

I read the *Times'* accounts of the preceding day's events with some apprehension. I knew even before I had read the newspaper the Mayor had an 8 A.M. meeting scheduled with Cassese at the Mansion that same morning. Later in the day, at one of my short meetings with the Mayor in his office when I was alone with him, I asked him how the meeting with Cassese went.

"I put it to him and Norman Frank [the public relations counsel to the Patrolmen's Benevolent Association]," Lindsay answered matter-of-factly. "I told them that if anything happened in New York—if there was a blow-up—they would be respon-sible. I think they were a little floored. I hit them where it hurt. I don't know if their position will soften any, but I asked them to give it a chance. I really socked it to them. We'll have to wait and see if it did any good."

As if the review board fight wasn't enough at this time, for reasons of which I was unaware, Lindsay decided to release a letter to Robert Moses firing him from his unsalaried job as Arterial Highways Coordinator—his last city job. At a late after-noon City Hall press conference, Lindsay denied there was any friction between himself and Moses—but everyone knew that for months the Mayor had been trying to deprive Moses of his power in New York. What the press did not know was that Lindsay had sent Arthur E. Palmer, his transportation adminis-trator, to try and persuade Moses to resign voluntarily, and that Lindsay had once gone himself to Moses' Gracie Square apart-ment in an attempt to avoid a public fight with Moses. However, when the exchange of letters was made public, they were viewed by the press as the culmination of months of feuding with Moses. The conflict had begun earlier in the year when Moses bitterly opposed the Mayor's proposed consolidation of the Triborough Bridge and city Transit Authorities. This would have deposed Moses as chairman of the Triborough Bridge and Tunnel Au-thority.

Even though the press was not particularly fond of Moses—he had barred reporters from his regular meetings of the old Slum Clearance Committee before it was abolished in 1960—they gave this story major coverage because it involved a confrontation between the young, forty-four-year-old Lindsay and one of the great old and powerful figures in New York, seventy-seven-year-old Robert Moses. It was a natural. I had mixed feelings about the publicity. It made the Mayor look good in one way—he was acting independently and knowing that he was the first Mayor in decades who was not afraid of Moses; but, at the same time, it also showed that he lacked the ability to work out a face-saving device for Moses and could not handle the situation graciously.

Lindsay had a second major confrontation that week with powerful and independent Austin J. Tobin, executive director of the New York Port Authority. The situation was not analogous to that of Moses, but Lindsay had been quarreling publicly with the two men in the past months and I found it ironic that both disputes should come to a head at once. Touching off the stories about the Port Authority was the fact that on July 12, Tobin had rejected the Lindsay plan to arbitrate the differences between the city and the Port Authority over the controversial World Trade Center. Negotiations had been going on—with Price representing the Mayor—for nearly five months over the amount of payment in lieu of taxes to be made to the city for the Trade Center site's 516 acres. The Port Authority had reportedly offered $4 million a year, while the city had been asking $27 million. Lindsay had proposed that the disagreement be resolved by a third party. Tobin had responded publicly that the proposal was "clearly, elementarily and legally out of the question. The only possible third party for negotiations between the city and the Port Authority would be the courts, and only then on certain matters of law," he said angrily. Tobin accused Lindsay of "public irresponsibility" and decried what he called the "shameful" five months of time-wasting delays which had held up construction of the new Center. Lindsay had been withholding permits for street closings during the months of bargaining and work had virtually come to a halt.

I was asked by the press for a reaction to Tobin's charges. After conferring with the Mayor, I told them that we were still "optimistic" that we could work out an agreement with Tobin. In the Mayor's name, I said: "We're not intentionally stalling on the Trade Center. We want to see the ground-breaking process go forward, but we must protect the interests of the people." This stilled further requests from the press, but it did not solve the problem with Tobin and the Port Authority. I was disturbed that

Lindsay's dealings with both Moses and Tobin had gone so badly and that, as a result, we had continuing public battles in the newspapers in addition to the review board conflict.

Lindsay left no doubt in my mind that he wanted to repair his relations with Austin Tobin when, at his regular Friday press conference on July 15, he told newsmen: "Mr. Tobin must have misinterpreted what I said to him." He denied that he had reneged on a promise to expedite construction of the center and he repeated his intention to go ahead as quickly as possible with construction. "I've done everything in my power to reach an agreement with them," he told reporters. "Under the law, the city and the Port Authority must reach an agreement before there is building. Austin wants me to build first and reach an agreement later. We want to continue talking. The door is open —wide open. The conference table is sitting there; all Austin has to do is to come in and sit down." He referred to Tobin as "Austin" several times, but at one point in the press conference, he said with a trace of a smile: "Of course, if we're willing to give away Manhattan, they could start digging up the city any time."

By this time in the summer, racial tensions had begun to break out into small street scuffles. Nobody had been seriously hurt yet, but there were signs—particularly in parts of Brooklyn and Harlem—that there could be a blow-up somewhere in New York during the summer. In 1964, there had been a major riot in Harlem and the police response had been to incite the residents of Harlem even further by firing hundreds of rounds of ammunition into the air. It had been a bloody, ugly spectacle and Lindsay wanted more than anything to avoid a similar outbreak. So he began to move around the city at night, without announcing his trips, on foot, and wearing only a short-sleeved summer shirt and slacks.

We had previously discussed the idea of Lindsay trying to keep the city calm by making these appearances. Sid Davidoff and Barry Gottehrer were in favor of it, but some of the other members of the Administration felt it would be too dangerous for the Mayor. I was one of those who supported the plan, but I worried every time he went out at night. Within a week after he started his walking tours, of course, the press found out about them and began to ask me about covering them with TV cameras and radios. I explained that this would defeat the purpose of his walks, but I agreed to let everyone have a shot at covering him exclusively on one of his tours. There would still be a problem with TV cameras present, but I indicated that one crew and one reporter might come along if they remained as inconspicuous as possible. The newsmen agreed and, as the tours continued, we usually had no more than one or two newsmen tagging along with the Mayor. Most of the time either Gottehrer or Davidoff, or both, walked alongside the Mayor. And, of course, there were the regular plainclothesmen who were assigned to remain with him at all times.

Many stories were written about these walks. The reaction was mostly favorable. People were glad to see their Mayor walking the streets, unafraid. I think it gave them confidence that the city was not as unsafe as most people thought. Lindsay, of course, loved it. He was the eternal campaigner and even if he got an earful of complaints in many places, he enjoyed the direct contact with people on the streets, especially in the black neighborhoods where he generally had a good reception. It also offered him an opportunity to do some direct campaigning in favor of the review board, which, I suspected, he thought would be in some danger of being defeated by the voters in November if it did get on the ballot as a referendum issue. The Mayor used every possible moment to sell himself and his programs and he even had some good laughs on these walks. I remember him telling me about a visit to a bar in Brooklyn, where he had stopped for a beer on a particularly hot night. He found himself beside a man on the next stool who was pouring out all of his problems to the Mayor. Lindsay listened for a few minutes, then put his arm around the man and without hesitation, declared: "You think you got problems? Just listen to mine for a while, will you?" The man and everyone around the bar broke out in laughter.

Lindsay had strong personal appeal and he was aware of it. He used it to advantage whenever he could. For example, on Tuesday, July 19, he was scheduled to give a talk at a dedication and ground-breaking ceremony for the Flatlands Industrial Park in Brooklyn about midafternoon. I arrived early to look over the area and found hostile crowds of Negroes awaiting him. They held placards indicating they wanted schools on this site—not an industrial park. They were restless and angry. It looked very much as if they intended to hold a demonstration which would disrupt the ceremony.

I quickly went to the nearest telephone and called the Mayor, who by now was en route to the site. I reached him on his car telephone and alerted him to the potential trouble awaiting him. A few minutes later I could see his black sedan pulling up about a block from the crowd. He stepped out alone and a dozen uniformed police began to close in around him, as if to form a protective cordon. He waved his hand at them, indicating he did not want them to accompany him. Then, much to the astonishment of everyone watching—including myself—he walked, smiling, right into the angry, shouting mob of some 1,000 people. Gradually, the noises from the crowd began to change from shouts of anger to cheers of enthusiasm and support. The frowns on their faces turned to smiles and, in a matter of minutes, several of the black leaders lifted Lindsay to their shoulders and carried him to the speaker's platform. He had turned the mood completely around by dismissing the police and taking matters into his own hands.

On Wednesday, July 20, we flew to Washington for the opening of the first New York City office in the nation's capital. Asked by a newsman at the press conference in the building on K Street Northwest if he would be looking more to Washington than Albany for assistance in the future, Lindsay responded:

"We'll have to. This is where the big breakthroughs in urban government programs are going. Let's face it. The big impetus is going to come from Washington." Accompanying the Mayor on this trip was Murray Drabkin, his principal tax adviser, whom the Mayor had named as head of the office. In addition, Senator Javits—who had been invited—came to the press conference and nearly usurped Lindsay by answering broad-ranging questions affecting the Congress. He spent more time talking to the TV cameras than Lindsay did. This did not particularly annoy the Mayor, however, because he knew he had a "good coverage" and didn't seem to mind sharing it with Javits.

On Thursday, July 21, just before a scheduled mayoral press conference, Bob Price had set up a picture-taking and interview session with Harry Golden, editor of *The Carolina Israelite*. Golden had apparently told Price he wanted to do some stories on the Jews in the Lindsay Administration. I was asked to pose next to the Mayor, along with Price and Harvey Rothenberg. This was supposed to show that three of the Mayor's closest aides were Jewish. I found Harry Golden an altogether pleasant fellow who asked questions unobtrusively and seemed to enjoy interviewing the Mayor. The interview lasted only a few minutes.

Later that afternoon and early evening, the Mayor had an "unscheduled" walking tour. It was during a tour of Brooklyn that night that he learned of the fatal shooting of an eleven-year-old boy, Eric Dean, from a sniper's bullet in East New York. He immediately went to the neighborhood where the trouble had occurred and was asked by spokesmen there to help ease the tensions between the Negro, Puerto Rican and white residents. "This has been a sensitive area for some time," the Mayor told newsmen that night. "I have talked with the community leaders here and asked them to try to work things out and I have told them I am available to help in any way." The Mayor remained on the streets with Commissioner Howard Leary, Chief Inspector Garelik and Human Rights Commissioner Booth until about 12:30 A.M. touring the tenement streets. It was a prelude to what was to become a major crisis in this community. Soon after the Mayor left the scene violence broke out—store windows were smashed and there were several street fights—but nobody was hurt.

By Friday night, tensions had risen so high in the East New York community that Leary had decided to station more than 1,500 policemen in the half-square mile area. Still reports of white and Negro gangs roaming the streets in search of trouble continued to spread. The Mayor grew more and more anxious as the hours passed. He was in touch with the Police Department about every thirty minutes. Lindsay had visited the mother of the Dean boy the night before and she had told him, according to one newspaper account: "You know, Mr. Mayor, the boy was on his way to see you when he was hit." Lindsay had been attending a meeting earlier that evening which the boy had evidently heard about. Several community leaders blamed the shooting on Lindsay himself because he had gone to visit one community group while allegedly ignoring others during his walks.[4]

Later on that night of July 22, violence erupted again. Two Puerto Ricans were shot, reportedly by four Negroes firing from a passing car. More than 150 cops, ducking snipers' bullets, Molotov cocktails and bottles, were rushed in to control a crowd of about 200 Negroes. Before the night was over, police had arrested 22 youths. The injuries might have been worse if the police had not been as well trained as they were. By showing restraint and good judgment, the police did not become directly involved with the angry crowds. Although they were taking a great deal of personal abuse, they stood their ground, silently. I knew that Leary had given strict orders to all policemen in his department to refrain from using overt force. He had previously briefed the Mayor and a few City Hall aides that this was his plan in case of trouble for the summer. "I have given orders," Leary calmly told Lindsay at an early morning City Hall meeting at which I was present, "that police officers must keep their billies on their belts and their guns in their holsters—unless their lives are threatened. That's my policy. It worked in Philadelphia and I have given orders here that there are to be no exceptions." The police did not like it, but they followed orders—and it kept the tensions down. Particularly in the East New York area, where there were so many conflicting ethnic groups, these tactics seemed to work, at least as a stopgap measure. In the 75th precinct where the Dean shooting had occurred, the mix was something like 56 percent white—mostly Jews, Italians, Irish and Polish—26 percent black and 17 percent Puerto Rican.

By late Friday night, it was clear that Lindsay had to take some additional action himself. Several of his aides suggested that he hold a "peace" conference in the community and go to East New York once again. Others felt he should invite representatives of all the factions to City Hall for a meeting. I was in favor of the City Hall conference, but I also felt it might appear to be Lindsay summoning the people to him instead of going to where the trouble was. In this case, however, he had made a visit there a few days before and it had not really done too much good. The decision was made: There would be a meeting called for Saturday morning at City Hall. The parley was arranged during the night and by 10 A.M. Saturday some fifty representatives from the community, including two dozen gang members and their feuding leaders—black and white— showed up. The Mayor began to talk, but he was almost immediately cut off by one of the youths in the meeting who verbally attacked him for "failing to do anything constructive." Lindsay, instead of losing his temper, merely told the youth: "That's what we're here for this morning. Let's cool it!" It was a difficult chore for the Mayor to try and bring harmony in a room filled with people who had been at each other's throats for years. I sat next to the Mayor as he fielded questions and tried to get to the root of the antagonisms between the youths. The gang leaders talked in terms of "our turf" and "their turf" and for a while it appeared as if the meeting would break up. At one point, several people were shouting at each other at the same time and a fist fight was narrowly averted as calmer people in the room stepped between two feuding youngsters. Lindsay had to forget he was the Mayor and he did. The people in the room that morning began, after the first hour, to bare their souls and Lindsay responded by dropping the formal pretenses which he had cultivated in previous meetings. After a while, people began to talk to him as a friend and he began to find out what was really troubling the community—long-standing racial and religious tensions which resulted mostly from a failure of each group to communicate with the other. After considerable patience and some persuasion, he convinced the people who attended the meeting to return to East New York and try and bring peace to the community. He agreed to be on hand at all times for telephone calls in case the uneasy truce was broken or was threatened. Three hours after it started, looking tired and pale, Lindsay turned to me and said: "Tell the press they can come in. I'll have a statement for them."

Surveying the crowd in the Blue Room, the Mayor told the reporters: "This meeting has resulted in some very important progress. These people have agreed to stretch out their hands and say, 'Let's put an end to this.' " Then, a few of the community spokesmen made statements and photographers swarmed over Lindsay for the pictures. He joined hands with two young men— a red-headed East New York youth, James (Sandy) McMenaman, and Vincent Jones, a Negro leader of the Warwick Avenue Block Association. These two had been particularly antagonistic toward each other when the meeting had begun in the morning. The hand-holding was a symbolic expression of the progress which had been made at City Hall. The next day the *Times* ran this headline on the top of page one of its Sunday, July 24, edition: MAYOR PLEDGES TO 'COOL' BROOKLYN UNREST. As I scanned the news story on that morning, I thought how capable Lindsay could be when he put his mind and energy to solving a serious problem between people. This was the same John Lindsay who spent much of his time posturing and arguing with people publicly through the news media. If he had only sat down and reasoned out his own differences with other people in New York the way he had used moderation to win over the various factions in East New York, he would be in much better shape at this mid-point in 1966, and so would New York.

10 *"You have to develop a thick skin in this business."*

DURING THE FIRST WEEK in August, one of the things I had most feared—a major controversy over our lagging antipoverty program—erupted virtually without warning. The spark which touched off the public scandal was an announcement by the Federal Office of Economic Opportunity that it had asked the city to return more than $10 million—half of the antipoverty funds it had received for the fiscal year ending June 30—because the city reportedly had failed to use it for the Head Start program. This was the national project to help poor pre-school children to be better prepared for learning when they enter school.

I suspected that one reason Washington was carefully scrutinizing our antipoverty program—aside from the fact that we had a group of young, inexperienced men running it—was that Robert J. Mangum, a former city deputy Police commissioner and deputy Hospitals commissioner, had not been retained by our Administration, but had accepted a post as regional Office of Equal Opportunity director (including the New York City area). It was public knowledge that he was not kindly disposed to us in the first place. In any case, Lindsay took the initiative in responding to the breaking story. On the last day of July, he had appeared on the CBS *Face the Nation* television program and charged that he had inherited "one of the worst" antipoverty apparatuses in the country and that the Federal government had "defaulted" on antipoverty money promised to the city. At the same time, however, he admitted that he was still reorganizing the city's antipoverty operations and that it would take "another six months to get it really in shape."

No matter how the Mayor explained the situation, however, the newspaper stories in early August added up to one clear impression: The city failed to properly use all of its antipoverty funds, regardless of the reason why. Taking advantage of the situation, Representative Adam Clayton Powell, speaking at a news conference in Harlem on the same Sunday that Lindsay was defending the program on TV, declared that "this is gross inefficiency on the part of Mayor Lindsay and his Administration." For several days, stories about the "unspent $10 million" dominated the front pages of the newspapers. The *Times* even went to the extent of interviewing scores of "poor" people and published a story telling of their frustrations. I was deeply concerned over this particular flap because I felt that we should have straightened out the antipoverty operation by August. And I knew, perhaps better than anyone, how inexperienced—even incompetent—our young antipoverty aides had shown themselves. Bob Price was right, I thought to myself in early August, when he had told me the previous December that housing and poverty would be the trouble spots in our Administration.

Just when I expected the poverty story to become a really large-scale scandal, it was moved off page one by a big plus: Lindsay and Price had come to a successful agreement with Austin Tobin of the Port Authority after six months of wrangling and bitter public statements. I scheduled a joint press conference at City Hall for Wednesday, August 3, at which it was announced that the city had agreed to go ahead with construction of the $525 million World Trade Center. The issue of how much the Port Authority would pay the city was settled by the introduction of a formula which was described as a major innovation in authority-government relationships, namely, that the size of the payment would be subject to annual review and would be increased or decreased as the official valuation of comparable property in the city rises or falls. For the first year, the agreement called for the Port Authority to pay the city $6.2 million. This new concept was a particular source of satisfaction to Bob Price, who had worked hard to reach an agreement, and to Donald F. Shaughnessy, an assistant to the Mayor for economic affairs, who had also played a role in the negotiations. A four-column photo of Lindsay shaking Tobin's hand in the *Times* with Price standing nearby, the next morning, did a lot to improve our public image at the very moment that it had been badly hurt by the poverty stories.

Another piece of good news for our Administration broke on August 5, when City Clerk Herman Katz ruled invalid the petitions of the Patrolmen's Benevolent Association and the Conservative Party asking for a referendum on the civilian-dominated police review board. Katz called the Conservative Party's petition "vague, indefinite, ambiguous and incomplete." He also said it failed to contain the necessary 30,000 valid signatures. Although the Patrolmen's Benevolent Association petition did contain 37,423 signatures, Katz said that the petition —which called for a City Charter Amendment—was "not, in fact," a real Charter Amendment, "but an addition to the Administrative Code." The Patrolmen's Benevolent Association and the Conservatives immediately announced they would challenge Katz's ruling in the State Supreme Court. Although I was momentarily cheered by Katz's action, it was predictable. I did not have a deep understanding of the law, but I suspected that the two groups pressing for a referendum would—in the long run—win the right to have the issue brought before the voters. And, even though I didn't want to see the Mayor lose this fight, I felt that it might be better settled by the voters. If they supported the Mayor, we would have an even clearer mandate which would strengthen our public explanation for creating the board, an issue that Lindsay had made part of his platform in the mayoral campaign.

Another troublesome issue at this time was our position on pay raises. For months, Lindsay had been saying publicly that it was his policy to raise city salary levels in order to attract top quality people and to compete with private industry. To a large extent, he was right and I agreed with the necessity to face up to the facts—even though it was not a politically popular thing to do. But once he recruited someone, he would frequently follow up with an immediate raise within a few months. This, I knew, annoyed the public and tended to contradict his campaign pledge of saving the city millions of dollars. On August 9, the *Times* took note of Lindsay's actions with a story headlined:

MAYOR CONTINUES
PAY-RAISE POLICY

The story reported that the Mayor had raised the salaries of Air Pollution Commissioner Austin Heller and City Renewal Commissioner Jason R. Nathan who had been appointed July 17 from $25,000 to $30,000. Another raise went to Murray Drabkin, assistant to the Mayor and the architect of our tax program, who had just been appointed director of the City of New York office in Washington. Drabkin, whose salary had been $18,000 up to then, was increased to $30,000. These raises, coupled with several others, led the *Daily News* to run an editorial accusing Lindsay of going back on his "economy" campaign pledge.[1]

For many months before the summer, I had felt that it would be good for Lindsay to gain citywide television exposure and to somehow come into direct contact with the voters. Dave Garth, who had been advising us as Lindsay's special consultant for radio and TV, helped me set up a program on WCBS-TV called *Ask Mayor Lindsay*. Garth made most of the arrangements. A smooth-talking public relations man who knew his way around the radio and TV industry, Garth had won several awards for handling other prominent political personalities. He knew how to joke with Lindsay—to loosen him up and show him off to his best advantage. On Sunday, August 7, Lindsay appeared in the first of a series of programs, along with eight top officials—including Police Commissioner Howard Leary, Fire Commissioner Robert Lowery and Parks Commissioner Thomas Hoving. There was time for about thirty questions from the public. One questioner in the studio publicly asked what had up to then been a rumor: Had Leary and Lindsay approved the use of Albert and Larry Gallo, Brooklyn gangsters, as peacemakers during the recent racial violence in East New York? And who does the Lindsay Administration plan on using next?

The Mayor replied that, "when things are as tense and dangerous as that, you call for help from any area." Leary said the city's arrangement with the Gallos "was done without the knowledge of the Police Department, but we take the position, in times like that, to take help from everybody we can get."

Despite this latest uproar and all the other pressures of my own job—arranging press conferences and trying to respond to the continuous barrage of radio, TV and newspaper inquiries—I decided to take Lindsay at his word when he told us at a staff meeting to schedule vacations for ourselves. I was slated to go away for three weeks in August when Lindsay, too, was planning to take some days off and remain at his Long Island home. I knew I needed the rest and I wanted to spend a little time with my family without worrying about the telephones for the first time in eight months. Just before I was about to leave, I received a call from Bob Price, who was in his office. He asked me to come in for a few minutes.

"Woody," he began, "you don't need this press secretary's job any more. All you've been getting is aggravation and trouble. How about taking the job we've been trying to fill for six months—chairman of the New York City Housing Authority? Would you be interested? It's 35 Gs and you know about housing from your reporting days."

I had been trying for months to help the Mayor find a new chairman for the giant city agency which builds and maintains all of the low-rent public housing in New York. I had never thought of myself as a candidate for the post. I looked at Price in utter surprise.

"I'm not sure I know enough about public housing to serve as chairman," I replied. "Besides," I continued, "despite all of the troubles we've had with the press, I really do enjoy the job I have and I want to remain in journalism. I'm a journalist and I think that's where I belong."

"You think about it," Price insisted. "You want to make some real money, don't you?"

I turned and left his office, somewhat bewildered. I wondered why he hadn't offered the job to me before. And did Lindsay know about the offer? Was Price really interested in furthering my financial interests—or did he have another candidate for my job? Lindsay had never said anything to me about being dissatisfied—on the contrary, he had been complimentary on several occasions. I went home and pondered the offer with my wife for a night. We decided to turn it down, mostly because I preferred to remain in the press area rather than move into housing as a career. As much as I cared about the housing problem, I simply did not want to cut my ties with the profession I had loved and worked at for fourteen years. I left with my wife and daughter for a few weeks on Cape Cod without giving the matter any further thought. Bob Laird became acting press secretary, and I assigned Al Troche and Joseph Polser, who was on loan from the Rent Administration, to back him up.

While I was away, the opening of a Little City Hall took place in the section of East New York in Brooklyn that had been the scene of the racial disorders. Robert Blum, a mayoral assistant who had been placed in charge of the Mayor's Little City Halls program, received a "good press" when he was quoted as saying: "The Mayor felt it was extremely important to do something more than just put policemen elbow to elbow here. We want to find out what the frustration was all about. This will serve as an office for all the city officials out here, and give us a neutral spot to sit down and meet with people without exacerbating the situation." Because the City Council was still blocking funds for the City Halls (many Councilmen charged these offices would be nothing more than Lindsay political clubs; some even said they feared these would turn into Lindsay-for-President bases), Blum said he was attempting, along with Commissioner of Public Events Bud Palmer, to round up private contributions to support the office and its staff.

Although I tried to disengage myself from what was going on in New York while on vacation, I found myself driving to the nearest newspaper stand early every morning anxious to find out what the *Times* was carrying about Lindsay. Once or twice I telephoned Laird and once the Mayor called me. I was in touch with New York at least twice each of the three weeks I was away. During this time, the State Supreme Court overruled

City Clerk Katz and upheld the legality of the petitions of the Patrolmen's Benevolent Association and the Conservative Party for a fall referendum on the Civilian Police Review Board;[2] and one of the young street leaders who had pledged himself to "cool it" in racially tense East New York, James (Sandy) McMenaman, twenty-five, was arrested for possessing and selling marijuana. It was the second time he had been arrested since the well-publicized City Hall conference; the first time he had been charged with burglary—and a City Hall spokesman (someone other than myself) responded by saying: "The Mayor knew that many of the young men in that room last Saturday had been in trouble before. He feels that was not the point—that much more meaningful is the fact that an agreement among those youths to keep peace in New York was reached." Following a story in the *Daily News,* the *Times* reported that the Patrolmen's Benevolent Association denounced as a "civic disgrace" the use of the Gallo brothers in helping to halt racial violence. The story pointed out that the "arrangement" had been made by Frank C. Arricale II, the City's Youth Board director. I knew Frank Arricale to be a sensitive, compassionate man who did what he thought was best and, although it proved to be embarrassing in some quarters, I felt he had done the right thing—despite all of the complaints by the police, the press and one or two community groups in Brooklyn, and even a charge from Brooklyn District Attorney Aaron E. Koota that the action taken by Arricale was "a deplorable abdication of official responsibility."

On August 18, in a column by Jack Newfield in *The Village Voice*—a widely read weekly newspaper in New York City and elsewhere—I was surprised to read that Bob Price (whom Newfield called "the power behind the throne") had reportedly asked Lindsay to let him quit as Deputy Mayor. He described Price as "psychologically dominating the Mayor"—a statement which I knew from my own vantage point was true. Newfield, an excellent writer and a reporter with political acumen, went on to state that Price's influence had declined and that "the slack" was being picked up by Barry Gottehrer, Bob Sweet and Jay Kriegel. Then, much to my surprise, I found my own name in the middle of his political gossip column as one of several

Lindsay aides "who appear to be in some difficulty and whose jobs are on the line." My immediate reaction was to dismiss the report as unfounded, but I did show it to the Mayor and asked him what he thought of it.

"Forget it," he said. "You have to develop a thick skin in this business, Woody. I told you that many months ago. Don't give it a second thought."

On August 18, Lindsay interrupted his own vacation to take a first-hand look at the new Little City Hall in East New York. The walk, although well intended, stirred some resentment in the community from a few people whom the *Times* quoted as charging that the Mayor's presence only served to remind the public of the racial tensions. Many residents were quoted as saying it would take more than walks by Lindsay to solve the basic problems of jobs, better housing and narcotics addiction. It was one of those attempts which made me wonder if the Mayor hadn't reached the point of diminishing returns with his street walks. Aside from the factor of safety, they could only serve to promote his image as a Mayor who "cares" for a certain amount of time. After that, the people would want—even demand—action.

While I was discussing with other aides a possible "new strategy" for the Mayor concerning his neighborhood walks, we began to prepare in some detail for his appearance before a Senate subcommittee chaired by Senator Abraham A. Ribicoff (Dem., Conn.) which was holding hearings in Washington on what had by now become known as "the crisis of the cities." There was some anxiety among a few Lindsay aides about this particular appearance because Senators Javits and Kennedy were outspoken members of the subcommittee. Lindsay's testimony, carefully worked out by Jay Kriegel with help from Mike Sviridoff and several other top Administration aides, was released from my office on the morning of Monday, August 22. The news lead, I felt, would be the Mayor's call for an expenditure of $50 billion more in Federal funds in the next decade to transform New York into what Lindsay described as "a thoroughly livable and exciting place in which to live." Much to my satisfaction, the *Times* reported it that way the next day—but the *Daily News* ran a headline which reflected the unexpected and surprisingly bitter confrontation between the Mayor and Bobby Kennedy which was aired throughout the nation on network TV. The headline read: LINDSAY, RFK CLASH ON CITY'S BILLIONS BID. The *Times,* in leading with Lindsay's estimate of the $50 billion need, made a reference in the subhead to Kennedy, but did not feature the verbal exchange between the two.

When Lindsay cited the $50 billion figure, Kennedy interrupted to say it was "totally unrealistic." The Federal government, he said firmly, "is not about to increase its aid to New York at that rate." The personal sparring continued throughout Lindsay's appearance. When Kennedy began to press Lindsay on how much the Federal government presently gave New York, the Mayor offered answers in terms of "capital" and "expense" budgets. "But what is the total Federal figure?" Kennedy pressed on. Obviously exasperated, Lindsay retorted: "All right, you do the addition." Kennedy did. He got $619 million per year. Lindsay agreed that an all-inclusive total would be "somewhere over $500 million and below $1 billion. "That's quite a margin," Kennedy observed acidly. At this point, Ribicoff eased the mounting tension by breaking in with his own estimate of $861 million and then added, in an obvious effort to make peace: "It's almost impossible for the Federal government to know how much it is giving or a city to know how much it's getting," he said. "That's the purpose of these hearings."[3] I was not present at the hearings, but when I saw the film clips on TV that night, I knew that Lindsay had once again been bested by Bobby. I felt a little frustrated and angry that he had permitted himself to have been trapped into virtually admitting he did not know how much money the city was receiving from Washington.

Only a few days later, however, some political fence-mending by aides of Lindsay and Kennedy enabled the Mayor to ask for— and receive—Kennedy's support in the fight for the Civilian Review Board. Dave Garth, who had been asked by the Mayor to take charge of the campaign to save the board, was able to persuade Kennedy aides that it would be in the best interest of the two men to join together in this issue. Senator Javits also added his support for the board in order to present a united front among New York liberal office holders, except for

Governor Rockefeller.[4] The battle lines were firmly drawn on August 26, when—in response to an appeal from the City Corporation Counsel—the State Appellate Division upheld by a 3–2 vote the legality of the petitions calling for a November referendum on the review board. And three days later, on August 29, Staten Island's Republican State Senator John J. Marchi came out strongly against the review board, blaming the City Council's "dereliction" and "do-nothing attitude" for its existence. He said he would call public hearings in the fall "on all aspects" of the Mayor's attempt to bypass the City Council by creating the Police Civilian Review Board with an executive order. Marchi, chairman of the Senate Committee on the City of New York, said the City Council failed in its duty to consider a referendum on the review board question.

The other lingering story—the Gallo affair—came back into the news on Friday, August 26, at a press conference, when Lindsay was asked by a newsman to comment on a statement by City Human Rights Commissioner William Booth that "the Gallo brothers did the job because they were in a position to do it. They have a right to do good. They did a fine service for the city." I had discussed the whole subject with the Mayor and he said he wanted to meet it head-on. He would not back down. As soon as the question was asked, therefore, Lindsay defended the Youth Board's use of the Brooklyn gangland figures and added: "I will certainly call on them again if the need arises. You can't always deal with people who are leaders in the Boy Scout movement," he added, as newsmen hurriedly scrawled on their pads. "Sometimes you must call upon individuals with fairly rough backgrounds. I, as Mayor, don't live in a cocoon. It was hot and dangerous at the time, and I am very thankful that all aspects of the neighborhood agreed to keep it cool." In making this strong—and unexpected—statement the Mayor backed up Frank Arricale who had contended that the Gallo brothers were the only persons who commanded enough respect among the gangs of East New York to persuade white youths to stop their forays against Negroes.

While Lindsay continued to be besieged on all fronts with problems, there was one area in which, I felt, we were beginning to make solid progress: preventing business from leaving New

York and attracting new business. For example, the Mayor was succeeding in his campaign to lure the movie industry to New York. Harvey Rothenberg and Barry Gottehrer had made some real progress in helping producers and small businessmen who had become tangled in red tape. Also, the Department of Commerce and Industrial Development had made a lot of headway in this area during the summer months.

Late in August, I heard that a small truck transportation company was about to move into the city from New Jersey. Rothenberg was busy and so were the officials in the Commerce Department, so I volunteered to meet the truck company on the New York side of the Holland Tunnel and offer them an "official reception" in behalf of the Mayor. The meeting was scheduled for 10:30 A.M. on a Saturday, but the convoy arrived about twenty minutes early and caused a major traffic jam. By the time I got there, the newsmen were smiling with glee over the fact that they had a good story—not the arrival of new business in Manhattan, but a monumental traffic jam because of an alleged "snafu" in arrangements. The *Times* carried a two-column 16-inch story in its Sunday edition about the mixup, which far overshadowed the arrival of a new business. When Lindsay saw the story in the Sunday paper, he merely smiled and told me: "Better you than me. Can you imagine what they would have written if I had gone down there and caused that traffic mess!"

In early September, the spotlight gradually lifted from City Hall and began to focus on the gubernatorial race, which had now become a four-way contest between the incumbent, Governor Rockefeller; Frank O'Connor for the Democrats; Franklin D. Roosevelt, Jr., for the Liberal Party; and Paul Adams for the Conservative Party. Aside from a routine endorsement of Rockefeller in mid-summer, Lindsay had managed to stay out of the campaign. And he had his own political battle to worry about—the Civilian Review Board. By September 11, he was publicly saying that "we are on the upswing, we have a fighting chance." Ironically, he officially thanked Frank O'Connor for supporting the review board and then chided Rockefeller and Roosevelt for not taking a public position. Lindsay, I felt, had at least two good reasons for optimism: First, five well-known

New Yorkers had agreed to serve as co-chairmen of the Federation of Association for Impartial Review (FAIR). These were: Herbert Brownell, a former U.S. attorney general and one of Lindsay's closest advisers; Bronx Borough President Herman Badillo; A. Philip Randolph, president of the Brotherhood of Sleeping Car Porters and vice president of the AFL-CIO; Morris Abram, president of the American Jewish Congress; and Theodore W. Kheel, the labor mediator who had been a top aide to Mayor Wagner.

And secondly, there was the hope that came with the emergence of the new *World-Journal-Tribune* on the afternoon of September 12.[5] Lindsay's statement on September 11 said he hoped the new newspaper would "make a major contribution to the life of our great city" and, although he did not say so publicly, I knew he was pleased that this also meant an opportunity for more publicity—and therefore a greater hope for victory—for his campaign to save the review board.

11 "Everything seems to be going wrong."

THE MAYOR FELT that in order to get Congress to pay attention to New York City's needs, it was necessary for him to enhance his own national stature. By September, the press was responding with articles comparing him favorably with other well-known figures in American politics. He was certainly the best-known Mayor in America after being in office for only nine months.[1]

He was now making more trips to Washington and appearing before more Congressional committees with well-prepared speeches, which drew a lot of attention in the Washington press. His favorite theme: The crisis of the cities deserves first priority in America. In his effort to talk on national issues intelligently, he needed a great deal of research and sharp new ideas. Most of this came from Jay Kriegel and Jim Carberry. Kriegel, a brash young man who was not at all personable, was nevertheless extraordinarily bright and quick. He understood what Lindsay should be saying in the national arena and he helped to draft many of Lindsay's most effective statements. Kriegel also was smart enough to recognize the inevitability of the local criticism—much of it petty—which Lindsay had drawn from the press in New York, particularly the reporters who covered him at City Hall.[2]

Lindsay's nationally oriented speeches were frank and to the point. In one talk to the Urban America, Inc., organization, for example, the Mayor predicted disaster for the nation's cities unless the Federal government recognized its responsibilities to plan and finance major reforms. "Everything that is wrong with New York City," he said, "will eventually become a failing of virtually every one of our cities. Congress has not organized itself to deal effectively with the cities of this nation." His pleas for New York were well reported—in the newspapers and magazines. But no matter how hard Lindsay tried to bolster his image with solid, genuine appeals for more funds for New York, the annoying everyday urban problems in New York continued unabated. For example, at one Cabinet meeting Lindsay declared that he would no longer tolerate double-parking and illegally parked cars; he directed Traffic Commissioner Barnes and the Police Department to crack down on all violators. The word went out: Tow away all cars and enforce the $25 fine for all midtown violators. But the new crackdown angered many people including doctors and diplomats, and brought forth charges from policemen that the Mayor was trying to bolster his drive for the Civilian Review Board by turning the public against the police for handing out parking tickets. The Mayor responded by defending his drive on illegal parking. "The motorists will appreciate it when they can cross town without getting stuck for an hour," he said.

Another example of a small but embarrassing development on the home front occurred in mid-September and the press made the most of it. There was a major foul-up regarding the signing of a $9 million bond issue by the City Housing Authority—which still was without a chairman (I had turned down the post and so had several other people outside city government). William Reid had retired as chairman on January 1, 1966, leaving Francis V. Madigan and Ira S. Robbins as the two remaining members. In order to make bond issues legal, two of the three members of the City Housing Authority must sign the bond issue. As it turned out, Robbins was out of the country at this time, leaving only Madigan. So Lindsay had to fill the vacant post of City Housing Authority chairman in a hurry. The Mayor decided to name Jason R. Nathan, already chairman of the Housing and Redevelopment Board, as the temporary chairman (at least long enough to sign the bond issue). He asked an aide to check the legality of the appointment with Lee Rankin first. But the aide failed to reach Rankin —and also failed to notify Lindsay of this fact. So Lindsay, believing it was okay, went on to swear in Nathan as city Housing Authority chairman in a quiet, non-publicized ceremony in Nathan's office. Nathan then presided at the Housing Authority meeting. It was at this point that Rankin advised the Mayor that the Public Housing Law prohibited the City Housing Authority chairman from holding two jobs at once. Since Nathan was needed at the Housing and Redevelopment Board, his appointment as temporary head of the City Housing Authority was rescinded and the Mayor picked Gerald J. Carey, the City Housing Authority's general manager since 1959. Nathan resigned and Lindsay swore in Carey. The *Post* reported in a headline: THE SHORT, HAPPY CHAIRMANSHIP OF JASON R. NATHAN.

Still another moment of major concern occurred about this time involving my own office. Lindsay called me in one day and asked me what I thought about each of the commissioners "sounding off on their own"—as he put it—without checking with him. He was speaking, in particular, of Moerdler, Booth and Hoving, although it had become the general practice by now for anyone to speak out without checking with Lindsay or myself.

"Hoving seems to be in the lead for the most-newspaper-stories derby," I replied.

"It's not Hoving who bothers me," he said. "He's doing a beautiful job. But some of the others just pop off without even as much as a telephone call to me. I have to find out what's going on by reading the paper."

"What do you want to do?" I asked.

"You handle it," he said. "The word should come from your shop. But I think we've got to get some of these guys in line. Moerdler, for example. He just makes announcements all over the place. That one recently about inspecting all the public schools and finding a bunch of violations; and calling the city the worst slumlord. Why doesn't he tell us what he's going to say?"

"Probably because he doesn't know himself," I replied, knowing Charlie Moerdler's tendency to shoot from the hip.

"Okay, Woody," the Mayor said. "It's in your lap. You handle it."

I did. I sent out a memorandum on September 13 to the heads of all departments and agencies and assistants to the Mayor, asking them to call the Mayor directly or confer with his Press Office regarding the release of all news through the media. "This is necessary," I wrote, "in order to establish clear policies throughout city government and to keep the Mayor informed at all times about what his commissioners and aides are saying publicly. . . . We will prepare all major releases when the Mayor and commissioners make joint announcements and will work closely with you and your top staff." Immediately, I was besieged with questions from Room 9 reporters.

Two days later, in the September 15 issue of the *Times,* a little story on page thirty-four appeared, headlined: CITY HALL TO CLEAR NEWS FROM AGENCIES. It published parts of the memo and included a denial from me that the memo was meant to suppress news. The story quoted me as saying: "We encourage commissioners to talk to the press. We merely want to be kept informed of what they are saying. Our purpose is merely to coordinate the flow of news. In fact, there is no change in our policy of making city government news fully available to the press." In retrospect, I realized, I would have been much better off not sending out the memorandum, but simply having the Mayor make a verbal request of his commissioners at a weekly Cabinet meeting. But in my desire to take the responsibility off his shoulders, I had risked criticism from the press.

Still another embarrassment—this time to Lindsay—came on September 16, when Austrian Foreign Minister Lujo Toncic-Sorinj, a tall, handsome, gray-templed dignitary, was scheduled to pay a 3:30 P.M. courtesy call on Lindsay. He arrived at City Hall on time and was shown into the ante-room next to the Mayor's office. Bob Laird went into Lindsay's office and notified one of the Mayor's secretaries that the Foreign Minister had arrived. During the next twenty-five minutes, Laird reminded the secretaries—and the Mayor—that his visitor was waiting. Nobody showed any unusual concern because it had been almost normal procedure for all appointments to run at least a half hour late. Nevertheless, when Mr. Toncic-Sorinj got up to leave at 3:55 P.M., saying he had a TV commitment, his departure became news. Reporters immediately heard he was about to walk out. One asked the Foreign Minister as he was leaving if he thought the Mayor's behavior was discourteous. "What do you think?" he replied. I heard about the situation moments after he had left and immediately told the Mayor. He shrugged his shoulders in dismay. "I was on the phone," he said. "I didn't realize he was waiting so long." He turned to his secretary: "Telephone his hotel suite and express my apologies. And send some flowers to his wife."

The following morning—Saturday, September 17—I arrived at Gracie Mansion at about 8 A.M. in order to brief the Mayor for a television interview later that morning. A few other aides joined us at the breakfast table as Mary Lindsay poured some coffee. Lindsay appeared drowsy and bleary-eyed. He had been up half the night at a party and he looked very tired. We began to go over the questions that might come up on the program. By this time, I had written down a list of our "accomplishments" since January 1 and I handed Lindsay a copy of the three-page outline on which 18 major points were listed (see Appendix, pages 311–312), including the Civilian Review Board, recruiting "top talent," the tax program and the opening of a Washington office. We went over all the possible areas of government and then turned to other stories in the news. Then someone mentioned the unintentional snub to the Austrian minister. Lindsay choked up.

"Oh, hell," he said loudly, as he got up from the kitchen table. "Everything seems to be going wrong." He then suddenly left the kitchen and walked quickly upstairs. We had been throwing questions and answers at him for nearly an hour when he suddenly bolted upstairs. I felt the tensions had finally caught up with him. A few minutes later, his eyes red and his face pale, he returned to the kitchen dressed and ready to go across town to the TV studios. We walked out of Gracie Mansion and started across East 86th Street on foot. I walked, almost ran, on his right side. I put my hand on his arm for a moment.

"Take it easy, John," I said, feeling inadequate to the needs of the moment. "Everything'll be all right."

He didn't answer. He just quickened his pace. He was his old determined self again and he was striding toward the television studios as if he intended to do battle and come out victorious. In a short space of time, I realized, he had momentarily given in to his emotions at Gracie Mansion, pulled himself together and then emerged as "tough" as ever. This was always his desire—to appear tough, determined and undaunted by adversity. He admired toughness in others and this was, therefore, a word which found its way into his vocabulary many times every day. Now he was determined to show even those of us who had gotten to know him well—and had seen him falter for a moment—that he could take it. We went to the program that morning and he put on a fine show. He answered all the questions with determination and certainty. He was particularly sharp. The incident about the Austrian Minister never came up again.

A few days later, the battle over the Civilian Review Board suddenly took a new turn. Patrolmen's Benevolent Association President John J. Cassese charged that "Communism and Communists are somewhat mixed in this fight. If they are not in the forefront, they are making hay while the sun shines." I was called by the press for a reply to Cassese's charges, which, of course, were "good copy" in the press, whether or not they were true. I advised the Mayor to use his regular Tuesday morning press conference as a means of answering the charge. He agreed. On September 21, he told newsmen: "My reaction is one of abhorrence. The community at large, that is interested in progress, is supporting the review board." The Mayor then cited the fact that the board was supported by Senators Javits and Kennedy. "For Mr. Cassese to make a unilateral statement that the review board is a Communist plot," Lindsay continued "is shocking beyond words."

After the press conference, City Investigation Commissioner Arnold G. Fraiman—who had been doing an extremely effective job since taking office in January—stepped into the limelight by telling newsmen that defeat of the review board in the November referendum could seriously cripple his agency. Fraiman called attention to the fact that there was a "sleeper clause" in the referendum which would limit investigation of complaints against police. "If this thing means what it says," Fraiman told reporters, "my office won't be able to handle any complaints against the Police Department." And, in reply to Cassese, Dave Garth, chairman of the Federation of Associations for Impartial Review (FAIR), responded in a statement: "Cassese's statement is outrageous and reminiscent of a time when smear and fabrication became the chief weapon of an irresponsible few. In his fight to destroy the Civilian Review Board which has functioned successfully since July, Patrolman Cassese has become desperate enough to ally himself with the John Birch Society and the American Nazi Party by employing the same witch-hunting tactics."

On top of the review board controversy, another bitter racial conflict had been simmering since the start of school earlier in the month. On September 21, it erupted when angry Negro demonstrators broke through a police barricade and attempted to prevent the white principal from entering Intermediate School 201 in East Harlem. The tensions arose when some East Harlem parents and community leaders demanded that the principal, Stanley R. Lisser, who was white, be replaced by a Negro principal to provide a "proper image" for the largely Negro student body. But their broader objective, they admitted, was to gain a voice in the school's operation as a means of assuring a quality education program. Late that night I spoke to the Mayor on the telephone.

"I'm going up there first thing in the morning," he told me. "Don't put it on the press schedule. I just want to appear there. There will be enough newsmen there from yesterday to see what happens."

"Okay," I replied. "But how're you going to handle it?"

"I don't think parents should have veto power over the selection in the city school system of principals and teachers. That is clearly a matter for the Board of Education. That's what I intend to say."

Arriving at the school at 127th Street and Madison Avenue at

8:55 A.M. the morning of September 22, that's exactly what Lindsay did say. Although there were some fifty demonstrators behind police barricades, he easily walked into the school and conferred with the teachers and staff. As he was about to leave, he told reporters:

"I think there have been some errors and mistakes along the way. There are some clumsy aspects to the handling of the whole problem. But control of the selection of teachers should be in the hands of the Board of Education."

Parents' groups had been demanding that the school be integrated by busing in white children from other localities, and that parents should have control over the selection of personnel and curriculum. In response, Lindsay said: "It is clear that the community at large should have a more meaningful role. There should be increased dialogue and communication between the community and the board. However, the ultimate selection of staff members should come from the board." By taking a middle-of-the-road position, Lindsay angered both the parents and the Board of Education.

Later that day, I joined Lindsay in Yonkers for a meeting of the Big Six Mayors of New York State, and returned to City Hall just in time to see him jeered and abused by a shouting, stomping crowd of demonstrating taxpayers who were repeatedly interrupting a Board of Estimate meeting. They shouted angry cries of "Nazi dictator," "dirty crook" and "Communist plot," as the Mayor tried in vain to gavel for order. The demonstrations were touched off by announcements that the Administration intended to increase the water and sewer charges. Bob Sweet had been sitting in for Lindsay, but had been unable to control the angry mob, which was led by Vito Battista and numerous other outspoken citizens claiming to represent small homeowners in the Bronx, Brooklyn, Staten Island and Queens. Lindsay became so furious at one point—I don't think I have ever seen him so angry in public—that he ordered a policeman to eject one of the hecklers, telling the offender: "I consider this a willful violation of the Penal Law." The man looked at Lindsay as if the Mayor was speaking a foreign language.

Things did not ease up the next day. Lindsay decided that he had to bypass the Board of Education and personally step into the IS 201 dispute, which was still volatile. He invited a committee of parents down to City Hall to meet with him in the Blue Room. I sat in. The parents did most of the talking. They complained about police treatment of school pickets and warned Lindsay that there would be more trouble if things did not improve. The meeting had been arranged by Human Rights Commissioner Bill Booth, a Negro, who felt that the Mayor could accomplish a great deal by direct discussion with the parents. Earlier in the day, Lindsay had extended his criticism of the Board of Education by accusing it of "building a wall of isolationism around itself" and he pledged that his Administration in the future planned a more active role in the city's school affairs. He said that City Hall was not trying to take over control of the city's schools, but was attempting to bring about closer cooperation between the system and the city government. He said that "jobs, economic well-being and education are all tied together. It is impossible," he added, "to have goals of this kind if the Board of Education and the whole apparatus is in separate orbit from the political government of the city." I thought Lindsay was absolutely right, but I wondered—after all we had been through—how we were going to take on the entire public school establishment. The *Times* helped the Mayor throw down the gauntlet for the troubles that were to come in the next months and years by running a page one story headline: MAYOR TO EXPAND HIS ROLE IN THE CITY'S SCHOOL AFFAIRS.

I spoke to Lindsay in his office right after that story appeared and asked him whether he really wanted to open a new battle on still another front with all we had on our minds at this time. He looked at me as if I had insulted him and replied in a firm voice, without hesitating for a moment: "Look, we either have to do what's right in shaping up this government or the hell with it."

A few days later, what I had feared most happened. The *World-Journal-Tribune* ran an eight-column headline across page one: SCHOOL BOARD SET TO FIGHT, with a subhead: Won't Let City Hall Interfere. The story, attributed to "top sources on the Board," indicated that there was some real bitterness toward Lindsay among several members of the Board of Education. The newspaper account quoted the source as saying: "He's been threatening us with City Hall domination of the school system ever since he came to office. His people have been putting pressure on us since last January, warning us that we would have trouble getting money for schools at budget time if we didn't cooperate." The story went on to describe the board's general unhappiness over Lindsay's handling of the integration dispute at East Harlem's IS 201.

While the school issue was still raging, Lindsay continued to battle furiously for the Civilian Review Board. A full-page advertisement appeared in the *Daily News* on Monday morning, September 26, showing a picture of a frightened white girl near a subway entrance on a darkened street with a legend below: "The Civilian Review Board must be stopped! Her life . . . your life . . . may depend on it. Send your contribution today." It was signed by the "Independent Citizens Committee Against Civilian Review Boards." That night I accompanied Lindsay to a meeting at the Overseas Press Club in midtown Manhattan of an ad hoc committee to defend the review board. We were late, and the tenth-floor meeting room was filled with smoke and a crowd of people were milling around. As we arrived, a cheer went up for Lindsay. He acknowledged it with a characteristic smile and immediately went to the small podium in front of the room.

"I see by the ad in the paper this morning," he began, "that they [the opposition] are playing on fear. It is an attempt to incite racial tensions," he added, jabbing and chopping the air for emphasis. "The ad is a distortion. And we must keep in mind that their campaign is well financed." Then, pausing for a moment, his face more serious and contemplative, Lindsay talked of this fight in terms I had not heard before. "This is an historic moment," he told the crowd of about 150 people, as they quieted down. "Perhaps the most important fight I have ever seen. I am appalled to discover, after passage of many civil rights bills, that many of the wonderful liberals are slightly doctrinaire, it appears. This fight is the guts of it. This separates the men from the boys. History has seen before established liberals not smart enough to see the importance of crucial fights. The result is that we are set back for many years."

The next day, at his usual Tuesday press conference, Lindsay swore in a new team of men to run the city's Department of

Water Supply, Gas and Electricity, headed by the Mayor's close friend, mayoral assistant James L. (Jim) Marcus. Prior to the formal press conference in the Board of Estimate chambers, I had passed out the usual press release giving Marcus' background and the backgrounds of three men who would serve as unpaid consultants to Marcus: Philadelphia's Water Commissioner Samuel S. Baxter (who had previously turned down an offer from Lindsay for the job he finally offered Marcus) and two other nationally known water experts. Marcus came into my office before the swearing-in and introduced his attractive wife, Lilly Lodge, to me and my staff. Accompanying him also was his father-in-law, former Connecticut Governor John Davis Lodge, the brother of Henry Cabot Lodge. Mrs. Marcus was friendly and charming. Marcus, however, was more nervous than I had ever seen him. Normally cool and in full control of himself, he seemed fidgety. He walked up to my desk and leaned over.

"What should I say?" he asked timidly.

"Just relax, Jim," I replied. "Let the Mayor do all the talking. And if you get any questions about the water supply, just keep your answers vague. Tell them you'll have more to say after you've taken a first-hand look at the situation."

"I have some graphs and statistics," he said. "Shall I use them?"

"Sure," I replied. "If they're simple and people can understand them." The charts showed how full the city's reservoirs were and clearly indicated that there was still a water shortage. This had been a major issue in the 1965 campaign and interest was still running reasonably high on the subject. Marcus thanked me quietly.

"Good luck, Jim," I said. "Just be yourself and you'll make out fine. There's nothing to worry about."

He turned and smiled at me as he went out the door. I returned his smile, thinking to myself that Jim Marcus was one of the most modest, decent and loyal men I had met in the Lindsay Administration. I had always enjoyed talking with him and I was happy that the Mayor had picked him for this key $30,000-a-year job. The swearing-in itself went smoothly. The Board of Estimate was packed with guests and the press. The Mayor spoke glowingly of Marcus' service to him as an adviser on all matters pertaining to water supply and its distribution since our Administration took office. Then Marcus accepted his new role with a few quiet words and proceeded to give his short talk, pointing out that the city's upstate reservoirs held 318 billion gallons, or 66.7 percent of capacity. The normal supply for this date, Marcus said, was 327 billion gallons, or 69 percent. He appealed for continuing water conservation. "I hope and urge that New Yorkers will conserve water to the best of their ability," he said quietly.

His first public appearance as commissioner had been simple and effective. I was impressed with the casual and almost nonchalant manner in which he behaved. He was consistently cool, calm, friendly, unflappable, dependable. After the ceremony, Marcus came down to my office and asked me how it went. I told him he had done very well and then suggested that he remain close by for interviews. Several of the reporters did talk to him, including Erwin Savelson, of the *World-Journal-Tribune,* who wrote a six-column story in the next day's edition quoting Marcus in detail about his plans for "a billion-dollar fight to insure New York's future water needs." It was an impressive story and Marcus sounded as if he knew his subject well. He was an instant success and nobody criticized the appointment, even though he was an amateur in the field and a personal friend of Lindsay's. His pleasing personality and his genuine modesty had won him many friends and the press recognized that he wanted to do a good job.

A few days later, another controversy broke over what the Mayor and I considered a trivial matter, but the press climbed on the story as if it were one of the most important muckraking crusades in decades. The *New York Post* learned that within a week Pan American Airways was scheduled to pay for a supper dance planned for top delegates of the United Nations at the New York State Theatre. The cost was estimated at about $15,000. The story raised the point that Pan American Airways' contract to continue controversial flights from its midtown rooftop building was scheduled to expire October 31. The paper quoted several City Councilmen as suggesting there might be a "conflict of interest" involved because Pan Am did business with the city. I was asked for comment by the *Post.* At the Mayor's request, I called John Bott, the paper's city editor, to try and inform him that the Mayor felt such a story would hurt the Mayor's long-standing campaign to involve private industry to help the city to under-write important public events. My request was unheeded and the *Post* broke the story with what it apparently thought was a shocker headline: PAN AM PAYS FOR CITY'S UN FETE.

When Lindsay saw the story, he lost his temper and urged me to telephone Mrs. Dorothy Schiff, the publisher. I told him I thought it would not be a good idea to go over the city editor's head. I knew from my own past experience that such a tactic only angered the editors and reporters and turned them more against you. Instead, we prepared a statement which said, in part: "I should think that persistent complainers should recognize and applaud the fact that the city and community of New York are recognizing the presence of this great institution [the United Nations] and celebrating the opening of the General Assembly." The Mayor's statement also noted that "any questions regarding the Pan Am heliport in which the city has jurisdiction will be decided strictly on the merits alone."

Three City Councilmen, nevertheless, called for an investigation into the matter and we found ourselves fighting on still another front. In this one, I issued the statements and tried to articulate our policy of private involvement; but I was still uncomfortable with the coincidence which the *Post* had turned up and I felt that our Administration would have been much wiser to have chosen another sponsor at this time. A brief flurry in the papers caused us to reconsider our position and the names of all private companies which had sponsored any public affairs were made public by Commissioner of Public Events Bud Palmer at the Mayor's request. The records showed Standard Oil Co. of New Jersey had paid for a dinner for Ferdinand Marcos, president of the Philippines; that Alcoa had paid for a reception for Harold Holt, prime minister of Australia; and that the Trade Bank and Trust Co. had paid for a party in honor of Zalman Shazar, president of Israel. In releasing the information, Palmer and Lindsay denied vigorously that there had been any trace of wrongdoing. Palmer added: "I'm doing no more than Dick Patterson and Grover Whalen [former official city greeters] did before me." No matter what statements we released, however, the Administration looked bad in the whole matter because of the Pan Am affair. Editorial comment was generally unfavorable.[3]

By the end of September, reporters began once again to request time with the Mayor for a series of "first nine months" stories. He started with Nat Hentoff, who was working on an article for *The New Yorker*, and, in discussing his duties as Mayor, he told Hentoff: "I think I've got a grip on the monster now. I'm much more certain now about how the structure should be changed, and I think I'm staffing the government as best I can. That's terribly important. I still spend a lot of time on it." Asked how he hoped to solve some of the city's problems with limited financial resources, the Mayor replied: "I keep saying the Federal Government has to reexamine its priorities. Instead of making cuts in appropriations for the cities, it ought to see what cuts can be made in all those funds pouring into Vietnam."

The *New York Post's* nine-month look at Lindsay consisted of a six-part series which began on September 26. Three reporters —Michael J. Berlin, Joseph Kahn and Anthony Prisendorf— offered a careful analysis of our performance to date. In the first article, entitled "Promise vs. Performance," the *Post* reporters wrote that Lindsay "had been an exciting Mayor, and he has been disillusioning. He has laid a foundation of change that could, some day, actually grow into all the promises that he has failed to keep. And he has left the distinct impression that there are only two things blocking his vision of New York City— money and Lindsay himself. To get elected, Lindsay (like any reformer) had to promise more than he could produce. Lindsay truly believes in the rightness of his promises—his friends say this with awe, his detractors with annoyance. 'But the Mayor of New York City,' says a professional non-partisan, 'requires the art of the politician.' And this is Lindsay's great flaw."

In the second article, dealing with finances, the *Post* chided Lindsay for promising to save money and then handing out generous pay raises. It complimented him for attracting new industry to New York, but it suggested that his plan to consolidate fifty different city departments into ten "administrations" might be costly to the taxpayers rather than save money. The third article, on labor, listed the transit strike and several other stoppages and threats, including one by city employees over the summer hours issue. "Labor hates his guts," it quoted one labor expert, and the article continued, "Lindsay's forthright style, carried to the collective bargaining table, has made his relationship with city employees, and with other unions who have come to turn to the Mayor as a mediator, one of the major failures of his nine months in office." The *Post* said transportation and traffic problems were still plaguing the city, but lauded the Mayor for his crackdown on parking violators and for retaining Henry Barnes as traffic commissioner.

The fourth article, on "Slums, Housing, Poverty," praised the Mayor for what it called "feeling the ghetto problems deep in his gut." The article continued: "Lindsay is pleased, and perhaps a bit surprised at the enthusiasms he engenders on his ghetto walking tours." On the poverty war, the *Post* pointed out how Lindsay had berated the Wagner Administration for delays and a "structural monstrosity" of a program, but said that he did not act fast enough himself, and noted that, by the end of the fiscal year, $10 million in poverty funds went unspent and was lost to the city. In the housing area, the *Post* pointed to Lindsay's campaign promise of 160,000 units in four years of low and middle income housing (a figure for which I and several other people had been responsible when we wrote the white paper during the summer of 1965) and correctly concluded that we would fall far short of this promise. But it complimented Buildings Commissioner Charles Moerdler, despite the fact that he turned out, the *Post* said, to be "a lover of publicity" and that his father-in-law was a slum owner. "There are more inspections than ever coming out of Moerdler's [Buildings] department; there was a crackdown on graft, and, as in most other city departments, a plan to reform that hasn't quite worked out." This article also complimented Human Rights Commissioner Bill Booth, as a "Lindsay-style action commissioner" and reported how he had tried to integrate unions and personally force cab drivers to pick up Negro passengers. Booth used his own city car one night to chase a cab driver who had not picked up a Negro passenger— an action for which he became known as "the Batman" of city government.

The fifth article was about parks, hospitals and schools. The *Post* praised Tom Hoving for doing his job "with ingenuity and a flair for promotion." It listed many of Hoving's innovations, including the "Happenings" for which he was to become nationally known (such as painting contests for thousands of children in Central Park). The article quoted Dr. Howard Brown, the health services administrator, as admitting that the services were "unacceptable" even if they were the best of any municipality in the country. And the *Post* indicated that little progress had been made in eight months.

It credited the Mayor with starting a war against air and water pollution and pointed out that "The Great Drought" had ended. "But Lindsay can't take credit for that one." (Actually, the Mayor often used the end of the water shortage as a humorous opening anecdote in speeches to show his listeners how much he had accomplished in such a short time.)

On the subject of schools, it described the strained relationship Lindsay had with the Board of Education and it raised the question of Moerdler's inspection of the public schools, which, to some observers, embarrassed the Board. (At the time, Moerdler told a reporter: "I'll get out of the schools when John tells me to, and when that happens he can look for a new commissioner." Lindsay's reaction was to decline comment and refrain from inhibiting Moerdler.)

The last article, like many others in other publications at this time, described a day with the Mayor. "In general," it said, "things are pretty hectic for the Mayor . . . but Lindsay seems to thrive on it. . . . Lindsay can't resist a friendly crowd. Maybe it's the Show Biz in him. Lindsay not only loves show people, he *is* show people (along with a lot of other things that his versatile personality envelopes). Besides his song-and-dance with Florence Henderson for the reporters, Lindsay did a stand-up comic monologue for the nation on the Johnny Carson show, and a New Act at Jane Morgan's Persian Room opening." Quoting Lindsay on what he might do if he ever left politics, the *Post* reported he said he "would think about" show business, but the Mayor added: "I don't think I'd be that good." The article commented: "He probably couldn't take the nightclub hecklers—and that's one of his political faults, too. Losing hurts too much, whether it's a touch football game or a tax program and he just can't bring himself to admit a mistake."

On a national scale, Emmet John Hughes wrote a column in the October 3, 1966, issue of *Newsweek,* entitled: "A Mayor for the Times." He commented: "He [Lindsay] is, most obviously, an impassioned activist and innovator. . . . Lindsay has defined his supreme purpose as the remaking of New York into 'The Proud City.' And he is a proud enough man to fight hard for nothing less."

After nine long and difficult months at John Lindsay's side, I knew that Emmet John Hughes was right. But I wasn't at all sure —as I had been at the beginning—that Lindsay's goal was really attainable.

12

"We did what we thought was right. It was worth fighting for, even though we lost."

As WE MOVED INTO October, the pace of the campaign for the Civilian Review Board quickened. However, the campaign was not being run from City Hall, but from a midtown hotel where Garth, Gottehrer, Kriegel and several other aides were running the daily routine and handling press inquiries. I had asked Martin Perlmutter to take on the public relations assignment for the FAIR campaign and he had obliged. In the meantime, I had been getting a great deal of assistance all summer and early fall from Joe Polser, who, like Perlmutter, was a former *Daily Mirror* reporter and had come into government after the death of that newspaper. Even with Laird and Troche working around-the-clock, I needed Polser's help so that one of the three of us regularly assigned to the Mayor's press office could take some time off. Polser responded beautifully and he was well liked by the press and the Mayor. I was fortunate, I thought, to have four good men to rotate at City Hall—Laird, Troche, Polser and Perlmutter.[1]

One of the public relations chores which I had not been assigned to, but which I gradually became a part of—working out an advertising program to promote New York City in conjunction with the business community—began to take up a lot of my time in early October. Young and Rubicam had been asked to work up a presentation on a theme for New York City which might attract more business. I accompanied the Mayor, Price and several executives of the Economic Development Council, including Paul Busse, its executive director, to a meeting at Y & R on Monday morning, October 3. It was a first-rate Madison Avenue presentation. The theme was entitled, very simply: "New York is New York" and it was carried out through the medium of one-page newspaper ads picturing the unique and varied aspects of New York. The idea was for the Mayor—if he liked the promotional campaign—to convince the City Council that it would be worthwhile to contribute some city funds for the literature and for making a movie. It was expected that large retail companies would pay for the ads in the newspapers and attach their companies' names at the bottom of the advertisement. This would be the first such joint city-corporate enterprise to my knowledge and it marked some very progressive and imaginative thinking on the part of the Economic Development Council and its membership. Lindsay was also impressed with the presentation, but tried to explain the political realities of getting funds from a Democratic comptroller and City Council president.

The businessmen reacted by saying that they understood the Mayor's political problems, but they suggested that the only way to find out if the other city officials would be willing to support the campaign would be to invite Mario Procaccino and Frank O'Connor to a similar presentation. That decided, we adjourned the meeting.

On the evening of October 6, I accompanied Lindsay to the Association of the Bar of the City of New York, where he gave a very good speech on the need to reform the method of selecting judges in New York City. "I believe," he told the group of 200 lawyers present, "the existing system for selecting judges—in New York City and throughout New York State—fails to produce jurists who fulfill Jefferson's exacting ideals. It fails because idealism does not govern the designation of our judges; it has been subordinated to the earthy practicalities of partisan politics." He urged the adoption of a "merit selection" and the appointments limited to recommendations of a non-partisan judicial selection committee. The Mayor received a standing ovation and, as I sat at the press table watching the reporters, I could see that even they, too, enjoyed his talk. It was one of the best I had heard him deliver. And, being a lawyer himself, he knew exactly how to capture his audience that night. The next day, Richard Witkin's account in the *New York Times* started on top of page one and was a major story headlined: LINDSAY PROPOSES APPOINTED JUDGES FOR COURTS HERE. I would have been happy that morning, except for another Lindsay story on the bottom of the page reporting an incident that had occurred the day before—and was blown way out of proportion. However, because it involved Lindsay and Senators Javits and Kennedy, it was page one news, too, with a large photo of all three men under a three-column headline which read: LINDSAY, KENNEDY, JAVITS IN SQUABBLE.

It grew out of a comment Senator Javits had made on October 5. Javits had told an interviewer that he had asked Kennedy and Lindsay to meet with him over the weekend to discuss their efforts to retain the Civilian Review Board. Javits had been quoted in the press as saying: "I don't think we've really gotten off the ground."

On the morning of October 6, several reporters wanted to know if the Mayor had any comment. I went in to see the Mayor and found he was angry about Javits' implied criticism of the campaign.

"Tell the press," Lindsay declared, "that 'the Mayor is glad Senator Javits has finally agreed to be of active help and hopes that Senator Kennedy also will take to the streets with him.' " I left his office and released the statement in that exact form.

About 11:30, I left with the Mayor in his car for Columbia University, where he was scheduled to talk to the National Conference of Editorial Writers. After the luncheon, we were driving down through Central Park when the car telephone rang. It was Al Troche, relaying a question from the reporters in Room 9: Would Lindsay meet with Javits and Kennedy over the weekend? I gave Lindsay the message while holding the car phone in my hand.

Lindsay seemed to relish the idea of continuing his battle with Javits. "Tell Troche to tell the press," he said with a slight smile, "that I am ready to meet with them and that Javits told me he would physically produce Kennedy. I'm waiting to hear from Javits concerning Kennedy, before I decide on my meeting."

Still holding the phone, I looked at Lindsay for a moment and replied: "I don't think you should say it in quite those words."

Lindsay glared at me. "That's exactly how I want to say it, damn it. Now tell it to Troche." He seemed genuinely disturbed at me for even questioning him. I decided not to argue with him any further and gave the statement to Troche, who then released the following to the press: "Senator Javits had promised Mayor Lindsay he would physically produce Senator Kennedy. Mayor Lindsay is waiting to hear from Senator Javits concerning Kennedy, before he decides on any meeting."

Three hours later—about 3:30 P.M.—Senator Kennedy (who I later learned was given Lindsay's comment while he was on the floor of the Senate) released a statement from Washington which read as follows: "Senator Javits spoke to me yesterday about a meeting on this matter and I agreed to meet on Saturday in New York City, provided the Senate was not in session. I was not informed at that time that I was to be 'physically produced' by anyone. My dealings with Senator Javits are always characterized by candor and decency. When and if similar good manners and courtesy are learned at City Hall, I would be happy to meet with the Mayor."

By this time, I was back in City Hall and I couldn't quite believe that the whole thing had been blown up into a major public fight. I had had a feeling that Lindsay was taking a risk in the car when he insisted on using the term "physically produced" —but he had intended a slap at Javits, not at Kennedy. When the reporters came to me with the Associated Press copy of Kennedy's statement asking for a further comment from the Mayor, I went inside and showed it to the Mayor. He looked at me and said bluntly: "You're the press secretary. Get me out of this one. Tell the press I never used the word 'physically.' "

Back in the press room I told the reporters the message had been garbled between myself and Troche and that there had been a "misunderstanding" between the Mayor and the Senator. In an effort to patch up the damage, I added: "The Mayor wishes to clear up this misunderstanding immediately. He is very anxious to get together with Senator Kennedy and Senator Javits and he has nothing but the highest esteem for them. His only intention here is to work closely and cooperatively with both of these out-standing Senators on the immediate and imperative goal." It was now about 6:30 P.M.

Without telling the press, I telephoned Washington and spoke with Kennedy's office. I told his aide that I had released the origi-nal statement and that the Mayor had not known about it. I said I would assume full responsibility. The aide said he would relay the message to the Senator. Then I went back into the Mayor's office and advised him to telephone Kennedy and to apologize to him. He did.

Meanwhile, Dave Garth at FAIR headquarters released this statement in an effort to minimize the conflict: "The whole thing is a problem of communications between three energetic men de-voted to the same cause."

At 7:45 P.M., a Kennedy aide in Washington telephoned a news-man and said: "The Mayor called Senator Kennedy and apolo-gized. The Senator was happy to accept his apologies."

On Saturday, October 8, Senators Kennedy and Javits came to Gracie Mansion for the meeting. I did not attend because I was busy taking care of the press outside of the Mansion. After a ses-sion that lasted about an hour, the three men emerged together and stood on top of the front stairway entrance. They said they were in full agreement with the need to save the Civilian Review Board. Lindsay seemed nervous; Kennedy seemed his usual sharp but reserved self; Javits talked more than either of the others and held a press conference of his own after the official conference was over. All in all, however, I was relieved that the event had taken place—especially after the kind of publicity the meeting had gotten during the previous week.

Lindsay subsequently took a walking tour in Brooklyn with Senator Javits. This was, by now, a daily occurrence for the Mayor, each walk in a different location starting about 5 in the afternoon. He always seemed happiest when he was walking among the people of the city. He once told me: "I can tell they are responding. I can see it in their eyes." I could see the joy written across his face as we moved from Spanish Harlem to Queens to Brooklyn. He needed to know how people reacted to him. It was, I had decided by this time, not only a necessary part of the "Lindsay mystique" to be seen on the streets, but also a vital part of his personality. He was a natural and highly successful campaigner. Prior to becoming Mayor, most of his time had been spent on the streets of midtown Manhattan. So these walks were, in effect, a continuing test of his own popularity in the other boroughs.

By now, his October schedule was beginning to grow so crowded that there was very little time for the Mayor to spend with his family or friends. I noticed as I traveled with him in his car and as I watched him in his office that he became more and more concerned about the outcome of the Civilian Review Board. One day in his office I asked him what he thought the chances were.

"Well, I don't know," he replied. "I am not at all sure that we're going to win. But one thing I am sure of—we're right. I have never been so sure of anything in my life."

Lindsay told me this just before going into a meeting in the new wing of the Mansion with some fifty businessmen whom he was entertaining in the hope of raising some funds for the campaign. This day was typical of the crowded calendar he was trying to meet. Harvey Rothenberg, himself under tremendous pressure to schedule the Mayor for ten times as many events in a day as time permitted, had been trying to pacify a demanding public. Each day two separate schedules—one for the Mayor and three or four mayoral aides, including myself, and the other, for the newsmen—were run off. I usually received them in the late afternoon from Edie Radley, Rothenberg's assistant, who originally had been my secretary. I tried to get the press schedule to Room 9 by 4 or 5 P.M. at the latest. Following are the Mayor's "confidential" and "press" schedules for a typical day—Tuesday, October 11, 1966. I usually disclosed to the media only those appointments which had immediate news value and which were not of a highly personal nature:

Confidential
JOHN V. LINDSAY
Tuesday, October 11, 1966

8:00 A.M. Dr. Howard Brown, Mr. Joseph Terenzio and Fred Hayes re: Bellevue Hospital-Capital Budget.
THE MANSION

9:00 A.M. Breakfast meeting re: Civ. Rev. Brd.—Jos. Willen and group of approx. 50 businessmen. Conference call from Javits and Kennedy to come in during breakfast.
THE MANSION—upstairs—NEW WING

10:00 A.M.   Launch telephone campaign for Civ. Rev. Brd.
             THE MANSION—downstairs—NEW WING
NOTE: Harvey R. to drive down with JVL to City Hall.
11:00 A.M.   Briefing prior to press conference at 11:30 A.M. Woody Klein.
11:30 A.M.   Press conference re: Announcement by JVL and Austin Heller re: Redirection/NYC Air Resource Management Program.
             BLUE ROOM
12:30 P.M.   Attends Mayor's Citizens Luncheon, Bud Palmer. Gasner's Rest.
             76 Duane St.   *Tele: RE 2–0879*
             (SECURITY has LIST of those attending)
2:15 P.M.   Col. Harold Riegelman.
2:30 P.M.   Gordon MacLachlan, Nuffield Provincial Hospitals Trust (England), and Dr. Sandy Robertson.
3:15 P.M.   Drop-in, meeting with Bob Sweet and John Rooney (PBA).
             BOB SWEET'S OFFICE
4:00 P.M.   Speak, promotion ceremonies-Police Department. Comm. Leary. Police Academy, 235 East 20th St. *Tele: OR 7–1311*
             (SECURITY has partial list of those being promoted).
5:15 P.M.   Holding for either D.A.C. or Walking tour possibly with Frank O'Connor re: Civ. Rev. Brd.
Arr. approx. 7:30 P.M.
8:30 P.M.   *BLACK TIE:* Speak, annual Columbus dinner sponsored by Columbus Citizens Committee, Inc., Fortune Pope, pres. Waldorf Astoria Hotel, Grand Ballroom, 50th St. and Park Ave., Manhattan.
             (SECURITY has FAX SHEET)   *Tele: EL 5–3000*
9:15 P.M.   Speak, 40th anniversary annual dinner-dance, Cocoa
Black Tie: Merchants' Association. Wm. I. Witkin presently Pres. N.Y. Cocoa Exchange and formerly Pres./Cocoa Merchants' Assoc. Hotel Pierre, Grand Ballroom, 61st St. and 5th Ave.
             (SECURITY has FAX SHEET)   *Tele: TE 8–8000*

Press Schedule
Mayor John V. Lindsay
Tuesday, October 11, 1966

11:30 A.M.   Announcement with Commissioner Austin N. Heller on Air Pollution Control Department activities. Followed by:
             GENERAL NEWS CONFERENCE
             BLUE ROOM

4:00 P.M.   Speaks, Police Department promotion ceremonies, Police Academy, 235 East 20th St., Manhattan.

7:30 P.M.   Speaks, Columbus Day Dinner, Waldorf Astoria, Grand Ballroom, 50th St. and Park Ave., Manhattan.

9:15 P.M.   Speaks, 40th anniversary dinner of the Cocoa Merchants' Association, Hotel Pierre, Grand Ballroom, 61st St. and 5th Ave., Manhattan.

The review board continued to occupy Lindsay's major attention. On Wednesday, October 12, Columbus Day, he met again with Javits and Kennedy at Gracie Mansion to plan more strategy. After marching in the parade from 45th Street up Fifth Avenue to the reviewing stand at 65th Street, he left on a walking tour for the review board with Bronx Borough President Herman Badillo. They met in front of Alexander's department store on East Fordham Road off the Grand Concourse and attracted large crowds as they walked side by side. Later in the afternoon, Lindsay returned to Manhattan and continued his walking tour from a new starting point in a new neighborhood: 72nd Street and Broadway.

The next day, we held a press conference announcing the names of an Executive Committee for FAIR at the Governor Clinton Hotel. Afterward, I sat in on a meeting the Mayor had with Judge James J. Comerford and a few other men interested in the Mayor's official statement that he intended to curtail public parades on Fifth Avenue because of the tremendous expense to the city. It was clear that by making this statement, Lindsay had alienated himself from Comerford, who had long served as chairman of the annual St. Patrick's Day Parade on Fifth Avenue. The meeting started with Comerford politely telling Lindsay that traditions like the St. Patrick's Day Parade were not viewed lightly by the Irish in New York. He made it clear that Lindsay would be making a major political blunder if he persisted in ruling out Fifth Avenue as the site and moved it to Central Park, which Lindsay had suggested several weeks earlier. As Comerford continued talking, Lindsay's mood softened. He realized that it would be foolish to try and change the tradition. After Comerford finished, Lindsay turned to the group and said:

"Gentlemen, I'm surprised that you have any doubts of my intentions. I wouldn't permit anybody to interfere with the Irish on St. Patrick's Day. Fifth Avenue is yours!"

Everybody broke out into laughter and the Mayor had won some new friends—or, putting it another way, avoided making some new enemies. That turned out to be a good day for the Mayor. At the Alfred E. Smith Memorial Dinner at the Waldorf later in the evening, where Richard Nixon was the main speaker, Lindsay shared the limelight with Rockefeller and Nixon.

On Friday, October 14, I helped arrange for a press conference in which the Mayor and Public Works Commissioner William Mattison announced plans for a $4.1 million program to improve and renovate Bellevue Hospital. The Mayor's announcement also paid tribute to his "new health services team" of Dr. Howard Brown, health services administrator, and Joseph V. Terenzio, Hospitals commissioner. The next day, Saturday, the Mayor went to Washington—at President Johnson's request—to attend a meeting of Mayors hosted by the White House. Before he left, I asked Lindsay why he was going. He looked at me with a smile and replied: "This fellow never tells you why he calls. But when he calls, you go. What am I going to do? Ask him what he wants?" As it turned out, Johnson wanted to brief the Mayors on forthcoming legislation for his Model Cities program. The fact that he did not tell them why he was calling them in was a typical Johnson maneuver and both the public and the politicians were familiar with the President's way of operating by this time.

On Sunday morning I accompanied Lindsay to St. George's Church at 207 East 16th Street where the Mayor gave a blistering talk in favor of the Civilian Review Board. It was the first time he had used a church pulpit as a platform for a talk on this subject and, as a result, there was considerable controversy the next day in the newspapers and on the radio and TV as to the propriety of Lindsay's move. I thoroughly enjoyed the talk and the minister, the Reverend Edward O. Miller, an old friend of the Mayor's from the days the Lindsays lived in the Stuyvesant Town housing complex nearby, was an impressive, outspoken clergyman who publicly defended Lindsay's right to talk about important social issues in the church.

On Monday, October 17, I accompanied the Mayor to the *Times'* publisher's dining room on the eleventh floor of the newspaper's building at 229 West 43rd Street. We had been invited to have lunch with Arthur Hays Sulzberger, chairman; John B.

Oakes, editor, editorial page; Clifton Daniel, managing editor; Andrew Fisher, and Monroe Green, vice presidents; Lester Markel, associate editor; Richard D. Peters, a member of the editorial board (and my former editor at the *World-Telegram and Sun*), and Daniel Schwarz, Sunday editor.

"Well, we're delighted to have you and the Mayor here as our guests," John Oakes said in a pleasant even-mannered voice, trying to put both of us at ease. A quiet-spoken man with whom I had talked several times during the year, Oakes began the discussion with the Mayor. Some of the other executives also asked questions. Clifton Daniel tried to arouse the Mayor by asking him why the city, instead of private corporations, didn't pay for entertaining foreign officials, but the Mayor responded:

"Mr. Daniel, I don't think either you or the taxpayers would be very happy if we used public funds to hold parties for foreign dignitaries while there is such a desperate need for money for schools, for housing, for so many worthwhile projects for the poor."

Daniel responded: "But, Mr. Mayor, we don't allow any of our people on the *Times* to accept any gratuities from anybody outside. We pay all of the expenses of all of our people. I think you should do the same."

"The difference between your management and mine, Mr. Daniel," Lindsay responded matter-of-factly, "is that I am a public official responsible for public funds and you are a private businessman responsible for private funds."

That ended the discussion on that particular point.

Lindsay handled himself well during the luncheon and impressed those members of the *Times* management who questioned him closely on political issues. We discussed everything from the transit strike to the Civilian Review Board. Later that day, Lindsay walked the streets of the Bronx, accompanied by Herman Badillo, in still another campaign pitch for the review board.

Every once in a while during the year, Lindsay would try and wrap up our acccomplishments to date in one major speech before a large audience. One such occasion was before the Audit Bureau of Circulations on Wednesday, October 19. In a memorable, well-written speech on "Our Cities and the Course of Our Country," Lindsay enunciated the theme which had won him national prominence: "The future of our nation will be decided in our cities." And, in calling for more Federal resources, he listed some of the programs and policies which his Administration had started to undertake in New York. "In New York City," he said, "we are trying to face up to the realities." And then he spoke about reorganization, community development programs and all the other steps we were taking. He also recommended that Congress establish a committee on urban affairs in both the Senate and House.

The rest of that day was spent in the streets campaigning for the review board. The pace was quickening and each day the Mayor was out of City Hall a little more. By now, he was beginning to leave his office about 3 P.M. and campaign outside until midnight, sometimes making as many as six different talks in as many locations. However, it began to seem clear to those of us at the Mayor's side during these walks that the people were more interested in other issues; that they did not thoroughly understand why he was spending so much time talking about a review board. Many asked him why he didn't trust the cops, why he wasn't spending more time on more pressing matters. On one particular day, Thursday, October 19, Lindsay and Bobby Kennedy campaigned together for the first time on the streets. I accompanied the Mayor as we drove to a platform on the northeast corner of 59th Street and Lexington Avenue. Despite a driving rain, a rush-hour crowd of more than 5,000 gathered around us to see Lindsay and Kennedy together. I stood within a few feet of both men as they took turns talking to the crowd on microphones that carried their voices above the sounds of the traffic. Lindsay was nervous and ineffective. He put on his raincoat and one of the detectives covering him held an umbrella over his head. Kennedy, meanwhile, remained coatless and hatless and seemed to be enjoying himself more than Lindsay did. After a while Kennedy struck up a give-and-take with the crowd. Although he was essentially a less articulate speaker than Lindsay, he knew how to reach a crowd better and he was proving it here. But when he asked for a show of hands, a majority of his listeners signaled they would vote against the board. He merely smiled, his teeth flashing and his mop of wet hair flying in the wind. Lindsay stood by looking grim.

After a few minutes both men descended from the platform and began walking downtown on the east side of the street. The crowd seemed to gather around Kennedy while Lindsay fell back. I turned to Lindsay and urged him to try and catch up with Kennedy, but Sid Davidoff, who was holding the Mayor's arm guiding him, kept Lindsay back. The Mayor turned to me: "How naive can you be?" He apparently didn't want to be seen with Kennedy any more and was willing to take his chances on collecting his own crowd. Davidoff then somehow steered Lindsay to his waiting car and, against the pull of a rapidly growing crowd, they disappeared into the car and were off to the next stop, leaving Kennedy on the street still signing autographs.

Later that evening, one group walked out on Lindsay as he was about to address a gathering of some 400 persons in the auditorium of Public School 213 in the East New York section of Brooklyn. Some 250 people marched out as soon as he started talking about the review board. The disgruntled residents, who said they wanted to talk about installing new traffic lights in the area, picketed in front of the school while waiting for Lindsay to finish his talk. The newspapers quoted one resident as saying: "We don't need a crown prince, we need a Mayor." Lindsay's reception at his next stop in Brooklyn was also hostile. He was met by anti-review board pickets at the entrance to PS 68 in Brooklyn. His speech was received with a scattering of polite applause and as he got into his car to leave, a group of teen-agers shouted: "Get the hell away from here and don't come back."

There were other signs of discontent around the Mayor inside government that were also beginning to disturb him at this time. His advertising program to promote New York had been virtually ignored by the City Council. And the reorganization plan was stalled. The Mayor had submitted to the Council leaders "confidential" copies of the 144-page omnibus bill to consolidate fifty city agencies into ten superagencies, but he had found out through aides of the City Council leaders that they were not even thinking of considering the bill until after the November 8 election and that the bill was virtually doomed in the form he submitted it. The master plan for government reorganization, already delayed, looked as if it would not get off the ground for several more months. At a City Hall press conference on November 19, the subject came up and I held my breath as the Mayor prepared to answer the question. He had become very testy in private toward members of the Council and I was hoping he would not attack them publicly as he had attacked the State Legislature.

"I don't really foresee any problems," he said calmly. "I am aware that certain aspects of the administrations will require legislation from both the city and state. My people are drafting such bills at present as you gentlemen know. In the meantime, I can carry out the intent of the reorganization by executive order for an indefinite period."

On Thursday, October 20, in an early morning press conference, the Mayor made an announcement which I felt was critically important to our long-range goal of making municipal government more efficient. He announced that he had enlisted a group of six leaders from private industry in a move to improve the administrative operations of city government. He named the six men to a new Management Advisory Council to work with Deputy Mayor–City Administrator Tim Costello. Lindsay asked them to infuse what he called "high efficiency management methods" into the governmental structure. The six executives were: Alfred E. Perlman, president of the New York Central Railroad; A. L. Williams, chairman of the executive committee of the International Business Machines Corporation; Fred J. Borch, president of the General Electric Company; Gilbert W. Fitzhugh, chairman of the board of the Metropolitan Life Insurance Company; Birny Mason, Jr., chairman of the board of the Union Carbide Company; and Philip D. Reed, director of the American Express Company. About three weeks before, the Mayor had named a seventeen-member Operations Research Council to work with Costello in introducing scientific techniques into the operation of city government. In announcing the new six-man Committee, Lindsay said: "My Administration is dedicated to the task of bringing to city government the streamlined, high efficiency methods of management that have revolutionized the business world."

The Mayor's announcement was a definite "plus," but it did not overshadow a troubling development which the *Times* had reported in the paper on that same morning. The newspaper disclosed that the alleged sale of promotions to supervisory posts in the Sanitation Department was being investigated by Investigations Commissioner Arnold G. Fraiman. The newspaper story said there was "a strong possibility that there may be indictments." The story reported that the promotion of some 55 men within the department due for increases from $1,600 to $3,000 had been blocked by Bob Price. According to the newspaper account, Price had directed Sanitation Commissioner Joseph F. Periconi to cancel a ceremony on October 3, scheduled for the next day, that would have installed the men in higher-salaried posts. Price was quoted in the story as saying, "An investigation is underway. No details will be released pending the conclusion of the investigation. However, after discussion with Commissioner Fraiman we believe that these are very serious charges. If these charges are sustained, it would appear to be an appropriate matter for referral to the District Attorney and the grand jury. Any further comment would be harmful to the investigation."

I had heard rumors the day before about such an investigation, but when Charles Grutzner of the *Times* had called I had referred him to Price, who had been conferring with Fraiman and the Mayor. But I was troubled because I did not know any of the details myself. Nevertheless, I realized that the Mayor didn't know much more and that, so far, the only paper to make an inquiry was the *Times*.

Saturday, October 22, was by far the most hectic weekend up to this point in the Civilian Review Board campaign. Five rallies were slated between 72nd Street and 110th Street on Broadway between 4:15 P.M. and 5:35 P.M. Accompanying Lindsay were Congressman William Fitts Ryan (in a rare show of alliance with Lindsay), State Senator Manfred Ohrenstein, State Assemblymen Albert H. Blumenthal and Jerome Kretchmer, and City Councilman Theodore S. Weiss. The following Monday morning, Lindsay continued to team up with Democrats who shared his strong feelings about the review board. His walk started at 10:30 A.M., from 145th Street and Harlem River Drive along with Borough President Percy Sutton.

Edward O'Neill's column in the *Daily News* the following Monday morning, October 24, didn't please me, but as I read it I realized he was close to the truth. O'Neill wrote: "In his all-out,

no-punches-pulled drive to save his civilian-dominated police review board, Mayor Lindsay has let himself in for real trouble.
City Hall Mayor-watchers, an astute breed, believe the Mayor may
have jeopardized his political future by his fiery campaign. And
because of the enemies he's been making, the very board he's so
strongly espousing may be toppled by voters as a protest against
the Mayor. There are those, even in the Lindsay camp, who are
beginning to feel he chose the wrong issue at the wrong time to
make a stand that will have an important effect on his political
future. . . . Here's the big question being asked by political
veterans and those Mayor-watchers: 'How can a guy who's just
raised everybody's taxes go before his own electorate and ask
them to do him a favor by voting for ANYTHING?' Come to think
of it, how can he?"

On the same morning, in the *Times*, Price was quoted in some
detail describing how the Sanitation Department bribe system
worked. He said some Sanitation men had been forced to pay
bribes for promotions and he charged that "this apparently has
been the way of doing business in the department for years."
Times reporter Michael Stern, a friend of mine and former
World-Telegram colleague, quoted Price further as saying that
the promotion-by-payoff system was the product of "years of cyni-
cism, apathy and bureaucratic decay." Price had issued his statement after conferring with Fraiman. Fraiman had telephoned me
at home to let me know that Price would be issuing the statement
and would give out some of the details of the investigation.

Between the sanitation scandal and the possible review
board disaster, I was beginning to feel uneasy about Lindsay's
public image once again. I realized that Price was playing the
role of chief source of information in order to protect Lindsay
from direct scandal, but I still did not like the situation. Price's
charge that the payoff system for promotions had been a "way of
doing business for years" was, of course, vigorously denied the
next day by two former Sanitation commissioners under Bob
Wagner—Frank J. Lucia and Paul R. Screvane. Lucia called
Price's charge "nonsense," and Screvane, who had himself worked
his way up during a twenty-eight-year career in the department
to commissioner, declared: "I was promoted through every rank
from truck driver to commissioner. I never had to pay anyone

for my job, nor do I know anyone who did. During my tenure as commissioner, where appointive jobs were available, I selected the most qualified men for promotion, based on my professional knowledge of their merits and ability to do the work. No payment was ever made or sought." Lucia went one step further and asserted that, in his opinion, it would be impossible for the practice to prevail without the commissioner's knowledge. Periconi, asked to comment, referred reporters to an aide who told the press that the commissioner was "cooperating with the Department of Investigation" and that Periconi would not be commenting. I felt that this was a mistake on Periconi's part. A former member of the Transit Authority, and later Bronx Borough President, Periconi had lost that post to Badillo in the November, 1965, election and was then appointed by Lindsay to the commissionership.

On the next evening, October 25, I delivered a talk to a membership dinner of the Men's Association of Congregation Rodelph Sholom on West 83rd Street. I had been invited to talk to the group by Rabbi Louis I. Newman, father of a former high school friend. I had not seen either man for twenty years, but when I received the letter from Rabbi Newman I willingly accepted because I felt it might help the Mayor in his Civilian Review Board battle. I was also aware that there was a certain amount of backlash among middle-class Jewish voters. This was confirmed for me personally when I spoke to this group. The questions centered around why the Mayor was "doing so much" for all the Negroes and Puerto Ricans and "deserting" the middle class. I could clearly sense that a good many people in the audience had no intention of voting to retain "Lindsay's Review Board," as it had come to be known.

On Wednesday, October 26, we had a pleasant change of pace. We flew, via a charter flight, to Philadelphia where Lindsay was to participate in a "Mayor's Panel" on urban problems sponsored by the Westinghouse Broadcasting Company. The show would be nationally televised and I thought it would be good exposure for Lindsay. Sid Gardner and I were the only mayoral aides to accompany Lindsay to the Warwick Hotel in Philadelphia for lunch and then to the broadcast. The Mayors of Phoenix, Arizona, Huntsville, Alabama, and several other major cities were present. Just before air time Lindsay asked me for a lined yellow pad. He had no prepared notes, but with about fifteen minutes to go he wrote down a few phrases to jog his memory during the program. He expressed himself with conviction during the show and was able to support his statements with facts. Later I glanced at his pad in the car on the trip to the airport on our way home and I noticed that it had these phrases scribbled on it: "National Crisis . . . total commitment . . . rhetoric . . . paper promises . . . community response . . . urban renewal funds . . . demonstration cities . . . quality of living. . . . People: streets, air, safety . . . estrangement . . . shaping up city government . . . city employees must live in city . . . regional tax . . . ghettos . . . housing: ⅔ apartment dwellings . . . housing and building code . . . decade of the city . . . ." The notes, scrawled in Lindsay's nearly illegible handwriting, gave me some insight into how his mind worked. He was able to reel off much information with just a few key phrases to set him in motion. I had always known that he had an unusual ability to retain facts—I had been briefing him for press conferences for ten months and he had never failed to remember what I had told him before each one—but this was a case where he had jotted down his own notes to organize his thoughts. I saved the notes and used them in drafts of later statements I was to prepare in his name.

When we returned to New York, we learned from Arnold Fraiman that the Sanitation Department inquiry had led to definite evidence of payoffs. He informed the Mayor that Vincent A. Starace, first deputy commissioner of the department, had refused to answer questions about the scandal. The next day, Lindsay called me into his office and we wrote out a statement[2] in which he explained the legalities of why he was dismissing Starace from the $17,500-a-year job. He also disclosed that another employee, a foreman, had been suspended. The following morning, October 28, the *Times* carried a three-column headline on the page one lead news story:

LINDSAY OUSTS A TOP AIDE
IN SANITATION FOR SILENCE
AT INQUIRY ON JOB SELLING

The story quoted Fraiman as revealing that payments of $500 or $1,000 had been extorted from "innocent victims" who had earned promotions through Civil Service examinations, but had been threatened by "higher ups" that unless they paid they would not get the higher-salaried posts and might even be given unpleasant assignments. Periconi, who had appointed Starace as his top deputy a few days after the Lindsay Administration took office, told reporters he was "deeply shocked by the disclosures involving our department." Although Starace was a long-time friend of Periconi's, nobody believed that Periconi himself was involved. And, in an effort to protect himself, Periconi told the *Times* in an interview: "Mayor Lindsay has told me he wants me to stay, and he has every confidence in me." I knew the Mayor had telephoned Periconi, but knowing politics as I did, I doubted seriously that Periconi would be allowed to stay on. Periconi came over to City Hall to see the Mayor several times and, on each occasion, he looked more and more haggard and dismayed. Joe Periconi was known to be a decent, hard-working man whom everybody liked. I tried to console him when I saw him and felt very sorry for him as I watched him sitting outside of the Mayor's office, apparently waiting for Lindsay and Price to decide his future. I did not know the facts of the matter—perhaps Periconi should have known what was going on in his department—but, in any case, I was certain that he himself was personally honest.

On the morning of the 28th at a press conference I arranged in the Board of Estimate Chambers, the Mayor released a statement based on a report from the Association of the Bar of the City of New York saying that the fight over the Civilian Review Board had now entered into a "new phase" and he issued a warning that "Question No. 1" on the ballot, as it was called, "would do far more than destroy the new Civilian Review Board. The language of the referendum," he continued, "would also prohibit the Mayor, the City Council, the Board of Estimate and the commissioner of Investigation from investigating complaints against members of the Police Department. We are no longer talking about complaints of brutality or discourtesy. We are speaking of the entire breadth of citizen grievances, including graft and corruption."

The pressure was now fully on Lindsay. With only days to go, he faced what still seemed an uphill battle on the review board issue. As a result of all of his walking tours, however, he had come down with a heavy cold and temperature on Friday and the doctors ordered him to bed. It was one of those rare times when the Mayor gave in. I spoke to Mary Lindsay at Gracie Mansion and she told me he had a very sore throat and a high fever and that he could hardly talk. As soon as word leaked out to the press, I was confronted by George Douris, a reporter for the *Long Island Star Journal* and president of the Newspaper Reporters Association, which was expecting Lindsay as its guest of honor at its annual dinner-dance the following night at the Hotel Roosevelt.

"Is Lindsay going to be able to make it?" he asked.

"I don't know, George," I responded. "It's up to the doctors. I certainly hope so."

"Look," he said, "I promised the boys that the Mayor would be there. We have a magazine with Lindsay on the cover in four-color. So I don't want to let the boys down, you understand?"

"Yes," I replied. "I'll do my best, George."

I telephoned Mary Lindsay late Friday night to see how the Mayor was feeling.

"Not so well," she said. "Look, Woody, those guys haven't done anything for John. Why the hell does he have to knock himself out getting out of a sick bed for them?"

"Because I promised them he would come," I said quietly. "And the party is built around him. He shouldn't let them down."

"Why not?" she said. "They are rude and impolite and all they do is give him a hard time."

"I know," I replied. "But it will hurt him if he doesn't appear."

"Well, he's going to speak on Sunday morning, you know, at the 200th anniversary of St. Paul's Chapel," she went on.

"The newspaper function is more important," I said flatly.

"No, it isn't," she said, her voice growing a little more impatient. "If he does anything, he'll go to church on Sunday."

"If he goes to church Sunday," I replied, "he goes to the Roosevelt tomorrow night. If he doesn't go to the Roosevelt, he shouldn't go to church on Sunday," I replied.

"Call me tomorrow and we'll see how he feels," Mary Lindsay said, apparently not anxious to argue any more.

I had rarely contradicted Mary because I knew that John wanted to listen to her and that she often played the part of the "spoiler" to make it easier for him to get away from meetings of social functions he didn't want to attend. I also knew that Mary had told Harvey Rothenberg that she wanted Sundays to remain relatively free so that he could spend more time with his four children.

"Time. Time is the problem," I had overheard Lindsay tell a newsman in his office during an interview about his personal life. "One night recently, Annie, my third child, who's ten, was trying to communicate with me. I just wasn't focusing. She turned to me and said, 'Mr. Mayor, do you hear me?' I felt a little bad. I must have more communication with them. Little snatches of time are all you can do. That, and what can be saved on weekends. And we'll have to get away every once in a while."

Mary Lindsay was a warm, friendly and strong woman. She had always been very courtous to Audrey and me, and I had always gotten along well with her. I respected her desire to save some of John's time for his children. In this instance, however, I felt compelled to try and persuade her to let the Mayor come— or at least keep him in bed Sunday if he didn't make it to the newspaper party Saturday night—mostly, I admitted to her, because of the pressure from George Douris.

The next morning I received a telephone call at my home from Douris again.

"Well, is he coming?"

"I still don't know."

"Listen, Woody, you better get him there one way or another. Those guys are going to be sore if he doesn't show. That's all I can tell you. He'd better show."

"I'll do my best, George," I replied, a little appalled that he should be putting such pressure on me. I understood it, however. Douris was the president of the Newspaper Reporters Association and it would reflect badly on him if he failed to "produce" the Mayor.

That afternoon I called Mary Lindsay again.

"He's sick and he can't talk. He's worn out. I don't see how he can go out tonight," she said. "If he's going to talk in church tomorrow, I really don't see how he can go out."

"Look, Mary," I said carefully. "You're in a better position to know the answer to this question than I am. Let me ask you this:

Will I be endangering his health seriously if he makes a brief appearance—say fifteen minutes—at the Roosevelt?"

"Damn it," she said, "if you want him to get out of bed, then you'll be responsible for what happens to him," she replied. "But I don't think it'll kill him if that's what you want to hear. Call me later and we'll decide."

By 7 P.M., when I arrived with Audrey at a pre-dinner cocktail party in a suite at the Roosevelt, I still did not know if Lindsay would make it. George Douris greeted me and asked me once again if the Mayor was coming. I told him I hoped so, but that I would be talking with him in a few minutes. I excused myself and went into another room.

"Okay," Mary said when I called. "I'll prop him up and put a monkey suit on him. You meet me at the 45th Street entrance to the Roosevelt and we'll stay for fifteen minutes. Is that a deal?"

"You have a deal," I said, and hung up.

Lindsay's appearance at the dinner was an anticlimax. He arrived in time for some of the entertainment and he could barely smile. He looked drawn and pale. I took one look at him and I was sorry that I had forced him out of bed. I felt terrible. I went over to him and told him I had to do it. He nodded, smiling a little, as if he understood. By this time, he was under heavy medication and I doubted whether he was completely aware of what was happening to him. I accompanied him to the ballroom and sat him down next to my wife and me.

The photographers gathered around, Douris posed with him, and several politicians came by to shake his hand. After fifteen minutes, Douris called him to the microphone to say a few words. Lindsay could hardly stand up. He thanked the newsmen for inviting him, but while he was talking the crowd failed to quiet down. They continued to talk and drink. It was a rude greeting for a Mayor who had just gotten out of a sick bed. I sat in my chair wondering whether it had all been worthwhile. I had my doubts. Within a few minutes after he spoke, I nodded to Mary that it was okay to leave if she wanted to. She got up, took Lindsay by the arm, and they disappeared for the evening.

The next morning, Mary Lindsay took John Lindsay to church. I had succeeded in my mission and she had completed hers. I knew very well that Lindsay put a great deal of faith in the way his wife managed his personal life. He had once told me during one of our car rides together how she kept things in perspective for him. "My wife's good at handling things. She's tough. Mary reminds me, whenever I get very upset, that I'm only here for a visit and I can't change the world."

November started off auspiciously enough with another press conference on Thursday, November 3, at Gracie Mansion with Senators Javits and Kennedy. The next day, November 4, a group of labor leaders—mostly representing smaller unions —came to City Hall for another special press conference in support of the review board. Over the final weekend before Election Day, Lindsay made a dozen more public appearances, including a talk at a church and a synagogue and a walking rally, accompanied by Senator Javits, through Washington Square and down into the lower East Side of Manhattan. In my concern for the review board issue, I had almost forgotten that Nelson Rockefeller was running for reelection against Frank O'Connor and Franklin D. Roosevelt, Jr.

The night of the election, November 1, I spent the early part of the evening setting up the necessary facilities for a major press conference in the library at Gracie Mansion. The Lindsays were entertaining a few personal friends in their living room—Mr. and Mrs. Herbert Brownell, Federal Judge Charles M. Metzner and a few others. About midevening, as the votes began to trickle in, a few newsmen arrived, mostly magazine and feature writers who had been assigned to do "color" stories on the Mayor's reaction. I accompanied the Mayor for a quick forty-minute trip to the FAIR headquarters at the Governor Clinton Hotel. The atmosphere there was subdued. I felt defeat in the air.

Soon after I returned to Gracie Mansion with the Mayor I went back into the new wing where two TV sets had been left on for newsmen watching the returns. After a few minutes, Walter Cronkite was saying, "The Civilian Review Board suffered a crushing defeat today." Then the TV screen showed Norman Frank, community relations counsel for the Patrolmen's Benevolent Association, addressing a jubilant crowd. "For your wonderful support," he was saying, "I only say God bless you. . . . It is a

mandate . . . constructive approach . . . joining hands . . . cooperation . . . dedicate our efforts. . . . The Police Department will
perform with dedication and persistence. . . ."

I walked away, followed by a pack of reporters, to the downstairs library where the TV cameras were set up. The camera
crews were wiring and adjusting lights and arranging microphones. I told the press corps that the Mayor would be arriving
in a few minutes. Then I went back into his living room to bring
him in. He appeared glum but not upset. Nobody said very much
as we prepared to leave the living room and go downstairs to
the library and the press conference. Lindsay was wearing a dark-
gray suit and a blue tie. As we appeared before the press, he
smiled and took his place in the glare of the lights. It was nearly
midnight now. Behind him, next to a wall of bookshelves, stood
Mary Lindsay, her hands folded; she was wearing a pink dress
with a gold pin. In one hand, Lindsay held a sheet of lined
yellow paper, at the top of which he had scrawled "Rockefeller"
underlined. He began to speak, slowly and deliberately:

"First of all, I'd like to express my heartiest congratulations to
Governor Rockefeller," he began, glancing down at his hand-
written statement. After a few words about the Governor, he
turned to the review board. "I wish to thank all those of you
who have worked courageously and tirelessly to sustain the review board, particularly David Garth, his colleagues at FAIR,
and the co-chairmen of FAIR, Senators Javits and Kennedy. We
think we have stood for an important principle and I should like
to thank all of those who had the courage to stand with us. I
have every confidence in our Police Department and in its commitment, with Commissioner Leary, to the maintaining of the
public safety and the improvement of community relations."
Then he folded the yellow piece of paper, put it away and stood
with his hands in his pockets, ready to answer questions.

"What do you think caused this defeat?" one reporter asked.

Lindsay's voice, turning somber and quiet, responded: "Emotion, and misunderstanding, and fear. But I don't really want to
go into that."

"Has this hurt you politically—has your prestige suffered?"
asked another newsman.

"I don't know," he replied. "I would regard that as irrelevant in any case. The important thing is that we did what we thought was right. It was worth fighting for, even though we lost."

The press conference did not last long. There wasn't much anyone could say. Lindsay smiled faintly as he thanked the reporters for coming to Gracie Mansion. Then he turned to go upstairs with Mary. It was the end of a long, confusing and complicated campaign and I was relieved that it was finally over.

13 *"I'm in trouble with the Republican Party, with the middle class voters... and with the press."*

IN THE AFTERMATH of the review board defeat, the *Times* ran a story on November 10 stating that Joe Periconi had tried to resign, but had agreed to stay on briefly to complete the reorganization of his department. The news did not come as a surprise to me because I knew that Periconi had been talking with Price and the Mayor. Whatever discussions the Sanitation commissioner had been having with Lindsay, it appeared to me that Periconi would not be remaining with us very long and that the sanitation scandal had been a real blow to the Lindsay Administration.

Lindsay, nevertheless, plunged onward into his work, meeting in the early days of November with business executives to discuss the need to attract more industry to the city; with health and welfare officials to discuss the growing welfare burdens; and with police and law enforcement experts to discuss alcoholism and what could be done about it. On November 14, he revealed the details of his reorganization plan in a talk to the Association of the Bar of the City of New York. He also stepped up his consultations with air pollution specialists, traffic consultants, and others in all fields of government. I knew that Lindsay wanted to make up for all the time he had lost campaigning for the review board. He was beginning to realize how much remained to be done if we were going to accomplish anything at all during our first year in office. That afternoon, November 14, Lindsay called me on my black office telephone and asked me if I could have breakfast with him at Gracie Mansion the following morning at 8 A.M.

"Anything urgent?" I asked the Mayor.

"A personal matter," he replied. "I'll go into details with you in the morning, okay?"

"Fine," I responded. As I hung up, I felt for a moment that ten-and-a-half months of tensions were soon to come to a close. That night when I went home I told my wife that my intuitive reaction to the Mayor's telephone call was that he was going to ask me to take another post in the Administration. I had heard rumors that Harry O'Donnell, who had handled the Mayor's press relations during the campaign, might be returning if Bob Price left. And, of course, rumors of Price's "impending" departure had been reported in the press for months.

I awakened early the next morning, November 15, and my driver, Joe Mandato, was waiting for me downstairs. As we made our way to the East Side Drive and up the highway toward the Mansion, I was quite certain of what was about to happen, but I wasn't sure how Lindsay would handle it. He had never said anything to me about our problems with the press all year. I decided that no matter what happened it would be for the best. We drove through the front gates and up to the main entrance to the Mansion. I stepped out and asked Mandato to wait for me. I rang the doorbell and walked in—this was a routine the Lindsays had come to expect. Mary Lindsay came down the spiral stairway and told me that the Mayor would be down in a few minutes. She was cheerful and friendly.

I walked into the dining room and saw places set for the two of us. As I looked around, I realized that after all of those months at Lindsay's side, this was the first time I had ever eaten breakfast alone with him. He came in, smiling, and asked me to sit down at the table. We chatted for a few minutes, drank our orange juice, and then he looked up at me and said softly:

"Woody, I've asked Harry O'Donnell to come down from Albany. I'm in trouble with the Republican Party, with the middle class voters, with the City Council and the Albany Legislature—and with the press. Harry's been around a long time. He knows Albany and he knows the Governor. I have to do something about repairing my relationship with Nelson. Harry knows Republican politics and he's needed now. I think you'll agree. Bob Price is leaving at the end of the year so Harry's agreed to come and join us. I want you to stay on, however, and be an assistant to me at City Hall."

I sat motionless. I looked at Lindsay and replied:

"Fine, John. It's okay with me."

"Nobody has been more loyal to me than you, Woody," he continued. "You're a friend of many years. I want you to remain close by. I know you can help me in the area of housing and attracting new business to New York. You have the background and the contacts. You can help Jay Nathan [City Renewal commissioner] reorganize the housing agencies and get that super-agency started. You are needed and I definitely want you to remain."

"Okay, John," I said. "I'll stay for a while, but I will be wanting to get back to journalism."

"Understood," he said.

"You know," I continued, thinking that this would be a good time to talk with him about some of the real problems at City Hall, "I've been disappointed, almost shocked, at the way some of the men we work with have just been looking out for themselves. All year I have tried to cooperate with them, but I am appalled by the way in which they use their office for their own interests. And many of them are not particularly interested in you, either."

He confirmed my thoughts. "It's been a difficult year," he said. "Much more difficult than anyone could have imagined. You're right about some of the fellows. I have known it. Now let's you and I continue working together and get on with the job. You can announce the change anytime—the sooner the better. And you'll probably want to tell Laird and Troche to look around for new posts, either inside or outside the Administration."

"Why don't we let Harry meet them?" I responded. "They're both good men. I have confidence in them."

"He'll probably want to bring on his own staff, don't you think?"

"I don't know. I'll talk to Harry about them. I think they should remain if Harry wants them."

"Okay," the Mayor said. "You work out the details of your announcement and what happens to Laird and Troche."

We shook hands, he patted me on the back and I walked out the door to my waiting car.

When I returned to my office I called O'Donnell, who was vacationing in Arizona. I told him I planned to announce his appointment the next afternoon. We agreed to have lunch when he returned and I told him I would recommend that he retain Laird and Troche, whom he had not met. He said he wanted to meet them and to discuss the transition with me. We agreed that he would take over on or about December 1—exactly one year to the day that I had been named by Lindsay to the job of press secretary.

I soon realized by glancing at the morning newspaper that my job was only one in a series of shifts that would change the line-up of the Administration. The day before, November 15, Lindsay had named Samuel J. Kearing to succeed Joe Periconi as Sanitation commissioner. Lindsay had said Periconi would continue to assist him on "legislative matters," but most of us around City Hall knew that meant very little. In fact, Lindsay had argued with Price in front of me about Periconi's future. Price had demanded that Lindsay retain him in some capacity, but Lindsay had demurred and said he would "see what I can do." It was a strange change of roles, I had thought at the moment. Price was the man who was anxious not to hurt Periconi, who felt that Lindsay owed him something; Lindsay appeared to be willing to just let him go.

The following morning, Wednesday, November 16, I picked up the *Times* and found, much to my surprise, the story of Price's planned resignation on page one. The story, which did not carry a byline, noted that Price refused to confirm or deny the report, but it went so far as to say that his resignation was scheduled to be announced Friday. This was news to me. Lindsay had a press conference scheduled on another matter that morning for 10 A.M. and I decided to ask him to announce his plans for me and Harry.

"Let's get it over with," I told him in his office about 9:30.

"Okay," he said. "I'll bring it up first thing and you can say a few words, too. You pull up a chair next to mine at my desk in the Blue Room. We'll just handle it like anything else we've done together." I realized the press would be asking Lindsay about the story on Price and that Lindsay would have to admit it was true.

Lindsay opened the conference by confirming immediately that Price was leaving because of "overpowering personal considerations." The Mayor noted: "My old friend Bob Price has advised me that he intends to stick to our old plan, that is, for him to remain for one year." He praised Price as a "tough administrator" and a "good trouble shooter" and added: "Our association is very close and continues that way." He made no mention of published reports that his relationship with Price had been strained in the past twelve months.[1] Then, turning to me, Lindsay said he had decided to ask Harry O'Donnell to come to City Hall. He praised the work I had done and informed the reporters that I would be taking on a newly created post of assistant to the Mayor for housing and urban development (a title Lindsay and I had worked out at our Gracie Mansion breakfast). It was a short press conference. There were no questions, except for one from an NBC correspondent who wanted to know how I felt. "Pleased that I will be working in an area I wrote about for a decade," I answered, "and happy that I had the privilege of serving as the Mayor's first press secretary."

In the next few days, other stories in all the press reported further shifts—the impending appointments of Donald H. Elliott to succeed William F. R. Ballard as city planning commissioner; of Jay Nathan to get the job Edward Logue turned down—housing administrator; and the removal of Richard Rosen as the Mayor's legislative aide in Albany.

In the closing days of November, I carried out my press secretary duties, but I began to ease off. I worked ten or twelve hours, instead of sixteen or eighteen hours a day, and I started to make plans for my new role as a mayoral housing adviser. I had left housing for more than a year and I had not really been in close touch with the details, except for occasional conferences with two Lindsay housing officials, Charles Moerdler and Eugenia Flatow. I had, of course, sat in on planning sessions about housing problems in the Mayor's office, but I had not had much time to become involved in daily decisions.

Logue's rejection of the Mayor's invitation to head up the attack on New York City's slums—after he had studied the city and authored the well-known "Logue Report"—came as a disappointment to the Mayor and to many of us interested in housing who knew that Logue was the best man in the country for the job. I had met Logue several times, during trips to Washington when he would accompany the Mayor, along with Mike Sviridoff and several other nationally known experts in poverty and housing. Lindsay had managed to convince Sviridoff that New York was the place to be at this time, but Logue's refusal to join hurt the Mayor and possibly the housing program. He had submitted his final report on October 2. It called for centralizing every function dealing with urban renewal and housing under a single administrator, and for the construction of 45,000 housing units a year for the next ten years. The reason for Logue's refusal was that he wanted the reorganization approved by the City Council before he took the job and he wanted a guarantee that the Federal government would allocate enough money to the city to enable him to succeed. Both demands were unrealistic and Lindsay could not meet them.

The week of November 21 started out badly, but it rapidly improved. On Monday morning, in a page one story, former Mayor Wagner was quoted summing up the Lindsay Administration this way: "A good deal of talk, not much action." He added: "The problems are still here—not solved as promised, and in some cases a little more exaggerated. He has certainly not set the world on fire by any means." In answer to questions from newsmen on a Sunday TV show, Wagner was asked how he would rate Lindsay. He replied: "Medium. Medium." Almost as if in response to Wagner's attack—though not planned that way—we announced several key appointments which gave some hope in the housing area.

On Tuesday, at a press conference in the Board of Estimate Chambers, the Mayor named Jason R. Nathan as the city's first housing administrator; Walter E. Washington, of Washington, D.C., a Negro, as chairman of the City Housing Authority; and Donald H. Elliott as chairman of the City Planning Commission. After Lindsay's formal press conference announcing these appointments, I called for a short five-minute break—as had been my custom—before the reporters asked Lindsay broad-ranging questions on all other topics. It was at this point that I took him aside and reminded him that it was November 22—the third anniversary since the assassination of President Kennedy. I suggested he open his remarks to the press with a few words in memory of the late President. Lindsay agreed to do so.

Over the Thanksgiving weekend, Lindsay took a few days off and flew to Bermuda with his family. Unfortunately, there was a three-day major air pollution crisis which reached the point of a near emergency. I remained in touch with the Mayor by telephone, but we agreed that despite the "alert" for the metropolitan area called by Rockefeller, and despite public attacks against him and his air pollution program from various Democrats, including City Councilman Robert A. Low, there was no necessity for him to return to the city. The pollution level reached a danger point, but after a telephone conversation with Austin Heller, commissioner of Air Pollution, I was assured that people's lives were not in danger.

When Lindsay returned on Sunday from Bermuda he refused to be drawn into a debate with Low, who had charged that the city was "dragging its feet" on enforcement of the law. "Why should I comment on that?" he told newsmen. "It's a political attack."

But this time I was thoroughly disheartened by the reaction of the City Hall Democrats to most of Lindsay's plans. These included Little City Halls, reorganizing city government, and many other major reforms which I still believed Lindsay was right in undertaking, but which I knew were becoming tougher and tougher to accomplish politically because of the great number of enemies—whether justified or not—Lindsay had made during those first eleven months in office. In any case, by the end of November, it was abundantly clear that if he was to carry out his promise of reform he would have to make more shifts in personnel.

Included among the scheduled changes were the appointments of Frank C. Arricale II to commissioner of Relocation (from executive director of the Youth Board); Donald F. Shaughnessy to president of the Public Development Corp. (from assistant to the Mayor); Richard M. Rosen, assistant to the Mayor for cultural affairs (from legislative representative in Albany); Harry J. Donnelly would resign as commissioner of Highways to accept a judicial appointment; and Gerard Weisberg to Markets commissioner (from top deputy in the department). One of the unfortunate side effects of all the shifts, however, was the addition to the already large staff of mayoral assistants which included Murray Drabkin ($30,000), Rosen ($20,000), Sweet ($23,000), Robert Blum ($21,000), James Carberry ($20,000), Barry Gottehrer ($20,000), Oliver Pilat ($18,000), Werner H. Kramarsky ($17,000), Harvey Rothenberg (unpaid volunteer), Jay Kriegel ($12,000), Robert Laird ($15,000), Alfonso Troche ($12,000), Sid Davidoff ($17,000), Dave Garth (unpaid), Constantine Sidamon-Eristoff ($18,000), James W. Smith ($17,500), John I. Ortiz ($12,500), Richard Buford ($20,000), Michael J. Dontzin ($17,-500). A story in the *Times* reported there were 23 mayoral assistants altogether earning a total of $400,000 a year.

When Lindsay saw this story in the paper, he called me in and told me he would prefer it if I transferred over to the payroll of the Housing and Development Administration. He said he wanted to move as many assistants off of the City Hall payroll as possible. After a few minutes in conversation, he turned to me and said he would also like me to help Nathan reorganize the city housing agencies and draw up a new reorganization plan. It would be necessary, he said, for me to join Nathan in an office at 250 Broadway, a new building on the West Side of Broadway across the street from City Hall. I agreed and, after a talk with Nathan, it was decided that I would move into the office at 250 on Monday, December 5, the day Harry O'Donnell was scheduled to take over my office at City Hall.

As my twelve months as press secretary to the Mayor of New York drew to a close, I began to clean out my desk with mixed emotions. I had shared some of the most intimate moments with John Lindsay on the first leg of a political journey and, in some ways, regretted leaving City Hall. I had answered thousands of inquiries from the press, put out 460 press releases, and acted as the Mayor's spokesman on many occasions. Yet, for me and for many others close to the Mayor, it had been a nerve-racking experience which had left us drained and weary. I felt completely spent. I had struggled, along with Lindsay, against what now seemed to be overwhelming odds. Lindsay's image had been severely tarnished. I had tried my best and yet the whole year had turned out to be disappointing and painful. It seemed like the end of a nightmare. And now that it was coming to a close, I knew that the change would be best for the Mayor and, even more important, best for me and my family.

14 *"The God damn bureaucracy can drive you crazy!"*

ONE OF THE LAST official functions I attended as Lindsay's press secretary was the funeral of Public Works Commissioner Bill Mattison on December 1 at St. Anselm's Roman Catholic Church in the Bay Ridge section of Brooklyn, where Mattison had lived with his wife and five children.

I was deeply saddened by the sudden, unexpected death of Mattison, from a heart attack, on Monday, November 28, as he was talking at a midtown dinner just one week before he would have celebrated his forty-ninth birthday. I had worked out at the Downtown Athletic Club with him only hours before that dinner; we had played ping pong and had taken a steam bath. He had told me during the workout: "I do the best I can for the Mayor. I am out every night and weekends. It's a rough pace, but it's the only way to do the job."

The following morning he was dead. At the early morning Cabinet meeting I attended at Gracie Mansion, Lindsay was pale and shaken. "Bill was going to be one of my top ten administrators," the Mayor murmured. "I was going to promote him soon." Bill Mattison never lived to know that the job for which he had been striving so hard had been earmarked for him.

On Monday, December 5, I began my new job. In reviewing the highlights of the housing program for our first year, I found that it had been a period of rallying new forces, of major policy change, and of planning and preparation for a broad attack on one of the city's grimmest problems—how to provide decent housing for all New Yorkers at prices they can afford. Of great importance were the policy changes. One was an increased emphasis on rehabilitation. This included a daring experiment, "instant rehabilitation," whereby a tenement would be gutted and new rooms lowered through the roof. And there was added emphasis on imaginative design of new buildings. But perhaps most significant was the shift in renewal policy. The Lindsay Administration had decided to concentrate its renewal resources on the worst slum areas—Harlem, Central Brooklyn and the South Bronx.

One basis for this new approach was the long-awaited report, "Let There Be Commitment," by a task force headed by Boston's renewal chief, Edward Logue. Crucial in the Logue Report was the reorganization and consolidation of housing agencies. And this was just part of the Mayor's plan for reorganization of city government, which had been formulated by Louis Craco, an attorney. The omnibus bill proposed to consolidate forty-nine city departments, agencies and bureaus into ten superagencies or "administrations." Six—including the Housing and Development Administration—had been set up by the Mayor's executive order even before the legislation was proposed, but the legislation went far beyond the executive powers of the Mayor.[1]

The reaction among City Council leaders was not warm, but one thing which, I thought, would help Lindsay in getting the legislation passed was his appointment of Robert Sweet as the successor to Price in the vacant Deputy Mayor's post. Sweet, who had been carrying the main legislative duties for the Mayor in his job as executive assistant to the Mayor during the year, drew high praise from many quarters as a man of good will and diplomacy.[2] His most important compliments came from City Comptroller Mario Procaccino and David Ross, the majority leader of the City Council.

The first housing officials appointed by Lindsay to Housing

Administrator Nathan's superagency included Mrs. Shirley Adelson Siegel, a lawyer who had been in charge of the civil rights bureau of State Attorney General Louis J. Lefkowitz's office since 1959, as assistant administrator for legal affairs. Her salary was set at $25,000 a year, making her the highest paid woman in the Lindsay Administration. The Mayor also appointed thirty-two-year-old Robert G. Hazen, an aide of Logue's in Boston who had written much of the Logue Report, as deputy administrator to Nathan at $30,000 a year; and he announced a new job for me as assistant administrator for public affairs of the new housing superagency, at a salary of $25,000 a year.

Meanwhile, I had been receiving many telephone calls and letters on all kinds of housing problems. Civic leaders, who had been good news sources for me as a reporter, were saying they felt Lindsay had not done much in housing for the first eleven months; that he had not been directly in touch with the long-standing organizations concerned with the city's urban renewal; that many of them felt ignored by City Hall, and ironically, by the man whom they had supported. So despite the vast programs, the crucial policy changes and the governmental reorganization, people were becoming impatient for visible accomplishment.

By the beginning of 1967, the press started publishing first-year reviews of the Mayor and some of the criticism was pretty harsh. Richard Reeves of the *Times,* writing in the Sunday Magazine section on January 1, 1967, declared: "Lindsay's campaign promises guaranteed disappointments." And, on January 7, the *Washington Post* commented: "Lindsay has proven to be a fighter—a stubbornly pugnacious one. Yet his celebrated zeal and reckless disregard for his own standing have often carried him to defeat—glorious, but defeat nevertheless." And author Nat Hentoff, after a lengthy interview with Lindsay in February, quoted the Mayor as saying: "My deepest satisfaction in this job so far is that I think we've helped to strengthen a change of attitude. We've shown, I think, that there is the possibility of a first-class government in this city by the way we propose to restructure it. After all, consider the quality of the people who have been willing to come aboard. They wouldn't have come if they hadn't believed in the possibility. It's true, though, that the machinery is still too slow. That's a constant struggle. The God damn bureaucracy can drive you crazy! Hell, even among the people close to me, some don't always move their butts as fast as they ought to."[3]

I recalled this comment of Lindsay's a few months later during the spring of 1967 as I began to grow impatient with our Administration's failure to clean up what had become known as "the mess on Macdougal Street" in Greenwich Village—the community in which I lived with my family. The previous summer—1966—had been noisy, crime-ridden and crowded in the Village. Now it was the spring of 1967 and the atmosphere was growing worse. Dope addicts freely wandered through the streets, the Bowery bum population had moved over to our section of the Village, and on weekends young mobs shouted and screamed throughout the nights, set off firecrackers, revved up their motorcycles and even attacked and robbed several local residents.

During the summer of 1966, I had sent Chief Inspector Sanford D. Garelik a confidential memorandum detailing the problems in the Village and urging him to assign more police to the area at night. He had responded, but the additional police failed to take any action. Now it was almost a year later and the police still refused to make arrests. When I complained about the noise one night to a patrolman on duty at the Sixth Precinct, he merely told me: "There's nothing we can do about this because we don't get any support from City Hall and the courts don't back us up."

As a result, I spoke out publicly about the conditions in the Village in a column I wrote for *The Villager,* a weekly community newspaper published by a friend of mine, William J. Williamson. I blamed much of the problem on what I viewed as the incompatible use of one small area: residents trying to live side by side with coffeehouses, hippie hangouts, a university campus (New York University) and various other commercial establishments. One of the nightclub owners, Art D'Lugoff, a friend of Lindsay's, wrote to the Mayor complaining about my column. Bob Sweet, the Deputy Mayor, called a special meeting of several commissioners, assistants to the Mayor and myself.

I described the chaos in the community to this group and told them that in my opinion neither the Mayor nor James

Marcus, the Mayor's special assistant for Greenwich Village affairs, had done much to solve the problems since we took office in 1966. We talked for a short time and then Sweet said, matter-of-factly:

"Okay, I've heard enough. I agree. We should make it look as if we're doing something in the Village. There's no doubt that we have a bad image there."

I left Sweet's office disgusted. Nobody in that meeting had really cared what was happening in the Village. Nobody had responded to the charge from community leader Emanuel Popolizio that many coffeehouses were operating without licenses and that the police were under orders from City Hall not to make arrests for disorderly conduct. I was even further upset when Sweet called me a short time later and told me to "lay off" writing about the Village in my column. Since I was still in the Administration, I had to comply with his request.

Meanwhile, Nathan was having a great deal of trouble making the new housing reorganization work. It was clear that his commissioners were resisting the plan and trying to retain their own public identities. This led Nathan to say to me one day, casually, "It won't be until this whole first group of commissioners has left and a new team brought in that we will have the kind of loyalty to a housing administrator that is needed if the Housing and Development Administration is to function as one single agency."

As the late spring weather turned from balmy to hot, officials at City Hall, the H.D.A. and other agencies as well were concerned about the possibility of violence in the ghetto. The Mayor's first summer in office had been relatively free of such incidents—except for the racial blow-up in East New York—but conditions were ripe for trouble, nevertheless. About this time, the H.D.A. announced the phasing out of Project RESCU (cq), a Federally funded antipoverty program, in which slum dwellers were paid to process complaints about housing violations. However, some of those on the payroll had criminal records, and the program generally had been disappointing. The Federal government was cutting off funds, while the city declined to pick up the bill itself.

About mid-May, the first of a group of demonstrators arrived to protest the closing of Project RESCU. They camped in the reception area of H.D.A. headquarters on the twenty-eighth floor of 250 Broadway. Police had been alerted and were posted on the floor, but were told to allow the demonstrators to remain. More protesters arrived and occupied other rooms on the floor, and finally, with Nathan out of the building at the time, they took over his luxurious, carpeted corner office with its sweeping view of City Hall Park and the East River. Bob Hazen, Nathan's boyish-looking, tight-lipped assistant, was in charge during Nathan's absence, and was concerned about the violence that might follow, not just in our building, but throughout the ghetto neighborhoods, if the sit-ins were forcibly removed from our office. Some had brought little babies with them, a tactic that had emotional appeal and helped deter police action.

They were prepared for a long sit-in. A few brought glass cutters, which could be used to cut holes in the sealed window panes when the building's air-conditioning was shut off at 5:30 P.M. They sent for coffee, sandwiches and milk for the babies. Hazen agreed to allow the food to come up. They seized control of the switchboard and several office telephones. They ransacked Nathan's desk and file cabinet, tossed food around the room and reduced the office to shambles. Nathan arrived and tried to talk to the group, which by this time totaled over 100, but was shouted down and threatened. He left with the help of police. Hazen drew up a compromise plan, but when he tried to present it he was met with shouts. He tossed his papers in the air and withdrew to his own office, which he had begun to refer to by this time as "the general's tent." The stalemate continued into the night. The scene calmed somewhat. The glass cutters were never used. And in the early morning, Hazen had worked out an agreement with the group whereby the city would take over some of the costs of the program and Project RESCU would be continued. It was an episode reminiscent of some of my hectic days at City Hall, but it attracted little press attention. By this time the press and public were becoming accustomed to sit-ins of this type in city agencies.

The Mayor, meanwhile, was beginning a second successful summer keeping the ghettos from blowing up. He was appointed by President Johnson as vice-chairman of the National Advisory

Commission on Civil Disorders; played a key role in the formation of the prestigious Urban Coalition; emerged in the fall as one of the nation's foremost advocates for cities in crisis and was increasingly mentioned as a possible national candidate for office in 1968. Still, some observers viewed Lindsay's housing program as a major weakness in his record. Writing in *Newsday* on September 23, 1967, for example, Political Editor Frank Lynn praised Lindsay for a number of new city programs, but then added: "Lindsay's record in combating slum housing is less apparent." And Charles Abrams, chairman of Columbia University's department of urban planning and chairman of Lindsay's first task force on housing, was quoted as saying that there had been neither progress nor brilliant innovations in the Lindsay housing program. "It's going along pretty much as it has," Abrams said.

With the help of Ed Silberfarb, Joe Polser, Claire McCarthy and a dozen more public relations people on my staff, we continued to announce new urban renewal projects, job opportunity programs in the ghettos, and vest pocket housing developments. Yet, in November, the H.D.A. sustained a bitter attack from the City Club of New York, due in great part to the fact that I. D. Robbins, a past president of the club, had become disenchanted with the Lindsay Administration. Robbins, a wealthy builder, charged specifically that the number of building permits for apartment construction had declined each year since Lindsay took office and that low-rent public housing construction had also declined rapidly. Depending on what set of figures one used, Robbins could be proven right or wrong.

By the closing weeks of 1967, the Mayor had officially appointed the full staff of the H.D.A. He had persuaded Eugene S. Callender,[4] executive director of the Urban League of New York, to join Nathan as deputy administrator, while appointing Robert Hazen, Frederic S. Berman, Frank C. Arricale and John T. O'Neill to the four major commissionerships. On the day he officially created the H.D.A.—November 29, 1967—the Mayor acknowledged that recent criticisms of the housing program had some justification. "We obviously have a long way to go," he told newsmen at a City Hall press conference. "We have large problems ahead of us and they are recognized."

At about this time, an incident occurred that far over-shadowed our housing problems. On Monday, December 11, 1967, Jim Marcus unexpectedly resigned as commissioner of Water Supply, Gas and Electricity. In a letter to Lindsay, Marcus told the Mayor that his investment business activities before he joined the Mayor were being investigated by New York County District Attorney Frank S. Hogan's office. "Please be assured the complaint [being investigated by Hogan] has nothing whatever to do with my official duties and that I am, in fact, free of any wrongdoing." Lindsay replied that he had no choice but to accept the resignation "with regret" and he told Marcus: "Your performance in office has been excellent and our friendship through government service and before has been close."

A week later, on Monday, December 18, Marcus was arrested on Federal charges of taking kickbacks on an $835,000 city contract along with Antonio (Tony Ducks) Corallo, whom the Federal Bureau of Investigation described as a reputed Mafia leader. The Federal grand jury which returned an indictment against Marcus charged that he had received a $16,000 kickback on a contract to refurbish the Jerome Park Reservoir in the Bronx. When I first heard the news on that Monday, I was in my office. I couldn't believe it. It seemed incredible to me that Jim Marcus, who had been designated by the Mayor to head one of the new superagencies, the Environmental Protection Administration, could have been so weak and stupid as to have involved himself with the Mafia. I thought that he might have been framed. Lindsay was so shaken by the news that he stayed in his office for six hours after the indictment was announced. The scandal reached higher into City Hall than any since James J. Moran, a deputy Fire commissioner under Mayor William O'Dwyer, had been convicted of conspiracy and extortion in 1952. By mid-afternoon, O'Donnell, speaking for the Mayor, merely passed out a statement that said: "There will be no comment on this new development. The Mayor has directed Investigation Commissioner Arnold G. Fraiman to examine all matters Mr. Marcus dealt with."

On the same day the indictment was carried in a four-column

headline on page one of the *New York Times,* Marcus' former close friend and colleague in government, Samuel J. Kearing, Jr., another one of the young men in whom Lindsay had put his trust, was also making front page news. In a smaller but equally brutal story headlined: KEARING SAYS CITY 'HAS BEGUN TO DIE,' the former Sanitation commissioner, who had resigned in November after a dispute with the Mayor, charged: "The condition of the city is not improving. Decay is everywhere. I know of no major city agency that is functioning better today than it was two years ago. Soon the bandaids will start popping off to reveal this hard truth."

As if his public break with Kearing had not been bad enough, the Marcus scandal virtually broke Lindsay's spirit, for the moment at least. The day after the indictment was announced, Lindsay held a tense, hour-long news conference. Looking tired and shaken, the Mayor stated: "If the charge in the Federal indictment is true, then it's clear to me that Mr. Marcus lied to me, lied to Investigation Commissioner Fraiman and lied to District Attorney Frank S. Hogan. To say, in that event, that I have been ill-served and the public also, is an understatement. Obviously, I consider this a betrayal of a personal and public trust." During the press conference, the Mayor was asked whether the Marcus scandal was the worst thing that has happened during his public career. He replied: "I've been through some rough ones. I guess this is about as rough. It has caused me great anguish and anger."

Despite the setback, I learned from talking with politicians of both parties that few people inside government blamed Lindsay for what his friend was charged with. The worst criticism I heard came from the news media, the *Times* in particular, which wanted to know why Marcus' background had not been checked out more carefully. Although I had left City Hall a year before as Lindsay's press secretary, I received a telephone call one night at home shortly after the Marcus story broke from a *Times* reporter asking me what had happened when I had sent out the initial press release announcing Marcus as an unpaid assistant to the Mayor early in 1966. I told the reporter of how Marcus had sat down in my office on a Saturday morning and typed out his own biography (which turned out to be highly exaggerated and inaccurate) and how Marcus had delivered the press release himself to the newspapers.

"But didn't you check out his biography before you wrote the press release?" the reporter asked me.

"No, I did not," I replied. "We were appointing dozens of new people to office in those days and it never occurred to me that a man as close to the Mayor as Marcus, the son-in-law of John Davis Lodge and a loyal Lindsay campaign worker, needed investigating by me. Lindsay had told me that Marcus was to be appointed and I was carrying out orders."

"You never suspected for a moment that Marcus had made up much of his background and that he was a phony?"

"No, I never doubted Jim Marcus for a moment," I replied. "Would you have challenged his credentials if you had been in my place?"

The reporter paused for a moment and then replied before he hung up: "Well, I guess you couldn't be expected to question him."

As we entered the early part of 1968, I was beginning to wonder how long it would be before housing became a full-fledged controversy in the city press. I knew we had made some changes, and perhaps a few innovations, but basically I felt that we had done virtually nothing about the problems of the worst slums in the city. Jason Nathan was not a popular administrator. His uncertainty about his relationship to the Mayor and his inability to listen to advice often got in his way. He also lacked political sophistication—he did not know how to talk with members of the City Council, for example. And so, the gnawing question in my mind after one year in the housing labyrinth was this: Can anyone really do anything about the one million New Yorkers who remain, year after year, trapped in incredible squalor? Perhaps, Mayor Wagner had been right, after all, when he had told me ten years before in an interview: "There's nothing you can do about the slums, you know that. They're always going to be that way."[5]

Thus, I was not really surprised when the Citizens' Housing and Planning Council, an influential civic group headed by Roger Starr, charged on January 20 that our Administration was "seriously deficient in developing the structural and political means" for building enough housing in New York. I issued a brief statement to the effect that we welcomed his views and hoped to do better in the future.

By the end of January, 1968, the annual assessments in the media about Lindsay's two years in office had been completed. Most were sympathetic to Lindsay, but in general the theme now was beginning to emerge: Was Lindsay going to be able to keep his promises or was time running out on him? Richard Reeves summed up 1967 perhaps better than anyone in a *New York Times* Sunday Magazine article entitled, "The Impossible Takes A Little Longer." Wrote Reeves: "For John Vliet Lindsay it was the best of years, it was the worst of years. In 1967 he became a significant American figure—the daring young Mayor who walked the mean back streets, the spokesman for the writhing cities, a possible President of the United States. But in the first weeks of his third year as Mayor of New York there were harsh questions. Was he really changing the city? Was he really so new, so young—or was he just another 46-year-old Mayor struggling for survival against the glacial flow of New York's eight million problems?" And columnists Jack Newfield and Leticia Kent, writing in *The Village Voice,* made this observation on November 23, 1967: "Mayor Lindsay's blow-up with Sam Kearing again dramatized what may prove to be the Mayor's Achilles' Heel—his inability to sustain close, long-term relationships with his aides. First, Lindsay broke with his political alter-ego, Bob Price. He then eased out firebrand housing boss Charles Moerdler. And now Kearing, one of his Administration's most effective commissioners, has been fired. City Hall insiders speak of Lindsay's rigidity of temperament as the cause of the splits. 'The real trouble with John,' one of his ardent former admirers said, 'is that he can't have an equal relationship with someone his own age, like Kearing. He can only relate to father figures, like Herb Brownell, or else all those teeny-boppers on his staff who idolize him.'"

These comments confirmed my own feelings about Lindsay, who had by now won a national reputation, but who—at the same time—had lost many friends and staff members. Bob Price had given me some insight into Lindsay at the end of 1966 which now came to mind: "The secret to Lindsay," Price had told me in late November, 1966, "is to make him come to you. Lindsay needs people who don't need him. Your mistake," Price had told me, "was that you always went to him, you tried to be helpful. You must not show your loyalty to him. He appreciates it, but he likes people who tell him what to do more. Lindsay is a guy who has to be told what to do. I know Lindsay better than he knows himself. I know what's good for him and what's bad for him. And I know that there are certain things you just don't tell Lindsay. But the important thing is you must make Lindsay come to you."

By the spring of 1968, I became totally discontented and disillusioned with public life. I began to be haunted by the realization that being part of a gigantic superagency and a municipal bureaucracy of 300,000 people was hardly what I had envisioned when I first joined John Lindsay. The fact is that government in New York would proceed at its own pace and there was very little that anyone—even the Mayor—could do about it.

Early that spring, I decided to test my theory that the reason little was being accomplished in housing was because of red tape, indifference and apathy on the part of public officials themselves—as well as community resistance. I decided to use as a test case, a building in the Metro North section of East Harlem, an area for which we had announced glowing plans a year before. In fact, as early as January 2, 1966, the second day of the Lindsay Administration, Metro North had been the scene of a much publicized visit by city officials, including Buildings Commissioner Moerdler, Parks Commissioner Hoving and Fire Commissioner Lowery. During the winter of 1967, I made several return visits to East 100th Street and to the house at number 311 because it was the setting for a book I had written on slum conditions three years earlier, the same book for which Congressman John V. Lindsay had written a foreword.[6]

On my first visit to this house in the summer of 1961, I had been appalled, almost sickened, by the stench of the building, the cockroaches running rampant, the rat holes, falling plaster, broken windows and stairs and ceilings, and mostly by the

Epilogue

"It was the best of times, it was the worst of times . . . it was the spring of hope, it was the winter of despair."
— CHARLES DICKENS, *A Tale of Two Cities*

FIFTEEN MONTHS after I left city government, John Lindsay was reelected Mayor in one of the most grueling and divisive campaigns in New York City's history. Immediately following his upset victory, many New Yorkers looked to him to head a new coalition from all political parties and to lead the city out of its turmoil.

For the first time since John Lindsay had been elected in 1965, I had the feeling that the mood of many New Yorkers— especially followers of Lindsay—had shifted from apathy to a new hope that perhaps there was a chance, after all, that the Mayor might eventually succeed.

At the same time, since he won reelection with only 42 percent of the vote, his victory could hardly be viewed as a mandate from the people. And the major problems in New York which had plagued him since 1966 still remained. During the first four years, most of John Lindsay's programs were slow in getting under way, many were ineffectively executed and almost all fell short of their goals: the streets needed to be kept cleaner, the traffic unsnarled, the air purified, the crime rate lowered, the welfare rolls reduced, the snow removed sooner, and the housing shortage alleviated.

As if to underline this last point, only two days after the Mayor was reelected, Jason Nathan—for whom I had worked for twenty-one months—resigned under fire, reportedly the victim of a political deal in which the Mayor had agreed during the campaign to remove him in return for support from the Reform Democrats. When it was announced that he was leaving, Nathan, apparently letting out the pent-up frustrations he had experienced since mid-1966 angrily told a State Senate Committee: "If the subject is housing, 'crisis' is an understatement. Disaster may be more appropriate." New York had, in fact, suffered a net loss of 21,000 apartments from 1965 to 1968— the first time in metropolitan history that the housing supply had decreased.

But Jason Nathan—and others such as Deputy Mayor Robert Sweet who have left since Lindsay's reelection—hardly represented the beginning of the exodus of officials from his Administration. The problem started in 1966. By the end of 1967, more than a dozen well-known political figures had resigned from Lindsay's Cabinet and, by the end of his first term, only a handful of people who had been with him in the beginning remained.

The first major city official to leave the Mayor was his number one aide and long-time friend, Deputy Mayor Robert Price. Although he never publicly talked about his premature departure at the end of 1966, it was apparent to those of us who were in City Hall at the time that the relationship between Lindsay and Price steadily deteriorated from the day we took office.

Price did help implement important changes in the Police Department (which Lindsay's political opponents characterized as "interference" in the department); and as chairman of Lindsay's committee dealing with the Port Authority, he was instrumental in settling the dispute over the World Trade

Center. Price was also an accomplished behind-the-scenes political strategist who often advised the Mayor. But he did not particularly enjoy trying to cope with the substantive problems of government—housing, poverty, welfare, for example, and he left for a much higher-paying job with a nationally known mutual fund in December. I had the feeling that the Mayor was not certain whether or not he could run New York without Price in the next office at City Hall. As soon as Price left, however, Harry O'Donnell came in to replace him as the number one political strategist in the Administration. Lindsay grew more confident and for a long time it appeared as if the changes were very advantageous to the Mayor. It turned out to be bitterly ironic, of course, that O'Donnell—on whom the Mayor leaned most heavily for political advice after Price resigned—left the Mayor himself in April, 1969. Officially, he gave reasons of health, but newsmen speculated that it was Lindsay's tendency to revert to some of his younger aides that caused the veteran political press secretary to walk out. In addition, O'Donnell had wanted to play a major role in the 1969 campaign, but felt rebuffed by Lindsay's choice of Richard Aurelio as campaign manager. In the end, it was this pattern of Lindsay's reliance on his so-called bright young men that drove many top officials out of the Administration. Lindsay believed that they and only they could overcome the traditional patterns of New York politics; that they had the energy, determination and talent to work twenty-four hours a day, seven days a week—totally devoted to him and his cause.

Like O'Donnell, Lindsay's chief speech writer, James Carberry, also quit in the middle of the 1969 campaign because he found himself gradually being replaced by other younger, more power hungry aides. Carberry, a taciturn man with a sharp sense of humor, resigned with praise for Lindsay. His official explanation was that he needed a rest from four years of "pressure writing." Nevertheless, he had teamed up well with O'Donnell and, after O'Donnell's departure in April, Carberry found himself being squeezed out of the Mayor's so-called Inner Circle.

Another major cause for many resignations was the Mayor's reorganization plan. Some of Lindsay's commissioners felt that his reorganization of city government downgraded their power.

Previously, they had enjoyed a closer working relationship with the Mayor, but with the reorganization they were faced with having to report to an "administrator" who would then discuss their problems with Lindsay. Perhaps the reorganization, which grouped some fifty city departments and agencies into ten administrations, will, in the long run, eliminate some of New York's massive bureaucracy; but its immediate effect was to demoralize many of his appointees.

For example, the resignation of Buildings Commissioner Charles Moerdler after eighteen months was directly attributed to his dissatisfaction with the housing reorganization. Moerdler resented Nathan because he (Moerdler) had worked for Lindsay since early 1965 and he thought he should have been appointed as the housing administrator instead of an out-of-towner like Nathan. Rent Commissioner Frederic Berman's resignation in 1969 was a similar situation. The former Democratic State Senator did not enjoy being overshadowed by Nathan. He returned to private law practice with praise for the Mayor.

Other high officials who left during Lindsay's first term included one of the nation's best known poverty experts, Mitchell Sviridoff. He had come to New York from New Haven at the urging of the Mayor who established one of the city's top salaries—$40,000—for his post as administrator of the Human Resources Administration, the agency which was to run the poverty and welfare programs. When he was still in his post, he had told a reporter: "There is no way to win in this job. The question is how rapidly you lose."

Sviridoff disappointed Lindsay by announcing in the middle of 1967 that he had accepted a job as vice president of the Ford Foundation, calling it an "even greater challenge" than the post with Lindsay. I later asked Sviridoff in an interview to explain his departure. "I'm not saying New York was an easy experience," he said, "it was a rough, exhausting experience. The city machinery proved to be an impossible mechanism, between the budget, the Comptroller and the Personnel Department, you couldn't hire, pay or move people or programs fast enough. I realize the system has many checks and balances, but I couldn't get enough production out of it. My second problem was with the state and Federal governments. In both cases, I felt a combination of distrust, dislike and competition with Mayor Lindsay, some of which he may have contributed to. I did not get the kind of instantaneous responses I needed; some of the reasons were political, and some had to do with the unwillingness of the state agencies to recognize change. Also, the press never stopped to understand our problems with the Office of Equal Opportunity."

Commenting on his relationship with the Mayor, he added: "I had a policy of not bothering the Mayor. I thought it was my job to take the responsibility off of his shoulders. Whenever I had a problem, I got his support. I had a good personal relationship and I enjoyed working for him. I had a great personal respect for him. Compared to other men in public life, he grasps things quickly and he does his homework. He is not superficial, although he is unquestionably concerned about his image. Of course, there were times when John Lindsay was overwhelmed by events, but who wouldn't have been?"

Thomas P. F. Hoving is another well-known and popular administrator who left Lindsay for a better professional post— director of the Metropolitan Museum of Art. Hoving, the city's administrator of Recreational and Cultural Affairs, made a name for himself early in 1966 by staging "happenings" in the city's parks and by exhibiting a sense of enjoyment and imagination which had not been seen in city government for decades. A brilliant, talented official, he resigned reluctantly, stating in December, 1966: "No job in the world other than director of the Metropolitan would have tempted me for an instant to leave the work that I have started this past year."

Thus, the resignations of Price, Moerdler, Sviridoff and Hoving and the Marcus scandal served to undermine the public's confidence in the Mayor in the first two years. In addition, Walter Washington, a Negro who had come up from Washington, D.C., to head the New York City Housing Authority, was enticed back to Washington by President Johnson to become Mayor of the nation's capital. Of all the resignations, besides Marcus', however, the dismissal of Sanitation Commissioner Samuel J. Kearing for "insubordination" was the most dramatic and volatile. In a parting blast in December, 1967, Kearing said: "We were held together by Bob Price, but with Price gone the communication was gone. It's hard to be close to Lindsay."

Among other officials who left, Timothy J. Cooney, who served first as Civil Defense chief and then as an assistant housing administrator, resigned in early 1968, charging: "I no longer have any faith that hard work within the government is going to make much difference in improving the slums." Cooney, who had spent a decade in city government, added: "Controversy, debate, confrontation and political pressure are absolutely essential. The boat has to be rocked." He joined a pressure group known as the Committee for a Confrontation with Congress.

Assistant Press Secretary Alfonso Troche, a Puerto Rican who worked for the Mayor until April, 1968, says: "I felt I was not used as much as I could have been by the Mayor and his staff on Puerto Rican affairs. I was shocked at how irresponsible leaders in the various fields could practically cripple the city because they didn't feel they were getting what was coming to them. It was for me a shameful and disgraceful situation, and as a result it left a real bad taste in my mouth for politics. . . . One thing I learned about New York City during those two years was that New York is not as liberal as it appears to be. . . . I think many of the problems John Lindsay faced during his initial period at City Hall were due to his lack of understanding of the press' role."

Oliver Pilat, a former New York newspaperman who had handled press relations for the Mayor during the 1965 campaign and then became an assistant to the Mayor, resigned after eighteen months because, as he puts it, "Bob Sweet wanted a private early look at *Lindsay's Campaign*," a book Pilat had written while still in the Administration. His main criticism of the Mayor: "JVL's unconscious tendency toward self-isolation."

There were, of course, many other officials who resigned. Frank L. Lazarus, a Wagner holdover as Real Estate commissioner, left in early 1966, accusing the Mayor of appointing "campaign workers and untried amateurs" to key city posts; City Narcotics Coordinator Efren Ramirez, who resigned in mid-1968 stating that among his major frustrations were "John Lindsay's incapacity to fulfill his commitments for financial and administrative support to the addiction programs." He called the Mayor "cool, too detached, lacking in capacity to install great enthusiasm for his programs among his commissioners."

The resignation of William H. Booth was, of course, somewhat unique because Booth, a Republican, had been a strong Lindsay backer and an outspoken civil rights advocate as Human Rights commissioner. Soon after the school strike, however, he was accused by Jewish leaders of being "insensitive to anti-Semitism" and, after some controversy, was removed by Lindsay and made a Criminal Court judge. Lindsay conceded publicly that Booth could have done a "better" job of looking into the anti-Semitism that "certainly surfaced during the school strike."

Dr. Howard Brown, the Mayor's first Health Services administrator, served for twenty-one months before he became disillusioned and frustrated. "John is a poor administrator," he says bluntly. Nevertheless, he adds, "I strongly support the Mayor, but I think he failed to understand the administrative requirements of city government. However, his gut instincts and goals are so right."

Mrs. Eleanor Guggenheimer, a member of the City Planning Commission, left the Mayor because she felt commission members were "downgraded and treated with contempt" when Donald Elliott, a close aide of the Mayor's, was appointed chairman. In an interview in early 1969, Mrs. Guggenheimer said: "John Lindsay is a fine human being . . . had he recognized his own lack of knowledge, experience and administrative deficiencies, he might have been the greatest Mayor this City has ever known. He has humor, charm, and integrity. On the debit side, he failed to appoint really competent people in key spots. . . . He is still too unwilling to listen to criticism which he always labels as political and still too interested in his own image, unable to relate to people as individuals, and still too petulant." Despite this criticism, Mrs. Guggenheimer eventually supported the Mayor in the 1969 campaign.

Other officials who resigned during Lindsay's first term included Murray Drabkin, architect of the Lindsay Administration's tax program and the first director of the New York City government office in Washington; Eugene M. Becker, Budget director; Arthur E. Palmer, Transportation administrator; Roy M. Goodman, Finance administrator; George Nicolau, commissioner of the city's Community Development Agency; Mrs. Helen M. Harris, chairman of the Mayor's screening board for antipoverty programs; Herbert Halberg, commissioner of Marine and Aviation; Carl Madonick, commissioner of Real Estate; Alonzo Yerby, commissioner of Hospitals; Joseph Periconi, commissioner of Sanitation; Herbert B. Evans, chairman of the Housing and Redevelopment Board; Michael Freyberg, member of the Tax Commission; Arnold Fraiman, commissioner of Investigation; Harry J. Donnelly, commissioner of Highways; Samuel Ganz, commissioner of Manpower; Dr. Donald F. Shaughnessy, mayoral assistant and president of the Economic Development Corporation; John Ortiz, assistant to the Mayor; Gerard M. Weisberg, Markets commissioner; Gen. Lucius D. Clay, chairman of the board of the Public Development Corporation; Joseph E. O'Grady, chairman of the Transit Authority; Louis Broido, commissioner of the Department of Commerce and Industrial Development; Mrs. Anna Kross, commissioner of Correction; Warren Gardner, assistant press secretary; William J. Diamond, acting Buildings commissioner and an assistant Housing administrator; Eugene Callender, deputy Housing administrator; Joel J. Tyler, commissioner of Licenses; Royal S. Radin, commissioner of Relocation; and Teresa Calabrese, assistant to the Mayor.

After serving in John Lindsay's Administration for thirty-three months, and having since observed him from a distance, I feel Lindsay is a man endowed with a great deal of idealism and sensitivity. However, despite his personal dedication, I don't think he shared enough of his inner feelings with the many people who worked with him every day, especially during that first traumatic year. John Lindsay wants to like people and he wants to be liked; but he often forms snap judgments and he does not always permit others to get to know him. He lavishes praise upon those whom he likes and tends to expect too much from them, as they do from him. As a result he—and those whom he appoints—tend to be disappointed in one another.

Lindsay still has a long way to go before he can hope to reverse the tide of steady deterioration in New York. For one thing, labor must be recognized for what it is: the single most powerful pressure group in the city. "This is a union town," former Mayor Robert F. Wagner was fond of saying, "and as long as I'm Mayor I intend to keep it that way." He did—for twelve years. The first lesson Lindsay learned—as a result of the costly transit strike and all the others which have followed—is that, whether Lindsay likes it or not, Wagner was right.

Another lesson that Lindsay should have learned during his first term is that unless the young men on whom he relies are more willing to serve the public and the Mayor—instead of themselves—he will not succeed. As James Wechsler of the *Post* once said, there was "an atmosphere of turmoil" in the early years of the Lindsay Administration; there were too many "internal bickerings and obstructions."[1]

My own view of the chaotic early months of Lindsay's first term about which I have written in this book is that they were crucial, exciting—and inevitable. John Lindsay had to prove himself and part of the process was to take the fire. And those of us who stood with him also had to endure the collective scrutiny of six New York newspapers and a galaxy of television and radio newsmen. Before we entered City Hall, I knew that John Lindsay had no administrative experience and so did he; I also knew that I had no experience as a political public relations man and that many of the young commissioners whom he named during our first year had no practical experience in their fields, either. At the time, Lindsay viewed this as an asset rather than a liability. He wanted to get away from the image of tired, middle-aged city officials from the political clubhouse; he wanted to inject youth, energy, idealism and imagination into city government. In retrospect, of course, it is easy to realize that we should have sought the advice of those who preceded us; we should not have launched so many reforms simultaneously; and we should not have assumed that we knew what was best for New York.

In addition, we should not have underestimated the power and importance of the press, especially the group of cynical newspaper, radio and television reporters assigned to City Hall. We expected a certain amount of critical scrutiny from the news media; a new Mayor with a team of young assistants was "fair game" for newsmen in Room 9. But, at the outset, the Mayor made it clear to close friends that he viewed the local City Hall reporters as less capable than the reporters he had known among the Washington press. He had enjoyed a generally "good press" in the nation's capital with reporters, columnists and commentators. For this reason, he found it difficult to learn to speak the language of the more down-to-earth reporters in Room 9, who were petty, blunt, and often crude. I sympathized with Lindsay because I, too, felt the sting of their criticism. I was also displeased with many of them because they did not treat the office of Mayor with enough respect. The problem was that they had been used to abusing Mayor Wagner for twelve years and they resented both John Lindsay's independence and my efforts to keep them at a distance from the Mayor. They had been accustomed to wandering in and out of Wagner's office and they were angered when Lindsay decided the Mayor should have privacy.

As the months and years passed, of course, the death of three major newspapers—the *Herald Tribune, World-Telegram and Sun,* and *Journal-American*—reduced the pressure on Lindsay and, unfortunately, also resulted in a lessening of competition among reporters. The *New York Times,* virtually alone in the field, cut its coverage from some fifteen reporters at the outset in 1966 to one or two in Room 9 by the end of Lindsay's first term.

Another major stumbling block to success in the early months of Lindsay's first term was the Mayor's uncompromising attitude on many key public issues. John Lindsay practiced the politics of confrontation, instead of the politics of mediation or conciliation. As a result, many of the changes for which we were striving failed to materialize. There was tremendous resistance among the many power blocs of New York to our suggested reforms, first because few people wanted change which meant any personal sacrifice, and second, because of the manner in which John Lindsay announced his reforms. He failed completely to take anyone who opposed him into his confidence; he failed to reach out and try to understand the opposition; he failed to admit his mistakes, even when they were blatant. It wasn't until the campaign of 1969 that he went on television and publicly stated he had, indeed, made some mistakes, that his credibility as a man who learned from experience was enhanced. It is this tendency, as many others have said, to display his puritan morality that has angered so many New Yorkers. "There's a New England stubbornness about him," Human Resources Administrator Mitchell Ginsberg once said, "and, I suppose, a certain stiffness, too. I expect there are very few people he relates to."

What is John Lindsay's future? If he leaves politics, "my options," Lindsay once told a reporter in my presence, "it seems to me, are superb. There's writing, for instance. I'd like to try that. I don't think I could succeed in it is a full-time occupation, but I'd like to see if I could. And if I did try, I'd like to do it abroad for a while. Also, there's always the law to go back to. I'd have to learn the tricks of the trade again, but I used to enjoy trying cases. And there's foundation work, and teaching, although university life has its drawbacks—and the more I see of it, the more of the drawbacks I see, especially in administration. I can think of nothing more exasperating than being Mayor of New York, except perhaps being a college president. Another option I find appealing is television work—news, running discussion programs, that sort of thing. Really, the variety of options is enormous."

As to Lindsay's political future, two things appear certain: First, he has shown that he has the ability to survive in New York's political jungle without the aid of either major party after four nearly disastrous years; second, as long as he retains a reservoir of goodwill and respect among the mass media and among other major political leaders, he will remain a prospect for higher office—Senator, Governor or President. He offered one clue about his Presidential aspirations in mid-1968 when the press asked him about the possibility of running as Vice President on the Republican ticket. "The Presidency," he replied, "is where the marbles are. I think the key is the top of the ticket, the candidate for President."

Meanwhile, despite his obvious inability to get along with Nelson Rockefeller—the two men simply do not trust each other or like each other personally—Lindsay will try and govern New York City with a new coalition of politicians, including many prominent Democrats. And while he remains Mayor, he will try to lend hope to New Yorkers and millions of others who live in cities across the nation that the quality of life can be improved. However, his hopes for the future have been tempered by the many crises which plagued his first term. In his second inaugural address in January, 1970, he said: "We are all human, we are all fallible. The test for this Administration and for this city is whether we have learned from mistakes. . . ."

And, in sharp contrast to the unrestrained optimism of his first inaugural in 1966, Lindsay declared: "It is best not to plan on promises and dreams. If we do all we hope to do in the next four years, there will still be too much of crime and poverty, too much of slums and pollution. There will still be a city that often seems determined to frustrate those who love it most."

As someone who grew up in New York and worked for its improvement, I have experienced this frustration. I look back on my time in public life more in sadness than in anger. I did not, as I had hoped, see Lindsay's promise fulfilled; I did not see the kinds of reforms about which I had always dreamed; I did not see many things happen around me that were either positive or lasting in the way of deep-rooted, meaningful changes. I did not meet many men of real courage and conviction in politics.

As a result of my experience, I am convinced that—at least in the foreseeable future—there is little anyone can do to revive a desperate New York. Not even John Lindsay.

Appendix

I   A BRIEF BIOGRAPHY OF JOHN V. LINDSAY, MAYOR OF NEW YORK

John Vliet Lindsay was born in New York City on November 24, 1921, one of five children of George Nelson and Florence Eleanor Vliet Lindsay. His late father was an investment banker and Chairman of the Board of the American Swiss Corporation. His grandfather had come to America from the Isle of Wight. The Mayor has an older brother, George N., a lawyer; a fraternal twin brother, David A., also a lawyer; and a younger brother, Robert F., a banker. A sister, Eleanor W. Schieffelin, died in 1965.

Lindsay received his early schooling at the Buckley School in New York City, graduating in 1935. Upon graduation from St. Paul's School in Concord, New Hampshire, he entered Yale University, completing the requirements for a Bachelor's degree in three years. In 1943, he joined the Navy as a Gunnery Officer on the destroyer Swanson. He served in the Mediterranean, the invasion of Sicily; in the Southwest Pacific with the Seventh Amphibious Fleet and in the Western Pacific with the Fifth Carrier Strike Fleet.

The end of the war found Lindsay a full lieutenant, the Executive Officer of his ship, and the holder of five battle stars. He returned to the Yale Law School in 1946 and obtained his law degree in 1948. The next year, he was admitted to the State Bar and joined the New York City law firm of Webster, Sheffield, Fleishmann, Hitchcock and Chrystie. He was named a partner in 1953.

On June 18, 1949, Lindsay married the former Mary Anne Harrison, of Richmond, Virginia. They have four children, Katherine, 19; Margaret, 16; Anne, 14; and John, Jr., 9.

In 1955 and 1956, Lindsay served in the U.S. Justice Department as Executive Assistant to U.S. Attorney General Herbert Brownell. He participated in writing the Eisenhower Administration's legislative program, was the Department of Justice's liaison officer to the Cabinet, Congress and the White House, and argued cases before the Supreme Court of the United States.

John Lindsay took an active interest in politics soon after his graduation from law school. He was one of the founders of the Youth for Eisenhower movement in 1951, and was elected president of the New York City Young Republican Club in 1952.

In 1958, Lindsay decided to run for Congress from Manhattan's 17th District. He won the Republican primary by 2,077 votes over the organization's candidate, Frederic R. Coudert, Jr. In the general election, Lindsay ran against Democratic-Liberal candidate Anthony B. Akers, a World War II hero and an experienced campaigner. Lindsay won by 7,718 votes. He won three Congressional elections after that:

In 1960, Lindsay defeated William vanden Heuvel by 26,148 votes, although Presidential Candidate John F. Kennedy carried the District.

In 1962, the 17th District was reapportioned so that it contained 35,000 more Democrats than Republicans. Congressman Lindsay, nonetheless, won reelection that year by more than 53,000 votes over his Democratic-Liberal opponent, Martin B.

Dworkis. He led the Republican ticket in New York City, doubling his 1960 margin.

In 1964, Mr. Lindsay won by 91,000 votes over Mrs. Eleanor Clark French, as Lyndon Johnson was carrying the District by 85,000 votes. Lindsay's plurality that year was the greatest of any opposed Republican candidate in the country.

This support by his constituency was a tribute to his six years of Congressional service, during which he earned a reputation as one of the effective advocates of civil rights legislation in the House of Representatives. He also worked actively for more humane urban renewal laws, for medical and hospital care for the elderly, fair, sensible immigration statutes, improved education, air pollution safeguards, middle and lower income housing, individual liberties, rehabilitation of narcotics addicts and advancement of the arts.

Mr. Lindsay was a Member of the House Judiciary Committee and was United States Delegate to the North Atlantic Treaty Organization Parliamentarians Conference. He was chairman of the Political Committee of the Conference.

John Lindsay has written several articles, about Congressional and urban affairs for such leading publications as *Harper's, The Atlantic Monthly, The Saturday Evening Post, The Saturday Review,* and the *New York Times Magazine.* He is also the author of two books, *Journey into Politics* and *The City.*

The 48-year-old Mayor is six feet four inches tall and has light brown hair and blue eyes. He enjoys skiing, ice skating, swimming, tennis and sailing. Lindsay is a member of St. James Episcopal Church, the Citizens' Committee for Children of New York City, The Council on Foreign Relations, Board of Advisors of the Young Men's Christian Association, the Board of Directors of the New York City Mission Society and The Yale Corporation (Board of Trustees). He is a member of the New York City, New York State and American Bar associations.

II INAUGURAL ADDRESS BY MAYOR JOHN V. LINDSAY, CITY HALL
PLAZA, NEW YORK CITY

For Release on Delivery
7:00 P.M.
Saturday, January 1, 1966

My fellow New Yorkers:
New York City represents all that is exciting about our cities
and everything that threatens to destroy them.

New York symbolizes the traditional aspirations of man—
power, fame and wealth. Yet it magnifies every adversity of city
living—the crowds, the noise, the dirt; the innumerable accommo-
dations and sacrifices exacted from those who live in an urban
society.

It is a city in which individuals have been characterized by
vigor and affluence; New Yorkers have always sought out the
newest and best in their own lives. As citizens, however, they col-
lectively tolerated a government possessing neither attribute.

Until now.

Last November 2nd, the people of New York decided that
their government was not good enough; that it must do better.
They voted for a change in leadership, one which would promise
to restore to this city the imprimatur of pride.

In keeping with this mandate, I affirm a dedication to a simple,
perhaps old-fashioned concept, drawn from the finest of American
political traditions. It is that the public interest must prevail over
special interests, the good of the community over the desires of
any group. This is the credo of responsible conservatism no less
than of modern progressivism; it was the spirit of Theodore
Roosevelt and Franklin Roosevelt, of William Gaynor and
Fiorello La Guardia.

It is the spirit of men who cared.

They cared about the malignant effects of injustice, intolerance
and indifference. And they dared to believe that men could rise
above the claims of party or class; that public service could offer
the largest satisfaction in life. They dared to assert that men
could find new answers to old questions.

The question now before us is whether men of conscience and

conviction can reject ignoble partisan intrigue and join in a massive effort to make real our dreams for New York.

If we fail, the implications of our defeat will be assessed throughout the nation, to be proclaimed by the cynics as proof that great cities are no longer governable.

If we succeed, we shall have demonstrated that independent government, free of the irrelevant dictates of party politics, can overcome the sickness and shame of our cities.

Divided, we can do little to meet the powerful challenges facing the city.

United, there is little we cannot do.

Together, we can open direct lines of communication between the people and their government. My plan to open Little City Halls in the neighborhoods of our city, manned by the people in those neighborhoods, will stimulate a new citizen involvement in the life of the city.

Their function will be in keeping with the oath taken by the young men of ancient Athens to "strive unceasingly to quicken the public sense of civic duty."

In this pursuit, a major objective is to destroy the assumption that those who serve their city are somehow compromised or demeaned.

I have undertaken to attack that premise by selecting men and women of known ability and stature to assist me in City Hall.

I hope that my appointments and reappointments will give tangible credence to my resolve to regard merit as the only test of service.

There will be tolerance for honest disagreement and human error within the offices of our government.

The New Yorkers of today will decide the destiny of the New Yorkers of tomorrow—by proving their readiness to accept the inconveniences and irritations, the hardships and responsibilities, that must accompany any transition.

I cannot predict whether—at the end of four years—this administration will be beloved by many. But I hope it will be respected by all.

As I speak, our city is crippled by a strike against the bus and subway system. It is an unlawful strike against the public interest, called even before the collective bargaining process had run its course.

It is an act of defiance against eight million people. I shall not permit the public interest to be flaunted, no matter how severe the stress.

The oath of office I have just taken requires me to uphold the law of the land. That I shall do—in the name of those eight million people.

I say to the parties to this dispute that theirs is the immediate responsibility for arriving at a swift and equitable settlement and I insist that they discharge that responsibility.

This is a time for reason; a time to serve the common interests of the city.

The current crisis is but one of the many which afflict New York. Let us move against each of them—now.

Let those who compile riches from the misery of slums hear this message as their eviction notice: There will be no compromise with the profiteers of poverty.

Let those who exploit human addiction hear me clearly: New York will no longer be your marketplace.

Those who would do business as usual may be distressed. Those wise enough to see the need for change will find that a city in rebirth will provide the healthiest climate for business and every other sector of the city.

We will combat terror in the streets. And we will do so with full respect for the rights and privileges of every citizen.

We will have the rule of law—and that means rigorous, diligent, corruption-free law enforcement. It also means that although wrong will be fought night and day, the Bill of Rights will remain a shield for all.

And so, my fellow citizens, I summon you to enlist in the fight for a better New York:

—The fight to revive the hopes of the downtrodden, the sick, the exploited.

—The fight for new and better employment.

—The fight against wretched slums, poisoned air, stifling traffic and congested subways.

—The fight for excellence and equality in our education—and for the integrity of our historic system of independent free city colleges.

—The fight for new parks and recreational facilities.

The New York for which we are fighting is as old as the vision of brotherhood. It is a city in which there will be new light in tired eyes, and the sound of laughter in homes. Our enemies in this battle are greed, ignorance, bureaucracy, prejudice and defeatism—in high places and low.

But no mayor and no city can go it alone. The rebuilding of New York will necessitate a close—and I hope fruitful—partnership with state and federal governments.

I am confident that our Governor, our Senators and our Legislators will help, realizing that our needs are in many ways the needs of the state and nation.

My administration will be a visible government. No longer will New Yorkers be obliged to seek out the distant, unfamiliar offices of their city; from this day on, their city will go to them.

Your mayor and his associates will be seen in this city. We will visit the slums and the waterfront. We will go into the schools, hospitals, and prisons.

We shall go forth with a selfless perspective;—with the knowledge that what we do here may gain us neither gratitude nor glory except in the judgment of a later age.

And if we transmit to another generation a city made happier and more beautiful by our endeavors, we shall take pride in our legacy.

Our commitment to New York is timeless; to our city we cheerfully devote our spirit and our hands, our energies and our skills.

We have faith that we can build what must be built . . .

Preserve what must be preserved . . .

Change what must be changed.

The fulfillment of that faith begins today.

III MAJOR ACCOMPLISHMENTS OF LINDSAY'S FIRST 95 DAYS IN OFFICE

The session on April 5, 1966, began with the Mayor outlining the major accomplishments of his first 95 days in office. He touched on the following points:

1. His has been a truly Fusion, Non-Partisan government.

2. He has pressed for tax reform.

3. His Administration has moved to halt the flow of small businesses from the city.

4. He has created a Sports Commission.

5. He has started the reorganization of city government, particularly in the areas of transportation, welfare and sanitation.

6. He has begun to introduce long-range budget planning.

7. He has made progress with the work of the City Commission on Human Rights.

8. He has launched an unusual experiment in housing, known as "instant rehabilitation."

9. He has begun to develop impasse procedures in city labor relations.

10. He has worked to select judges through a Judiciary Nominating Commission.

11. He has begun a program of vest-pocket parks.

12. He has begun to work to preserve green spaces, especially the preservation of Staten Island greenbelt.

13. He has introduced a New York City Youth Olympics, and recreation programs in parks, park concerts, and restoration of Prospect Park boathouse.

14. He has launched the Sviridoff and Logue studies in poverty and housing.

15. A New York City office in Washington will be opened and an office staff signed up by early summer.

16. Local Mayor's offices would be opened soon.

17. The new Expense Budget was being prepared.

IV SUMMARY OF CORPORATION COUNSEL'S OPINION ON THE LE-
GALITY OF THE CITY COUNCIL'S TRANSFERRING MONEY TO THE
TRANSIT AUTHORITY

*Following is a summary of the opinion as released to the press on
Monday, July 4, 1966:*

"The opinion clearly states first that the State Constitution
gives the State Legislature the power to create authorities and by
reason of that power no other body can create authorities, grant
powers to them or take powers from them. The opinion further
states that the City Council does not have the power to grant or
to take away any of the Transit Authority's powers under the
State Authorities Law.

Secondly, the opinion states that the $84 million claims of the
Transit Authority have not been presented. But, from information furnished to the Corporation Counsel by the Transit Authority, the opinion states, such claims, if presented, would fall
into the category described by the Corporation Counsel as "equitable" but not "legal." The only body that can allow equitable
claims is the Board of Estimate, according to the Corporation
Counsel. Under the City Charter the Board of Estimate cannot
allow equitable claims if they are barred by the statute of limitations, even if they should be presented.

In this instance the statute of limitations has run out on the
possible claims adding up to $84 million, according to the
opinion.

Thirdly, the opinion states that the bill attempts to usurp the
budget-making powers of the Mayor as created by the City Charter. If the Council wishes to modify the powers of the Mayor, the
opinion states, it can do so only with a referendum.

Fourthly, the opinion states there is no basis in law for the
payment to the Transit Authority or for use of any payment by
the Transit Authority even if received because:

a) No budget item has been adopted fixing such an amount as
part of the City budget.

b) The Transit Authority has no right to use it because of the requirement that the Transit Authority be self-sustaining under the New York State Public Authorities Law.

Fifth, the opinion states that the Home Rule Amendment of the State Constitution does not permit the City Council to enact local laws changing the powers and duties of the Transit Authority."

V ACCOMPLISHMENTS OF THE LINDSAY ADMINISTRATION, JANUARY
   1—SEPTEMBER 15, 1966.

1. Civilian Review Board
2. Government Reorganization
       Human Resources
       Health Services
       Transportation
3. Top Talent
       Hayes
       Heller
       Leary
       McGrath
       Nathan
       Ramirez
       Rankin
       Sviridoff
4. Washington Office
       Federal Aid Survey
5. Tax Reform
6. Program—Planning—Budget System
7. Attract New Business
       (A) EDC
           Public Development Corp.—Clay
       (B) Cut Red Tape
           1 Stop Service—4,000 Businesses Helped
           Movies
           Cabaret-fingerprinting
8. First Neighborhood City Hall—East New York
9. Economies
       Job Freeze
       Civil Defense
       Cut 100 Committees
10. Parks
11. Police—"Cool Summer"
       400 New Cars
       Minority Recruiting

12. Non-Political Appointment of Judges
      Mayor's Committee on Judiciary
13. Summer Youth Olympics
      City Sports Program
14. Urban Corps—1,000 kids
15. Welfare Reforms
      Satellite Centers
      Affidavit
      Birth Control
      Employment Incentive
16. Proposed Office of Collective Bargaining
17. Fire Department
      False Alarms
      Reallocation of Manpower
18. Traffic
      Crackdown on Scofflaws
To Come
 1. Parking in Midtown
 2. Housing—Logue Report
 3. Air Pollution
 4. Reorganization—Legislative
 5. Police Communications
 6. Traffic Crackdown
      New Proposals for Keeping Traffic out of the City

VI CITY HALL PRESS RELEASE CONTAINING EXCHANGE OF LETTERS BETWEEN JOHN V. LINDSAY AND WOODY KLEIN

Office of the Mayor   John V. Lindsay   City Hall   New York City

Tel: 566-5090   265-68

Immediate Release
Thursday, July 25, 1968

Mayor John V. Lindsay released today the following exchange of letters between himself and Woody Klein, Assistant Administrator for Public Affairs in the Housing and Development Administration:

July 25, 1968

Mayor John V. Lindsay
City Hall
New York, New York 10007

Dear John:

I am respectfully submitting my resignation to you, effective August 19, after having served your administration for more than two-and-a-half years.

In November, 1965, you asked me to join you to launch many long-overdue reforms in New York City. I felt committed to try and help you combat the tremendous problems, particularly housing, because for many years as a newspaper reporter I had written about the need for improved living conditions in our city.

I have enjoyed working with you in municipal government. Now, however, I feel it is time for me to return to my profession as a writer and editor in the private sector. Since we have been friends for 10 years, I am sure you understand my desire to get back to journalism.

Earlier this year, I decided to seek a position in private industry. Recently, the International Business Machines Corporation responded with an offer of an excellent job as a writer and editor in the company's communications department.

I want you to know it was a great privilege to serve as your first press secretary. I will never forget those early days when we shared so many new challenges. I think it was one of the most worthwhile experiences of my life. I also derived much satisfaction as an assistant administrator helping to run the city's first superagency, the Housing and Development Administration, under Jason R. Nathan. I have told Jay of my decision this morning.

I am proud to have been closely associated with you and this Administration and I hope I can always be of assistance to you in the future.

With warmest personal regards to you and Mary from Audrey and me.

Sincerely,

Woody Klein
Assistant Administrator
for Public Affairs

July 25, 1968

Dear Woody:

I enjoyed our visit this morning, and I appreciate your giving me your generous letter in which you advise you are taking a position with IBM as a writer and editor in the Corporation's Communications Department.

You are joining a distinguished organization, one that is increasingly assisting our City Government and our City in a number of ways. As I told you, I believe there are approximately forty young IBM urbanologists and systems men working full time on city problems. This means you are transferring your talents to another institution which is actively engaged in the urban situation.

As an old friend, it has been a matter of pride and pleasure to have worked with you; and I shall always treasure the early days in this Administration when we shared many battles, won some, lost some, and gradually shaped up the Administration.

The Housing and Development Administration, of which you have been a key part, is now on the track both structurally and in the production line of housing. There are now more housing units under construction in 1968 than in any time in the past ten years in our City. This is no small accomplishment, particularly in the area of Mitchell-Lama middle-income housing where the pipeline was virtually empty.

Good luck in your new endeavors, and I look forward to working with you at all times in the future. Mary joins me in sending our very best to Audrey and you.

Sincerely,

John V. Lindsay
Mayor

Notes

1. Aurelio returned to Senator Javits' office after Lindsay's victory. He rejoined the Mayor once again in 1969 as campaign manager in charge of the Mayor's reelection headquarters, and was named a Deputy Mayor by Lindsay after his victory.

2. After Lindsay became Mayor, he subsequently assigned Barry Gottehrer, a former *New York Herald Tribune* reporter, these duties.

3. Two months later, William V. Shannon, writing in the *Harper's* January, 1966, issue, commented: "Lindsay never made any single issue the dominant theme in the campaign. Many suspected this would be a weakness. Stevensonian liberal Democrats complained that his campaign was too much image and too little issues. But, at the end, it was clear that his real theme was not an issue but a promise—the hope of

change. A stalemated, weary cynical city decided on November 2 to give the fresh-faced new boy a chance."

CHAPTER 2

1. Ironically, Gribetz, who first returned to private industry, was later named regional administrator of the Federal Department of Housing and Urban Development by President Johnson and, in 1969 with Price no longer in the Administration, he was appointed by Mayor Lindsay as impartial chairman of the Rent Conciliation and Appeals Board, a privately sponsored board.

2. Quill identified one of the alleged "meddlers" as John B. Oakes, editor of the editorial page of the *New York Times*. He said, "Mr. Oakes, the publisher of the new Bible, has been trying to advise Mr. Lindsay on the direction of his programs, his appointments and the amount of money he should spend. I know exactly how much money Mr. Oakes has told Mr. Lindsay to O.K. for a settlement." Replying to this charge, Mr. Oakes said: "I have no comment on Mr. Quill's fulminations except to say whatever advice the *New York Times* has had to give the Mayor-elect Lindsay about transit or any other matter has been openly expressed in its editorials. And that is just where it will continue to be expressed."

3. The editorial pointed out that New York City's bus drivers and subway motormen were paid more than their counterparts in other major cities —Boston, Chicago, Cleveland and Philadelphia. Bus drivers in New York received $3.22 per hour and motormen $3.46 per hour. The editorial suggested the mediation panel, not Lindsay or Wagner, should make some recommendations for a settlement. "If more time were needed for an equitable settlement based on the mediators' proposals, the present contract could be extended under a guarantee of retroactivity," the editorial stated. "But the city should be prepared to take a strike rather than capitulate to the unbridled exercise of union power in defiance of the Condon-Wadlin Act and a court injunction. Mr. Quill cannot be allowed to triumph over the rights of the people of New York."

4. On December 30, I received a letter from James A. Wechsler, editorial page editor of the *New York Post*, with some suggested revisions on Lindsay's inauguration speech, which he had helped to draft. A confidant of many well-known political figures, Wechsler was generally regarded as one of the nation's most articulate and most liberal newspaper editors.

5. In handing down his ruling, Judge Tilzer had stated: "This threat hangs ominously over the lifeline of all the citizens of the City of New York, and should there be a strike called at 5 A.M., as threatened, general paralysis of the activities of the inhabitants of this city will ultimately ensue. . . . The effect of a strike would tragically and disastrously affect the people of the City of New York. . . . The staggering effects of a

strike at this time on the inhabitants of this city far outweigh the
rights of these defendants."

CHAPTER 3

1. The *New York Times* selected his appeal to all New Yorkers "to enlist in
   the fight for a better New York" as its lead in reporting the inaugural
   speech, under the headline: INAUGURAL ASKS FOR A BETTER CITY.

2. The Mayor's response to Quill's attacks drew this comment from the *New
   York Post*'s James A. Wechsler the following day: "Lindsay has never
   underestimated the possible dimensions of the conflict. He was also
   keenly sensitive to the human equations; that is why he carefully
   denied himself the luxury of an angry retort to Quill's personal taunts.
   On a smaller scale, and without seeming to liken the issues involved,
   Lindsay has approached this clash in the style that John F. Kennedy
   employed during the Cuban crisis. He would not let Quill degrade him
   by an exhibition of muscle. But neither would he let vanity provoke
   him into exercises which might deny his adversary the chance of
   honorable face-saving."

3. With reports of Quill's release circulating, Lindsay and Price decided that
   Price should visit Quill at Bellevue Hospital that night. The mission
   was such a well-kept secret—nobody else at City Hall knew about it,
   including me. The fact that the visit took place was not revealed until
   January 22, when New York *Journal-American* columnist Victor Riesel
   reported he knew about the visit during the strike. Price had cleared
   the plan with John O'Donnell, the Transport Workers Union lawyer,
   and Mrs. Quill, before going to Quill's hospital room. Price listened
   while O'Donnell told Quill that the membership was standing solid.
   Price said Lindsay wanted to keep the settlement figure "held to $50
   million," according to Riesel, "but there was no talk of money or any
   specifics at the bedside." Riesel's account of the meeting continued:
   "Mike was alert. So was the ever-present doctor. Then Price spoke up.
   He and Lindsay were concerned over the imprisonment of Quill and
   the others, he said. They were sorry he was jailed. It was insinuated
   this could be easily remedied. Price wondered aloud, after talking of
   chaos in the city, if Mike would try to expedite the settlement. Mike
   replied he would agree only to what the men would accept."

4. The *Times* editorial the following day, January 11, entitled "War on the
   Power Brokers," firmly supported the Mayor's stand. It read, in part:
   "With his bold speech last night, Mayor Lindsay has struck at the
   fiction that the paralyzing and illegal transit strike is in its essence just
   another normal dispute. . . . Mr. Lindsay's televised report, with its
   inspiring blend of courage, reason and resolution, was just what was
   needed to rally the community against this sinister attempt to club it
   into surrender through the reckless abuse of union strength."

   On January 12, *Times* reporter Richard Witkin, in a news analysis
   on page seventeen entitled "The 'Power Brokers,'" took up the same

theme and asked the question: "Who are the power brokers?" Witkin had called me in my office for a reply to the question. After talking with Lindsay, I called Witkin back with this answer: "They know who they are." He pressed me for more information and I replied: "The Mayor doesn't have to say any more than he wants to. He does not want to name names or identify anyone at this time."

CHAPTER 4

1. According to a New York City Health Department report dated January 17, 1966, the number of deaths and death rates in the first two weeks of 1966 (ending Friday, January 14, 1966) compared with deaths and rates for the corresponding two weeks period of 1965 and in 1964 were as follows:

Year	Number of Deaths	Death Rate*
1966	3,499**	11.5
1965	4,055	13.5
1964	3,766	12.6

* Per 100,000 population.

** The reason for the drop in the first 14 days in 1966, according to Karl Pretshold, the department's public relations counsel at the time, was "good weather" during that period.

2. Some months later, Mary Lindsay recalled in an interview with writer Nat Hentoff: "A week or so after the transit strike was settled, John and I took a Saturday afternoon walk from 14th Street down Broadway to City Hall. People stopped him, of course, but everyone—people looking out of coffee shops, kids looking out of windows—had a smile for him. That felt good. And, you know, during the transit strike, when he'd be walking downtown to the office, there'd be people at the doors of restaurants holding out a cup of coffee for him. So when he gets discouraged at a particularly bad morning's mail, I tell him the people who write are usually only the angry ones. I like to see what people are saying. I get 25 to 30 letters a day here, and I read them all. And others are addressed to me at City Hall. If someone doesn't like something, and if the complaint is something I can answer, and if there's a return address, I answer. I said he sometimes gets discouraged, but actually he gets more worried and concerned than discouraged. I'm sure, though, that little by little, things will become more workable. Being Mayor may never be *fun*, but it will be something he'll be able to cope with. It will take time."

3. Soon after, in the "Notes on TV" column of *Cue* magazine, writer Joan Walker described the scene at City Hall, noting that on occasions previous to the "fireside chat" when the Mayor had appeared on TV from the Blue Room, the cameras had caught him and one leg of the portrait of President James Monroe that hangs on the wall behind him. The article reminded the press of how Robert Montgomery, the actor, used to advise Dwight D. Eisenhower about makeup; how the debates be-

tween John F. Kennedy and Richard M. Nixon hinged on TV appearance; and how General Charles DeGaulle changed his TV image in
order to appear "folksy" instead of "austere."

"Apparently," the article continued, after describing the press coverage of the event, "some people would prefer it if Mr. Lindsay used a
disembodied knee as a backdrop, or, in wild sartorial disarray, glowered
into the cameras. We don't get it."

4. Mrs. Shainswit later became an assistant administrator in the Housing and
Development Administration and, at the outset of 1970, was named
first assistant to City Council President Sanford D. Garelik.

5. A short time later, one of Room 9's more enterprising reporters, Joseph
Fitzpatrick of the Associated Press, interviewed the Mayor privately on
the subject of Vietnam as part of a series of interviews I had set up for
members of the press who regularly covered the Mayor. The outcome
of Fitzpatrick's interview was a story in which Lindsay spelled out his
views on Vietnam. The *Times* picked up the interview and ran it on
page one under the headline: LINDSAY PROPOSES 'SOLID DIPLOMACY' BY
U.S. IN VIETNAM. The story quoted the Mayor as saying that bombing
cannot end the "most unwanted war" in the nation's history. It was
the Mayor's first extended comment on the war since he had announced his candidacy for Mayor in 1965. His views were really a re-
statement of a speech he had delivered in Oakland, Michigan, in April,
1965, written by James Carberry. who had urged him to speak out on
Vietnam.

6. The Mayor's City Hall staff coordinated the letters and telephone messages
with an elaborate staff system worked out by Rothenberg and Werner
(Wynn) Kramarsky, a Democrat and son-in-law of New York *Post* publisher Dorothy Schiff. Kramarsky had worked for Milton Mollen during
the campaign. He now handled all the mail and routed much of it to
mayoral assistants and other top members of the Administration for
draft answers, sometimes for the Mayor's signature. (A signature machine signed most of the letters, but each day the Mayor would put his
"John V. Lindsay" on two dozen or so highly personal or important
letters.) Meanwhile, responding to the many thousands of calls to the
Mayor which went through the City Hall switchboard was the Mayor's
Information Center, headed by James W. Smith, a Negro, who had also
worked in the campaign. This staff worked closely with a small volunteer night staff, which, in turn, assisted the "Night Mayor"—a city
official assigned to stay at City Hall all night in case of an emergency.
Oliver Pilat had been put in charge of the "Night Owl" program, as
it had come to be known.

CHAPTER 5

1. Deputy Mayor Timothy W. Costello was soon to publicly express his own
displeasure with the Night Owl program. After serving all night February 16—two days after the program started—Costello told newsmen:

"I'm not at all convinced of the usefulness of this practice. And I'll tell the Mayor I am less than enthusiastic about it. I'm exhausted." Less than two weeks later, on February 27, in a radio interview, former Mayor Wagner called the Night Owl watch "silly." He said he thought most of Lindsay's commissioners agreed with him.

2. "The office of Mayor needs a lot more dignity than it has had in the past," Lindsay told writer Nat Hentoff in an interview in February which was later quoted in the October 7, 1967, issue of *The New Yorker* magazine. "I think the Mayor of New York has usually tended to be kicked around, and he's accommodated himself to being treated that way by saying yes to everything without delivering. You have to lift up the joint. How? By the way you handle the press conferences, for one thing. By the way you use television. By sometimes refusing to say yes, even if it's going to make people angry. The Mayor has to walk a little taller than he ever has before." Lindsay also offered this view of how a Mayor should act in public: "Being Mayor involves your having to do three things simultaneously. I'm a public symbol and therefore must do enough symbolic things that will produce a feeling of leadership. That means being seen around the city at poverty hearings, walking in the neighborhoods, at the schools. Two, I have to resolve the clashes and collisions between people that are constantly going on while I'm also deciding on appointments, budgetary matters and all sorts of daily problems. Third, there is the matter of developing long range plans for New York. Where do we go in five years? In ten years?"

3. In 1955 and 1956, Lindsay had served as executive assistant to Brownell. He had worked on the Eisenhower legislative program and, as a young lawyer in the Justice Department, Lindsay had acted as that agency's liaison officer with the Cabinet. Other members of the Mayor's "Kitchen Cabinet" included Bethuel M. Webster, a prominent New York attorney; Gabriel Hauge, a banker; Walter N. Thayer, a lawyer and investment banker and president of the *New York Herald Tribune;* Alex Rose, vice chairman of the Liberal Party; David Dubinsky, a Liberal Party vice chairman and president of the International Ladies Garment Workers Union; Charles M. Metzner, a Federal judge; the Mayor's three brothers, and his wife.

4. Peluso later became an aide to City Council President Frank D. O'Connor and, in early 1970, executive assistant to Comptroller Abraham D. Beame.

5. The color painting is the official portrait of the late Mayor Fiorello La Guardia. It was painted by Sidney E. Dickinson in 1948 from a photograph and shows La Guardia dressed in a mayoral pinstriped suit with his tortoise shell glasses dangling from his left hand. Lindsay, in talking about the portrait to a reporter inside his office one day in February, said of La Guardia: "His was the first government in the flesh I ever saw. I think I was 12 at the time; that would have made it 1934, La Guardia's first year in office. Somebody arranged for me and my twin

brother, David, to come and visit the new Mayor in his office. He was using the big room for his office, the one we call the Blue Room now. The room was noisy and very crowded when David and I were ushered in. The Mayor was sitting behind that huge desk of his, with his glasses up on the top of his head. He was yelling at everybody and people were coming in and out of the room and yelling back at him. Then he stopped yelling for a minute and shook our hands. The whole thing was over in two seconds, but it made a deep impression on me."

6. Garelik resigned from the Police Department in 1969 to run for City Council President on the Liberal Party ticket with John Lindsay. He also won designation as the Republican candidate in a party primary. Although he was a registered Democrat, he was elected as City Council President as the Republican-Liberal candidate.

7. Sealy remained in that post until September, 1969, when he resigned to become an associate professor at John Jay College of Criminal Justice. At the time of his resignation just before the 1969 mayoral election, he was commander of all uniformed police in Brooklyn North—a racially tense area. He had served for twenty-eight years in the Police Department.

8. Steadman later became press aide to Comptroller Mario Procaccino during his 1969 campaign as the Democratic candidate for Mayor.

9. Former Representative John H. Rousselot, national director of public relations for the John Birch Society, was a Congressman from 1960 to 1962, from California. He had served in the House of Representatives at the same time as Lindsay and had taken advantage of his past contact with Lindsay by writing the Mayor a "Dear John" letter several days before he arrived at City Hall, suggesting a meeting between himself and Lindsay "so that you could have a more inte'ligent understanding of The John Birch Society." The letter had concluded: "I shall look forward to seeing you again next week."

10. There was one ironic result of the *News'* story. On March 9, in the letters-to-the-editor column, a Brooklyn reader referred to the "I am the Mayor" quote attributed to Lindsay and said: "How come he did not say that to Big-mouth Quill, when Quill publicly insulted him during the transit talks?"

11. The issue of October 14, 1967.

12. Murray Kempton, commenting on this disclosure in a column entitled "The Virtue Mongers," wrote: "The news that Buildings Commissioner Charles Moerdler and his first deputy are both related to owners of slum properties raises no question of morals and every question of taste. It will be useful only if it instructs the Lindsay people in humility. That happy result is unlikely. People who parade their vices occasionally reform, but people who parade their virtues are incurable."

13. The *Herald Tribune* ran an editorial on April 6 which complimented Lindsay on practically everything the Mayor had done up to that time. It was entitled, "Lindsay: The First 95 Days," and it read, in part:

"The Mayor, of course, has made only a start. But the important thing is that City Hall is imbued with freshness. We have new people with new ideas for making this a better city."

CHAPTER 6

1. The Board of Estimate in New York City is composed of the Mayor; the Comptroller (then Mario A. Procaccino); President of the City Council (then Frank D. O'Connor); and the Presidents of the five boroughs of New York City: Manhattan (then Mrs. Constance Baker Motley); Bronx (then Herman Badillo); Brooklyn (then Abe Stark); Queens (then Mario J. Cariello); and Richmond (then Robert T. Connor). The Mayor, who is the chairman, the comptroller and the City Council president each have four votes, and the borough presidents have two votes each—a total of twenty-two votes.

2. An editorial which appeared in the April 28, 1966, issue of *Town and Village*, published by Charles G. Hagedorn, was entitled, "Good Move, Mister Mayor," and read, in part, as follows: "This newspaper, while guarding jealously its independent role, has endorsed John Lindsay in every one of his political races. We mused on this Monday, as we watched the Mayor conduct himself at a press conference set up especially for weekly newsmen. To the best of our knowledge, Lindsay is the first Mayor to do such a thing. . . . It was no small feat to round up the top-level Commissioners, aides and administrators of the Lindsay Administration for the benefit of the weekly newsmen. And an immense amount of good staff work went into the careful preparation of answers to the questions submitted by the weekly newsmen. . . . So a pat on the back for Mayor Lindsay (who once lived in Stuyvesant Town) along with his many outstanding assistants who worked long and hard and effectively this week in behalf of local communities."

3. After a considerable controversy in the press, Dr. Bench's appointment was declared illegal. The decision came from the city's Corporation Counsel's office and was based on the fact that he was not a United States citizen, as required by the provisions of the State Public Officers Law. However, in order to retain his services, the Administration later listed him as a "counseling management systems" consultant. A story in the *Times* on October 2, 1966, reported he was working as an $80-a-day consultant while two special bills introduced by Senator Jacob K. Javits, a Republican, and Representative Emanuel Celler, a Democrat, to hasten his citizenship were awaiting approval of both Houses of Congress.

4. Lindsay met with the leaders of the ten unions in the newspaper industry at City Hall on Tuesday, May 3, at 2:30 P.M. My office put out a statement saying: "The Mayor believes it is in the public interest to explore at this time all possible approaches in order to attempt to achieve a settlement in the newspaper strike." However, little was ac-

complished as a result of the meeting. The strike continued with no end in sight.

5. Writing in *Newsday,* a Long Island newspaper, Political Editor Frank Lynn said that after five months in office, "Lindsay's overall performance has been criticized by many politicians and civic leaders, (but) most of them agree that the public is still in his corner. The man in the street apparently believes that Lindsay is an honest, sincere politician trying to battle the long-entrenched lethargy of the city. On the outcome of that battle hinges the city's fate and Lindsay's political future."

6. On the same day, the *New York Times* editorially chided Governor Rockefeller for refusing to support Mayor Lindsay's tax program. Under the headline, "Knifing Lindsay in Albany," the *Times* said: "Instead of being in the Mayor's corner, he [Rockefeller] is joining the pack of half-hearted, the politically timid men in the Legislature who are putting the knife to the Mayor."

CHAPTER 7

1. In a news analysis in the *New York Times* on Saturday, June 11, reporter Richard Witkin had summarized the importance of the event: "Some of them will not even be present. But all of the big names of New York politics—Rockefeller, Lindsay, Kennedy, Javits, Rose, Price and assorted Democratic contenders for Governor—will be subjected to new tugs and strains when the Albany talks get underway Monday on New York's tax crisis. . . . And the outcome seems at least as dependent on the interplay of politics and the personalities as it does on the fiscal merits of the matter. . . . Of the Republicans in the local struggle, Governor Rockefeller is generally conceded to be on the hottest spot. Mayor Lindsay, his chief antagonist at the moment, has a city to keep financially afloat. But most observers expect something viable to come out of the Albany talks, and the Mayor does have to run again in 1969."

2. The $283 million tax package consisted of the following new or increased taxes:
   * A personal income tax ranging from four-tenths of 1 percent to 2 percent on city residents, to yield $137 million.
   * An earnings tax of one-fourth of 1 percent on gross wages of commuters and a levy of three-eighths of 1 percent on the earnings of self-employed persons who commute from the suburbs, yielding $23 million.
   * A new business income tax to replace the city's gross receipts tax and to bring an extra $58 million.
   * A 25 percent increase in the stock transfer tax to yield $35 million.
   * Increased water charges to yield $30 million.

3. Despite this appearance of optimism, the Mayor was later to tell writer Nat Hentoff in the fall during an interview that the "roughest time"

during his first nine months in office was, as Lindsay put it, "Those last days and nights in Albany when we were trying to get an agreement on the city income tax program. It was a brutal, bloody show, with little groups in different rooms caucusing and caucusing. That was a rough three days."

The Mayor's twin brother, David, who had served as one of his closest advisers during the first year's crises, also told Hentoff in an interview: "It was rough in Albany, in June. During those last days and nights in the Governor's mansion, there were times when if you'd struck a match the whole place would have blown up. Not that there weren't some moments of relief. One of the Governor's aides was giving Frank O'Connor a tour of the paintings when John happened by. John knew that O'Connor was surely going to run for Governor, and so he said, 'Frank, you know the paintings don't go with the house.' John's humor hasn't been affected by all these pressures."

4. In an editorial dated June 17, the *Times* supported this contention by headlining its editorial: "A Victory in Principle." It read, in part: "Mayor Lindsay and his Democratic allies returned from the long talks in Albany with a negotiated agreement on a tax program for New York City that can be regarded as a half-victory. But on principle, and this is highly important for the future as well as the present, the Albany compact with Governor Rockefeller and legislative leaders was a great and bona fide victory for the Mayor. He established for the first time, as a dependable and productive revenue raiser, the graduated personal income tax. He won recognition, faulty and short of equity though the formula is, for the principle that the commuter who earns his livelihood in the city should make a financial contribution to its operation. He replaced the gross receipts tax, so long criticized as unfair, with a business income tax—a reform sought for many years. He added banks to the list of new taxpayers. This is no small achievement, this broadened, reorganized tax system, for a man in office only six months and up against a horrendously difficult political situation."

CHAPTER 9

1. Fox later left the Police Department to join the *New York Times*.
2. Algernon D. Black, the senior leader of the Ethical Culture Society, had been an ethics teacher at the Fieldston School in the Riverdale section of the Bronx when I was a boy in that school in the early 1940s. I had first met him there and I had remained on friendly terms with him ever since.
3. The other six members of the board were: civilians—Dr. Walter I. Murray, a Negro who was professor of education at Brooklyn College; Manuel Diaz, Jr., chief consultant and acting executive director of the Puerto Rican Community Development Project; and Thomas R. Farrell, a lawyer who was the former president of the Bronx

chapter of the Catholic Interracial Council; policemen— (appointed by Commissioner Howard Leary) Edward McCabe, a deputy commissioner in charge of the division of licenses; Franklin A. Thomas, a Negro who was deputy commissioner in charge of legal matters; and Pearse P. Meagher, deputy inspector, a twenty-five-year veteran of the force. All the civilian appointees had been recommended by an eleven-member panel, headed by former United States Attorney General Herbert Brownell, Jr. The panel had been appointed earlier by the Mayor to suggest candidates for the review board. Thomas and McCabe were holdovers from the old review board, which had been composed entirely of policemen.

4. Several months later, Nat Hentoff, in an interview which appeared in *The New Yorker* on October 14, 1967, asked Lindsay about his frequent walks through the ghettos of the city. Said Hentoff: "What if you're just raising hopes in the ghettos when you're out in the streets—hopes that will turn into even deeper frustration if movement doesn't lead to visible change?" According to Hentoff, the Mayor replied: "I've done a lot of thinking about that, but I honestly believe people are reasonable. They don't expect miracles. They do expect some understanding and knowledge of their troubles. And when I'm around they do see some signs of visible change on some level."

CHAPTER 10

1. The *New York Daily News* chided the Mayor with the following editorial: "There are still about 116 shopping days until Christmas, but John 'I am the Mayor' Lindsay can't wait to give out goodies to his favored few. This new raid on the municipal cupboard comes right after John's handsome cooperation with the City Council in granting whopping 'lulus,' or expense allowances, to its members. Now John is handing out raises to the immediate family. The first deputy hospitals commissioner gets an added title—and $5,000 more per year. A Mayoral assistant's post is reactivated and the $18,000 salary upped to $30,000. For no particular reason, the Air Pollution Control Commissioner and Housing and Redevelopment Chairman enjoy $5,000 raises, bringing each of them to $30,000 per. Yet only yesterday in his Mayoral campaign, it seems, John was preaching economy, economy, economy. Tell us, Mr. Mayor, don't you love the taxpayer in August as you did in November?" Later, in an interview with the *Times*, Lindsay defended the pay raises, saying: "If I have to catch hell for paying good men good salaries, I'll just have to catch hell. I have to do what is right for the city."

2. Supreme Court Justice Irving H. Saypol, in upholding the legality of the petitions on August 12, stated: "It is completely within the prerogative of the electorate of the City of New York to initiate

legislation in this area." He questioned Katz's competence to adjudicate such legal matters and said this was an area "commonly reserved to lawyers and judges."

3. The next day, August 23, in an attempt to clarify the record, the Mayor asked his budget director for a detailed report and he released these figures at a City Hall news conference: the city's expense budget included $507.6 million from the Federal government while the capital budget contained $332.6 million—a grand total of $840.2 million.

4. Governor Rockefeller refused to be drawn into the controversy all summer, declaring it was not a statewide issue. "I strongly believe in home rule," he was quoted as saying in the *Daily News* on September 14, "and I will not campaign on this issue."

5. Although Typographical Union No. 6 had settled in May, the Newspaper Guild remained on strike. The shutdown continued through the summer, resulting in a decision not to reopen the *Herald Tribune* and to merge what was left of the *Tribune* with the afternoon combination to form the *World-Journal-Tribune*.

CHAPTER 11

1. Writing in *The Village Voice*, Jack Newfield said on September 1, 1966: "Compared to former Mayor Wagner, or Daley of Chicago, Locher of Cleveland, or Yorty of Los Angeles, John Lindsay is Pericles. But measured against his enemies in an ocean of urban disintegration, Lindsay seems more like Hemingway's solitary tragic hero, displaying grace under pressure against a hostile universe." Further analyzing Lindsay, Newfield commented: "If there is another quibble with Lindsay up to now, it is in the murky terrain of personality and psyche; it is his exasperating squareness, his puritan innocence, his boy scout pep talks. Lindsay sometimes seems not to grasp fully the terrible tangled social problems, to foolishly think that old-fashioned good will and high-minded decency will make the ghettos vanish and the unskilled learn employable skills. . . . His mind appears to be too literal and conventional to perceive the ragged edges of reality. His is not introspective, and thus lacks the friction between the real and the unconscious that gives Robert Kennedy his brooding extra dimension."

2. In an interview with Nat Hentoff which appeared in *The New Yorker* on October 14, 1967, Kriegel was quoted as saying: "I think we're on the way up. The first six to eight months were the lowest point that John is going to have. The press *had* to knock him down—the Ajax knight on the white horse. And, in a way, he and some of his aides deserved it. They did think they would change the world right away. But we came to learn the value of planning, and of time. You

have to know what to wait for. You have to learn the need to set priorities. You don't try to change the whole city at once. You decide what you're going to change first."

3. Typical of the editorial reaction was the following editorial in the *World-Journal-Tribune* on Friday, September 30, under the headline: LINDSAY PASSES THE HAT. It read: "It's just about time Mayor Lindsay quit acting like a petulantly defensive little boy every time one of his offbeat capers comes under criticism.

"Latest exhibit was the disclosure, through journalistic digging, that Pan Am was bankrolling City Hall's dinner-dance for U.N. delegates. Cynics were quick to note that contract renewal for the controversial helicoptor service atop the Pan Am Building will shortly be up for municipal decision.

"Lindsay angrily slapped down any unworthy inferences. His official greeter, Bud Palmer, said gosh, he hadn't even known about the contract. Both Lindsay and Palmer defended the new Administration's practice (of which the Pan Am incident is only one example) of not merely accepting but soliciting contributions from individual private corporations to finance official municipal receptions, parties and assorted formal festivities.

"Inherent in this brainstorm is a naivete bordering on stupidity. Is the practice, after all, really much different from such discredited dodges as buttonholing businessmen to buy tables for political dinners or advertisements in unpublished political journals?

"Put yourself momentarily in the position of a corporation executive importuned by a top city official to kick in several thousand dollars to underwrite a municipal soiree. You might regard it as a glorious civic opportunity. Then again, especially if you have been around New York very long, you might interpret the request as an implicit promise of favor—or threat of complications.

"Lindsay insists there has been no conflict of interest or 'wrongdoing' in passing the municipal hat to Pan Am and other companies.

"We don't challenge that assertion.

"What eludes Lindsay, however, is the need to avoid even the appearance of impropriety, lest eyebrows begin to arch and tongues to wag.

"The issue is not venality but dopey judgment."

CHAPTER 12

1. In addition, I had the help of Simeon Baker, a friend of Bob Price's who specialized in the American Jewish press and the Israeli press. When we first came into office, Price had told me that Baker had helped Lindsay in the campaign and that he (Price) wanted to put Baker on the payroll to do the same kind of work—promote the names of Lindsay's Jewish city officials in the Jewish press. I objected

at first on the grounds that we did not need a specialist just for one ethnic religious group; but Price insisted, so I added Baker to the City Hall payroll at a salary of $50 a week. He responded immediately, much to my embarrassment, by placing stories about Price and myself in several New York-based Jewish-language newspapers.

2. The statement, issued as press release number 414 from City Hall, read, in part, as follows: "Commissioner of Investigation Arnold Fraiman has reported to me the results of his investigation into alleged irregularities in the Department of Sanitation. On the basis of his report, and pursuant to the provisions of the City Charter, I have sent the following telegram to Vincent A. Starace, First Deputy Commissioner of the Department of Sanitation:

THIS WILL ADVISE YOU THAT FOLLOWING REPORT TO ME BY COMMISSIONER OF INVESTIGATION AND PURSUANT TO CHAPTER 49 SECTION 1123 OF THE CHARTER OF THE CITY OF NEW YORK YOUR EMPLOYMENT WITH THE CITY OF NEW YORK IS HEREBY TERMINATED.

JOHN V. LINDSAY, MAYOR

CHAPTER 13

1. In an interview with Nat Hentoff which was published in the October 14, 1967, issue of *The New Yorker*, the Mayor clarified his relationship with Price. He made it clear that after Price left he made his own decisions and no longer needed his former Deputy Mayor. "I've heard that said, of course, about my having been very dependent on Bob," the Mayor told Hentoff. "But nobody seems to know that there were increasing disagreements between us—on how you pick people for the administration, on policy, on how you run a government. Bob tends to be a fixer. I don't mean that pejoratively. I mean he looks for ways to manipulate problems so that they'll be smoothed over for a time. That's good in the short run, but it's not the way to build a whole new structure of government. You see, there is a difference between government and politics. Sure, they're intertwined, but government can't be all politics. It can't be entirely a matter of keeping yourself in the clear. Occasionally you have to take stands on pure, lofty principles, even though you know the stands are wrong politically. The Civilian Review Board was an example. So was the city's fiscal problems for a year or so without the income tax, but they wouldn't have run true. Not for the long run."

CHAPTER 14

1. The legislation proposed to amend the City Charter by substituting ten chapters for those sections already describing existing city agencies. The plan was developed in the interval since Mayor Lindsay was elected in November, 1965, by a panel headed by Louis A. Craco, a lawyer. The bill that was introduced in December, 1966, was the

fifth draft. The *New York Times*, endorsing the plan in an editorial on December 15, 1966, declared: "The bureaucratic maze of the existing structure delays vital information from reaching the Mayor in time to head off crises before they develop. The city lacks adequate machinery for cooperating with the state and Federal governments. The Mayor's reorganization plan is a considered attempt to remedy these and many other municipal weaknesses."

2. In an interview with Nat Hentoff at City Hall earlier in the fall, Sweet expressed his attitude toward Lindsay and the Administration's goals. Hentoff quoted Sweet, then serving as executive assistant to the Mayor, as saying: "John is a loner. Anything this Administration has got so far has been by main strength and awkwardness. But I'm quite confident you'll know at the end of four years that we've been here. I can't believe men of good will can't accomplish *something!*"

3. Nat Hentoff's article appeared in the October 7, 1967, issue of *The New Yorker* magazine, beginning on page 58.

4. Callender resigned in 1969 to become president of the New York Urban Coalition.

5. Former Mayor Robert F. Wagner made this comment to me in his office at City Hall during an interview on December 15, 1958, when I was a reporter for the *New York World-Telegram and Sun.*

6. *Let in the Sun,* published by The Macmillan Company in 1964, was the profile of one tenement in a block in East Harlem which had become the symbol of the worst slums in the United States. The block had been visited by many public officials including Mayor Wagner, Attorney General Robert F. Kennedy, and Governor Mark Hatfield, of Oregon. I had written the book when I was still a housing reporter for the *New York World-Telegram and Sun.*

EPILOGUE

1. *The Progressive,* December, 1967, p. 14.

Index

Index

About the Author

Woody Klein served as Mayor John V. Lindsay's first press secretary in 1966, then as assistant administrator for public affairs in New York City's Housing and Development Administration. A former award-winning newspaper reporter with the Washington Post and Times Herald, *the* New York World-Telegram and Sun, *and a former television correspondent with WCBS-TV in New York, Mr. Klein is the author of* Let in the Sun, *a book about politics and slums published in 1964. He is a graduate of the Fieldston School in Riverdale, New York, Dartmouth College, and the Graduate School of Journalism at Columbia University. A native New Yorker, he has taught journalism at New York University and is adjunct associate professor of Journalism at the University of Bridgeport. In addition, he writes a column for* The Villager, *a Greenwich Village weekly newspaper. Hs is now an editor and writer with IBM and he lives with his wife Audrey and daughter Wendy in Westport, Connecticut.*